Power Markets and
Economics

Power Markets and Economics

Energy Costs, Trading, Emissions

Barrie Murray

Electricity Market Services Limited, UK

John Wiley & Sons, Ltd

This edition first published 2009
© 2009 John Wiley & Sons, Ltd

Registered office
John Wiley & Sons Ltd, The Atrium, Southern Gate, Chichester, West Sussex, PO19 8SQ, United Kingdom

For details of our global editorial offices, for customer services and for information about how to apply for permission to reuse the copyright material in this book please see our website at www.wiley.com.

Library of Congress Cataloging-in-Publication Data

Murray, Barrie.
  Power markets & economics: energy costs, trading, emissions/Barrie Murray.
     p. cm.
  Includes bibliographical references and index.
  ISBN 978-0-470-77966-8 (cloth)
1. Electric power. 2. Power resources. I. Title. II. Title: Power markets and economics.
  TK3001.M87 2009
  333.793'23–dc22   2008044492

A catalogue record for this book is available from the British Library.

ISBN: 978-0-470-77966-8

Set in 10/12.5 Palatino Roman by Thomson Digital, Noida, India.
Printed in Great Britain by TJ International Ltd, Padstow, Cornwall

To my dear grandchildren Ella, Harris and Henry

Contents

Foreword   xiii

Preface   xv

PART ONE INDUSTRY INFRASTRUCTURE   1

1 Approach to Restructuring   3
  1.1   Introduction   3
  1.2   Industry Physical Structure   5
  1.3   Introduction of Competition   8
  1.4   Restructuring Options   9
  1.5   Comparison of Structures   14
  1.6   Summary   16

2 Market Mechanisms   19
  2.1   Introduction   19
  2.2   Market Participants   20
  2.3   Market Mechanisms   23
  2.4   Market Implementation   29
  2.5   Price Analysis   33
  2.6   Summary   37

PART TWO THE COST CHAIN   39

3 Basic Generation Energy Costs   41
  3.1   Introduction   41
  3.2   Cost Components   42
  3.3   Practical Operating Efficiencies   46

3.4   Impact of Utilisation on Costs   48
3.5   Comparison of Generation Costs   49
3.6   International Comparisons   53
3.7   Summary   54

4 Alternative Energy Sources   **55**
4.1   Introduction   55
4.2   Competing Sources   56
4.3   Current Production Europe   59
4.4   Incentive Schemes   62
4.5   Market Pricing   64
4.6   The Economics of Alternative Sources   65
4.7   Comparisons   70
4.8   Summary   72

5 Emissions   **75**
5.1   Introduction   75
5.2   Emission Trading Schemes (ETS)   76
5.3   Large Combustion Plant Directive (LCPD)   77
5.4   Generation CO_2 Emissions   78
5.5   Production Costs   79
5.6   National Allocation Plans   80
5.7   Market Operation   82
5.8   Impact of Capacity Mix   83
5.9   International Approach   84
5.10 Summary   87

6 Transmission   **89**
6.1   Introduction   89
6.2   Impact of Transmission Constraints in Markets   90
6.3   Transmission Charging   93
6.4   Derivation of Use of System Charges   95
6.5   International Tariff Comparisons   97
6.6   Transmission Investment   98
6.7   Interconnection Investment Appraisal   100
6.8   International Practice   104
6.9   Summary   106

7 Distribution   **107**
7.1   Introduction   107
7.2   Market Status   108

7.3   Commercial Arrangements   109
7.4   Metering and Balancing   110
7.5   Cost of Distribution   111
7.6   Distribution Tariffs   112
7.7   OPEX Regulation   115
7.8   Capex Regulation   118
7.9   Business Risk   119
7.10 Distributed Generation   120
7.11 Summary   121

8   End User Charges and Prices   123
8.1   Introduction   123
8.2   Price Comparisons   124
8.3   End User Energy Prices   125
8.4   Total End User Prices   128
8.5   Tariff Development   130
8.6   Customer Switching   133
8.7   Summary   134

PART THREE MARKET OPERATION   135

9   Market Trading   137
9.1   Introduction   137
9.2   European Markets   138
9.3   Developing Markets – China   139
9.4   Market Power   140
9.5   Trading Arrangements   141
9.6   Bilateral Trading   143
9.7   Balancing Market   144
9.8   Exchange Trading   145
9.9   Supplier Risk   146
9.10 Generation Risk   147
9.11 Market Interaction   150
9.12 Arbitrage Spark Spread   150
9.13 Summary   153

10 Market Analysis   155
10.1 Introduction   155
10.2 Modelling Overview   156
10.3 Dispatch Market Simulation   158
10.4 Load Duration Model   159

10.5   Hydro Generation   160
10.6   Interconnection Modelling   163
10.7   Predicting Demand Data   163
10.8   Generation Data   165
10.9   Calculations   167
10.10 Price Duration Curve   169
10.11 Statistical Forecasting   170
10.12 Predicting New Entry   172
10.13 Summary   177

11 Ancillary Service Markets   179
11.1   Introduction   179
11.2   Ancillary Service Requirements   180
11.3   Market Volume   182
11.4   Procurement Process   186
11.5   Cost of Providing Services   189
11.6   Predicting Revenues   194
11.7   Summary   197

12 Cross-border Trading   199
12.1   Introduction   199
12.2   Governance   200
12.3   Cross-border Capacity   202
12.4   New Investment   204
12.5   Managing Operation   206
12.6   Capacity Auctions   207
12.7   Security   209
12.8   Charging for Wheeling   210
12.9   International Trading Development   214
12.10 Summary   220

13 Investment Appraisal   221
13.1   Introduction   221
13.2   Overall Analysis   222
13.3   Analysis of Options   224
13.4   Plant Costs   225
13.5   Predicting Revenue   229
13.6   Bidding/Contracting Strategy   232
13.7   Evaluating Risk   233
13.8   Summary   234

PART FOUR MARKET DEVELOPMENT   235

14 Market Performance   237
    14.1   Introduction   237
    14.2   Performance Criteria   238
    14.3   Market Shortcomings   239
    14.4   Performance Assessment   242
    14.5   Performance Improvement   246
    14.6   Summary   251

15 Market Developments   253
    15.1   Introduction   253
    15.2   Generation Developments   254
    15.3   Future Plant Mix   260
    15.4   Transmission and Distribution Grids   263
    15.5   Carbon Capture and Storage   265
    15.6   Market Implications   268
    15.7   Summary   269

16 Long-term Scenarios   271
    16.1   Introduction   271
    16.2   Emissions   272
    16.3   Alternative Energy Sources   274
    16.4   The Nuclear Option   276
    16.5   Fuel Prices   277
    16.6   Fuel Supply Security   279
    16.7   System Security   280
    16.8   Clean Coal Technology   281
    16.9   Network Developments   284
    16.10 International Commodity and Freight Markets   286
    16.11 Competition   287
    16.12 Conclusions   288

Glossary   291

References   295

Appendix   297
    Conversion Tables   297

Index   301

Foreword

Dr Murray was a former colleague for over twenty years at National Grid, UK (and its predecessor, Central Electricity Generating Board) until 1998. He had been a key senior manager whilst at National Grid, responsible for establishing the processes and systems necessary to support system and market operation at the National Control Centre, including scheduling and dispatch, operational planning and system planning. He played a lead role in enabling restructuring in the UK, having been involved since the inception of the market in 1990.

Since 1998, Dr Murray has worked on the design and operation of liberalised electricity markets. He provides consultancy services to utilities, banks, regulators and government agencies throughout the world in the area of liberalised energy markets, including regulation, commercial agreements and market and system operation. He has also played a key part in the implementation of markets and the Independent System Operator (ISO) function. He leads on the development of the business processes to support system and market operation, settlement, the promotion of competition and the accommodation of privatised operations.

When I started my role at the University of Bath as the Course Director for the Electrical Power Systems MSc Programme by Distance Learning, I noted the distinct absence in the market place of textbooks on the subject of Power Markets from a practitioner's viewpoint. I approached Barrie and encouraged him to embark on this book so that all his invaluable and precious knowledge could be passed on. I am therefore most delighted that this has come to fruition. I have no doubt that my students, engineers, economists, analysts, consultants and many others would find this an excellent reference book on the subject, written by an internationally recognised expert.

Dr Henry Lu
MSc, DIC, PhD, CEng, MIET,
DMS, ACMA

Course Director, University of Bath, UK
www.bath.ac.uk/elec-eng/eps/dl

Preface

It is now almost twenty years since liberalisation and the introduction of competition was proposed for electricity utilities. Some form of restructuring has been widely adopted around the world to suit local objectives. This book is designed to provide insight into the structure of those markets and the economics of power systems. It also covers basic generation, transmission and distribution costing and pricing. The performance of markets and their current status and problems is reviewed. The industry now faces new challenges associated with global warming, rising prices and escalating energy demand from developing countries such as China and India. The industry will have to cope with:

- the impact on fossil fired generation resulting from restrictions on emissions and the costs derived from the European Trading Scheme;
- the costs and competitive position of alternative energy sources and associated incentive schemes;
- a resurgence of interest in nuclear but concerns over who will finance and underwrite the risk;
- escalating fossil fuel prices and the reaction of generators in bringing forward improvements in efficiency;
- the security of fuel supplies with increasing dependence in Europe on imports from Russia;
- the impact on system security of the management of large tranches of variable generation output from wind-farms disturbing cross-border flows;
- the potential for clean coal with carbon capture and storage enabling conventional sources to compete with subsidised renewable sources;
- the advent of distributed generation and actively managed distribution networks;

- the impact on world commodity markets and freight costs of the burgeoning Chinese and Indian markets;
- the impact of mergers and acquisitions on market liquidity and competition.

The first wave of restructuring was designed to promote competition in the expectation that this would reduce prices. It is now necessary to consider how the various market structures that have been adopted have performed and how they will address some of these new issues and what further changes might be necessary.

The book is split into four parts covering the following:

Part One The Industry Infrastructure

This describes the infrastructure of the industry and the various structures that have been adopted to effect market operation and how they have performed. It introduces the various entities involved in the process and how they interact.

Part Two The Cost Chain

This develops the cost chain that contributes to end user prices. It covers the costs of conventional and renewable generation and the impact of emission restrictions. The basis for transmission and distribution costs is developed and how these contribute to the charging structures is illustrated. Finally it is shown how all the cost elements combine to make up end user prices.

Part Three Market Operation

This part focuses on the operation of markets and covers the trading arrangements and price forecasting. It introduces the mechanisms used to trade ancillary services and illustrates their costing. The process for cross-border trading is described and the auctioning of inter-connector capacity. The final section deals with the process of investment appraisal and risk assessment.

Part Four Market Development

This part discusses the performance of markets in operation, the techniques used to monitor performance and improvement measures. It describes some of the technological developments that are likely and how these might impact on market operation and development. It discusses the new issues that need to be addressed and how they might be managed. The section concludes with some scenarios that may materialise in the longer term through to 2050.

The analysis is illustrated with examples based on typical costs for fuel, plant and capital. This basic input data would have to be updated to current values for any new appraisal.

Dr Barrie Murray

August 2008
barriemurray.ems@btinternet.com

One

Industry Infrastructure

This part describes the infrastructure of the industry and the various structures that have been put in place to effect market operation and how they have performed. It introduces the various entities involved in the process and how they interact.

Chapter 1 Approach to Restructuring

This describes the motivation behind restructuring and the various stages of liberalisation. The different approaches taken by countries and the rationale behind them are discussed.

Chapter 2 Market Mechanisms

This outlines the different market structures that have been applied and explains their operating arrangements. It covers the Pool, Single Buyer, Multi-Market, Nordpool and Balancing Markets and their approach to pricing.

1

Approach to Restructuring

1.1 INTRODUCTION

The last 20 years have seen restructuring of the electricity sector spread around the world with the expectation that the introduction of competition would lead to a more efficient industry with lower prices. Starting with simple mandatory Pool models, some countries have progressed to the complete liberalisation of both generation and supply with competition at each stage of the cost chain. Other countries have opted to introduce competition in generation with a Single Buyer market model. The approaches have been tailored to meet the developing needs of each country with varying degrees of success in meeting their objectives. In some circumstances it has been an essential prerequisite to encouraging new investment; in others it has been to improve operational efficiency.

The industry now faces a new set of challenges and it will be important to review how well the structures in place are able to meet them. Escalating fuel prices and the impact of emissions on the environment and global warming bring the industry into the forefront of political debate. Attempts to encourage the development of renewable energy sources based on 'feed in' tariffs and requirements placed on suppliers for a percentage of their energy to be derived from renewable sources have met with limited success. The introduction of emission trading schemes has sought to establish a market price to realise the least cost abatement approach to reducing emissions. The early phases have not been effectively managed and have had poor results.

Power Markets and Economics: Energy Costs, Trading, Emissions Barrie Murray
© 2009 John Wiley & Sons, Ltd

The burgeoning energy demands of the Chinese and Indian markets add dimension to the problems faced. Concerns over security of fuel supply and the prospect of a revival in nuclear energy raise concerns at a political level. Will the structures put in place be robust enough to deal with these issues or do we need to rethink the approach? The management of some of the risks requires the resources of large organisations rather than a fragmented industry. The results of mergers and acquisitions has seen the European sector moving from the industry being structured on a national basis to being controlled by large multi-nationals like EdF, RWE, E.On, ENEL and Iberdrola. At the same time several national markets have merged and moved towards providing the prime cover for several countries: Central Europe, including France and Germany; Benelux embracing the Netherlands and Belgium; Iberia covering Spain and Portugal and an all Ireland market covering the Republic and Northern Ireland. The coverage of the power exchanges has followed suit with activities being merged. It is timely to review the current status of the industry and its fitness to meet the needs of the future.

This chapter provides an overview of the approaches that have been taken to restructuring and the market designs that have been adopted. It discusses:

- the reasons for promoting restructuring of the industry to introduce competition;
- the different market structures that have been applied;
- a comparison of the market models illustrating their strengths and weaknesses;
- some of the results of restructuring.

The initial step in the unbundling process was usually to split off generation from transmission. A further step would be to break up the generation into separate competing generation blocks. The transmission would be regulated as a monopoly business and it is often required to separate out the system operation function to establish a totally Independent System Operator (ISO). The distribution companies may be retained as an entity supplying a franchised customer base or split into a wires ownership organisation and a supply business, managing supplies to customers. The wires business would be regulated as a monopoly while supply would be open to competition. The general approach has been for supply competition to be introduced gradually starting with large consumers and working down to the domestic market. In the EU the target date for completion of the process was mid 2007.

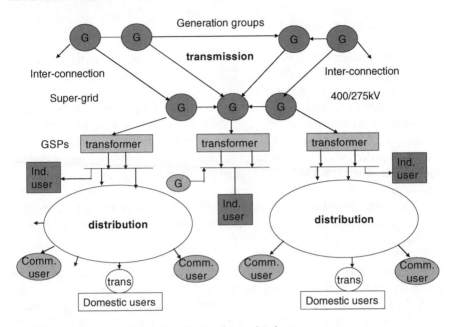

Figure 1.1 Basic physical infrastructure

1.2 INDUSTRY PHYSICAL STRUCTURE

A simple schematic of the physical infrastructure of the industry is shown in Figure 1.1. It is made up of generating stations connected to an inter-connected super-grid operating at system voltages[1] of typically 275/400 kV and enabling the pooling of generation. The generation voltage is typically 11–22 kV and is transformed up at the station to 275 or 400 kV for connection to the grid. Nearer the load centres transformers at the grid supply points (GSPs) reduce the voltage from the super-grid level to 132 or 33/11 kV.

These voltages may be used to supply larger industrial consumers as well as local distribution rings operating at 11 kV. These may also feed larger commercial premises as well as local substations transforming from 11 kV to 415 V that are used to connect to domestic premises supplied from one phase operating at 240 V. There may also be inter-connection to adjacent systems connected at the super-grid level and also smaller generation embedded within the distribution network.

---

[1] System voltages in three-phase systems are normally referenced by the line or phase to phase voltage and equal 1.732 times the individual phase to neutral voltage.

The physical entities involved are:

- the **Transmission Owner** who plans, builds, owns and maintains the super-grid system typically made up of 275/400 kV transmission lines, transformers and reactive compensation equipment;
- the **Distribution Owner** who plans, builds, owns and maintains the distribution network made up of the 132 kV network and lower system voltages and associated transformers and switchgear;
- the **Generators** who plan, build, own, operate and maintain generation that may feed into the super-grid network or, if smaller, be connected into the local distribution network;
- the **System Operator** (SO) who manages operation of the power system so as to maintain stability and the security of supplies from minute to minute.

Until around 1990 the industries in most countries were operated as monopolies in state ownership with the generation and transmission under the control of one central authority (the Central Electricity Generating Board in the UK) supplying distribution companies with a geographically defined franchise for customers in their area. This was the general arrangement, although in some countries the local distribution was under the control of the municipal authority. The central authority managed the development of the generation and transmission to meet expected load and operated the system so as to minimise the cost of production whilst maintaining security. The authority procured fuel and recovered its costs from the sale of energy to the distribution company against a bulk supply tariff (BST). This tariff was structured with an element related to the maximum demand together with an energy component. In the UK the maximum demand, referred to as the triad, was the maximum demand occurring during three non-consecutive half hours separated by more than 10 days. The fixed element, related to maximum demand, was designed to cover the costs of capital for the investment in generation and transmission required to meet the demand. The energy part of the tariff was designed to reflect the marginal costs of production with cheaper charges overnight and at weekends and higher charges during the weekday working hours. For example the 88/99 UK BST prior to liberalisation was structured as below.

Capacity charges
    Peak £23.5/kW based on triad demand
    Base £20.0/kW based on average demand of 300 half hours

Energy rates p/kWh
  Night 1.57 (2400–0800 hrs)
  Day 2.16 (0800–2400 hrs)
  Surcharge 1.0 at peak
The total charges would be made up of:

- the peak capacity charges times the recorded triad demand (the average of three recorded peaks separated by 10 days);
- the base capacity charge time the average demand of 300 half hours;
- the night energy rate times the total energy recorded between the hours of 2400 and 0800;
- the day energy rate times the total energy recorded between 0800 and 2400 with a surcharge added to the recoded energy for the peak hour.

The industry was controlled by external finance limits set by government and was at that time set to be negative, requiring debt repayment. Defined levels of coal were also required to be burned without the freedom to choose fuel sources. It was subject to frequent government interference and used to support general fiscal policy. The industry was driven technologically to achieve improved production efficiency but in operation the dominant influence was to maintain security rather than to minimise cost. Despite this, cost improvements were realised through the development of larger more efficient generation and higher voltage transmission systems. The development of generation capacity in Western Europe is shown in Figure 1.2. It shows the recent and projected trend in capacity with oil and coal declining, while renewable and gas are increasing. The emphasis on security sometimes leads to over investment to avoid shortfalls in capacity during worse than average weather or exceptional plant failures. The lower dotted line of Figure 1.2 shows the demand, while the upper shows the expected available capacity allowing for outages. It can be seen that the margin of spare capacity is expected to be at a much lower level than that planned by the state controlled utilities.

Energy prices were set reflecting average costs rather than the marginal cost of production. The distribution companies managed the development of the distribution system for which they had a franchise. They bought energy from the CEGB and sold to end consumers against a set of user tariffs. Although ownership arrangements varied this was the norm around the world with geographic regulated monopolies.

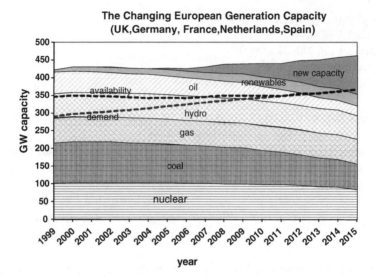

Figure 1.2   Developing plant mix Europe

1.3 INTRODUCTION OF COMPETITION

There was no competition in generation or supply and this was considered to be inefficient. The distribution companies had no choice but to buy from the central generating authority at the prices declared in the BST. End users had no choice but to seek a supply from their local distributor and pay the declared tariff. Various economic advisers suggested reform was necessary because:

- the model gave no incentive to operate efficiently;
- it encouraged unnecessary investments;
- the cost of mistakes were passed on to the public without recourse;
- it was too easy for governments to interfere, creating a stop/go policy.

It was argued by advocates of deregulation that market disciplines would lead to lower prices and benefit consumers and the country. It was recognised that the industry had some special characteristics but that these did not present insurmountable problems.

There were opponents to the proposals who saw counter issues including:

- the need to maintain strategic control of a key part of the country's infrastructure;

- the need to coordinate investment planning centrally to establish adequate levels of capacity;
- the need to maintain a plant mix by fuel and type;
- the ability to finance large high capital cost investments;
- the need to fix responsibility for maintaining system security.

The opponents argued that these factors were more important than any benefits that might accrue from introducing competition. Despite these misgivings, it was proposed that a path of liberalisation should be pursued in the UK as well as elsewhere. A number of factors needed to be addressed to ensure a successful outcome including:

- the structure to be put in place to facilitate competition;
- the number of separate owners necessary to realise competition;
- the mechanisms to recover the costs of the transmission/distribution monopolies;
- the mechanisms that needed to be put in place to establish competition through a liquid market with many participants including the demand side;
- the mechanisms to ensure that security was maintained;
- the mechanisms to enable the System Operator to balance the system and maintain the security and quality of supplies;
- the realisation of the optimum levels of investment;
- the implications to equipment suppliers.

Of these, establishing a liquid market where the transaction volume exceeded the physical volume was kernel to establishing effective competition.

There was no universal answer to all these issues and each country that chose to pursue restructuring adopted a different approach tailored to meet their priorities. In most cases the first step was to un-bundle ownership. This meant separating ownership of transmission from generation, splitting up the generation into a number of competing blocks and establishing an Independent System Operator to manage dispatch to meet end consumer needs. Secondly restructuring would put some form of market structure in place to facilitate trading and competition.

1.4 RESTRUCTURING OPTIONS

Various restructuring options have been proposed and applied in different countries including the following.

1.4.1 The Gross Pool

This is the model originally applied in the UK in 1990 where it was mandatory for all energy to be traded between generators and suppliers through the pool shown schematically in Figure 1.3. This model was adopted by other countries such as South Africa. The price paid by participants or the market clearing price was set in advance, based on a unit commitment study. This was based on an optimisation algorithm with the objective function of minimising the total cost of production based on the prices submitted by the generators. In the UK model transmission constraints were initially ignored and generation was selected in cost order irrespective of whether its use would violate a network security. It was argued that network structure was not the responsibility of generators or suppliers and the same energy price should apply irrespective of physical location. A separate operational study was then used to determine the practical generation utilisation taking account of the effect of network constraints. The additional generation costs incurred were shared between all suppliers. Most players hedged against the volatility of pool prices by striking two-way hedging contracts (contracts for differences – CfDs) to adjust pool payments to a pre-agreed contract price. This model has been used in South Africa, Singapore and Spain.

The supply side of the business has also been liberalised with the franchise of the local distribution companies being progressively removed, enabling consumers to have a free choice of suppliers. The free choice was initially given to those consumers with a demand greater than 1 MW followed by an extension to those with a demand greater than 100 kW in 1994 and for all consumers by March 98. This pattern of progressive liberalisation of the supply side has been mandated by a European Union Directive for completion in 2007.

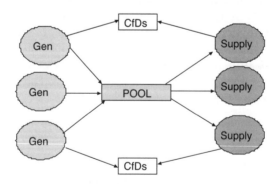

Figure 1.3 Mandatory pool

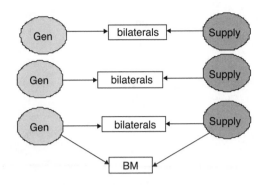

Figure 1.4 Bilateral trading plus balancing market

1.4.2 Multi Market (Bilateral Trading + Balancing Market)

This model is widely used across Europe with most of the energy traded directly between generators and suppliers through bilateral contracts as illustrated in Figure 1.4. These may be established though OTC trading or through a tendering process. Nearer the event, positions will be adjusted by trading on exchanges for the day ahead. Finally, since in practice the level of demand and the availability of generation cannot be accurately predicted, a Balancing Market (BM) is used to clear the residual energy and any un-contracted demand. It has been argued that full competition is not realised through this process as the bilateral contracts are not visible publicly to enable price discovery. The process will also be sub-optimal in that although individual generators will be able to optimise their particular running arrangements the opportunity to establish a national optimum is lost and overall costs will generally be higher. This arrangement, sometimes called the net pool, is widely used across Europe with most of the energy traded bilaterally with exchanges used to adjust to meet short term needs and a Balancing Market used to enable the System Operator to effect real time balance.

1.4.3 The Single Buyer

With this approach a nominated authority acts on behalf of all registered consumers to collate demand predictions and negotiate with generators to buy energy and services as indicated in Figure 1.5. Agreements will include the purchase of existing station outputs and establishing contracts for the output of new stations. The arrangement has been criticised in that the authority represents a monopoly that is not in itself subject to market forces. However, it does realise competition in generation and enables the

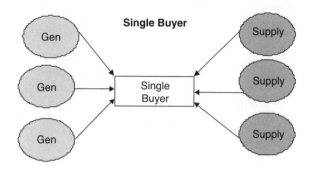

Figure 1.5   Single buyer market

development of generation and transmission to be coordinated and optimised in both the planning and operational timescales. A progressive introduction of the single buyer model is possible with a mixture of state and independent generation in varying proportions. The buyer should not own generation to avoid a conflict of interest and to maintain impartiality. Countries such as China, Abu Dhabi, Oman, Egypt and Namibia operate single buyer models. This model is popular where there is significant system development being undertaken that needs to be coordinated centrally.

1.4.4 Power Boards

In this arrangement the price of energy is set for defined geographical zones that are tightly coupled by transmission and dominated by a vertically integrated company as illustrated in Figure 1.6. This means that generation within

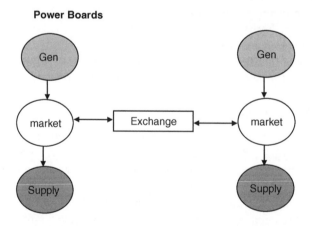

Figure 1.6   Power boards

the zone can usually be used freely without limitations due to transmission. Trading is effected between zones depending on the level of interconnection capacity and price differentials. This approach introduces additional complexity but highlights the importance of transmission and creates an incentive to invest. It is therefore appropriate where the existing network is weak and the introduction of more inter-zonal transmission capacity would bring consumer benefit. The capacity of the interconnecting transmission is usually auctioned and can be bought by parties on both sides of the link. The trading could be between the pool authorities or directly by generators who have bought capacity to enable them to bid into adjacent areas/pools, as happened with Scottish and French generation who bid into the UK pool. Where generators are also allowed to register as suppliers they may acquire local distribution and supply companies and become vertically integrated power boards.

1.4.5 Open IPP Access

With this arrangement the main body of generation is retained with a state interest but the system is required to enable the entry into the market of a proportion of non-utility generation (NUGs). The benefits of integrated planning are retained and a measure of competition is introduced to the utility generation. The system provides a useful intermediate step to introducing full competition in generation but it is claimed that the utility always favours its own generation and true competition is not realised while the buyer owns generation. The French introduced a system whereby external parties could contract the output of EdF generation capacity to meet their supply commitments. The Republic of Ireland adopted a system to encourage new entry through the provision of prices for 'spill' and 'makeup' energy. This enabled independents to balance their position by buying 'makeup' energy to meet their commitments when their own output was restricted or selling excess 'spill' energy when in surplus.

1.4.6 State Utility

This model is essentially a fully integrated utility where all the generation is under state ownership together with transmission and sometimes distribution. In this model the government sees the need to retain a national champion to safeguard its strategic infrastructure. The absence of competition may lead to inefficiencies but this can be in part offset by introducing a proportion of financing through the private sector to exert influence. The main advantage is that it enables integrated generation and transmission planning and can create a relatively stable environment in which to encourage investment. For a developing country it has many advantages and allows the state to adopt a tariff policy that encourages the development of the infrastructure of the country as well as supporting the financing of major projects like hydro schemes. Some new investment may be encouraged through the establishment of long term Power Purchase Agreements but subject to central control.

1.5 COMPARISON OF STRUCTURES

It is difficult to draw quantitative comparisons between the various market models because the outcome depends on the structure of the utility to which they are applied and its state of development. However, a qualitative guide is shown in Table 1.1, illustrating the strengths and weaknesses of each option. The table columns shown make comparisons assuming the following.

1. Competition in generation gives cost saving through the introduction of more efficient generation such as combined cycle systems and CHP reducing the fuel bill.
2. Integrated planning saves in avoiding excessive capital costs by ensuring the ideal plant margin and generation mix with no excess capacity.
3. A monopoly results in inefficiency and additional costs resulting from higher staff levels and a reluctance to use generally available standard equipment.
4. The cost–benefit rating indicates the combined effect of the key factors affecting costs.
5. Column five gives a subjective view on the implications of the chosen market structure on the likelihood of securing new investment.
6. Column six gives the likelihood of the chosen model maintaining system security.

Table 1.1 Market comparisons

Structure	Generation competition	Integrated plan/ops	Efficiency	Cost–benefit rating	Invest. rating	Security rating
Gross pool	VG	M	M	B	Low	Low
Multi Market	VG	B	M	G	Low	Low
Single buyer	VG	VG	M	VG	Med.	Med.
Power boards	G	M	B	M	Med.	Med
Open IPP access	M	M	M	B	High	High
State utility	VB	VG	VB	VB	High	High

Table 1.1 uses these factors to provide an indicative comparison of the different market structures ranging from: very good (VG); good (G); medium (M), bad (B); very bad (VB).

The **gross pool** realises price competition in generation by splitting up the state generation. This assumes that sufficient competing groups are established to ensure competition but in practice this is sometimes difficult to achieve. Central control and coordination is maintained at least for the operational process if not planning. The culture of the state utility will continue to operate and the removal of inefficiency and excess staff will be slow.

The **Multi-market model** enables bilateral trading with a Balancing Market and also realises competition in generation and, whilst losing some central operational coordination, it shifts the culture to a more efficient competitive level. Participation in a day-ahead market and the BM is optional.

It can be seen that the **Single Buyer** model scores high with a very good cost–benefit rating in that it enables the benefits of competition in generation and the coordination of central planning whilst removing a lot of the inefficiency of a state utility monopoly culture. A difficulty with its application is in managing operation against a contractual framework based on PPAs. It is sometimes difficult to apply the strict terms of a complex contract into the management of day to day operation of the plant.

Power Boards introduce competition between each area through trading across inter connectors. Each Board may operate as a vertically integrated utility internally so generation competition is not complete nor is central planning globally coordinated. Each Board will operate within its area largely as a monopoly with limited improvement in efficiency.

Open IPP access introduces limited generation competition to the residual state generator but IPP entry is sometimes difficult to attract because of the market domination. Some central planning is retained and some improvements in efficiency can be expected.

The **State Utility** maintains the benefits of optimal central planning and coordination but this benefit is largely offset by the inefficiency of the monopoly in operation. There may be some small benefit derived from enabling access to a few IPPs that set benchmarks.

The best model for a particular country will depend on the state of development of the network and the need for new investment in transmission and generation. It may also be influenced by the perception of risk in the country and the need to encourage electrification of under-developed areas.

A number of countries such as South Africa have adopted a Pool-like model as a relatively simple transition with a view to further development as experience develops. The Multi-market model is the one most widely applied in the developed countries of Europe where the emphasis is on improving the efficiency of systems that are largely established. In developing regions, such as Africa, there is often a need to encourage inward investment and this may be more easily realised if Power Purchase Agreements (PPAs) can be put in place. This can be best undertaken by a Single Buyer acting on behalf of the end users and able to underwrite the contract. In some small states in the Middle East there may be insufficient generation to establish a viable competitive market and the Single Buyer model has been adopted.

1.6 SUMMARY

This chapter has described the motivation behind the introduction of competition into the power sector with the expectation that it would drive prices down and provide customer choice. Opponents to liberalisation argued that the loss of central control would undermine the investment process and endanger system security but on balance it was decided that the potential benefits outweighed these disadvantages for the UK. Some countries followed the UK approach but others pursued different approaches. The various market models that have been applied have been outlined and a coarse comparison is drawn between them. It is recognised that there is no universally correct model but rather that the needs of each country need to be analysed to establish the objectives. The state of development and size of the sector, the need to encourage inward investment and finance large projects are all relevant issues that will influence the optimum design.

Looking to the future it is difficult to see how all of the challenges can be met with some market structures. A key weakness of market based structures over a central planning approach is in the coordination of investment. The market will have a tendency to keep plant margins low when shortfalls can be expected, driving up prices. This can also result in insecurity with a higher probability of loss of supply when multiple failures result in insufficient generation to meet demand. The other area that presents problems is in coordinating the developing mixture of plant to maintain diversity and some hedge against fuel supplies being interrupted. The Single Buyer model does address these issues and allows the Buyer to place tenders for new capacity, thereby controlling the volume and type of generation. There are a number of other concerns as outlined below.

- The development of renewable sources has been subject to government intervention in the market and it would not have happened without incentive schemes.
- The Emission Trading Schemes have so far failed to deliver the target reductions.
- The absence of price stability is a problem for industry that has led to the establishment of consortia to establish long term supply contracts.

It remains to be seen if governments will tolerate these adverse effects in the hope that the market structure will eventually deliver or if they will seek to exercise more direct control.

2

Market Mechanisms

2.1 INTRODUCTION

Irrespective of the type of market structure that is adopted, business processes have to be defined that enable energy trading while at the same time securing physical operation of the power system. On the one hand, the trading community would like to regard the grid as infinite and has no interest in the complex physical aspects of the plant. On the other hand the System Operator has to focus on balancing supply and demand and managing the network so as to maintain a secure stable system. The marriage of these two diverse requirements requires detailed attention to the design of the interface between the two activities and the timing of the handover of data and responsibilities. This is best achieved through the application of standard business process design methodologies that detail data flows and the associated processes. Lack of clarity in the definition of the interface could jeopardise the security of the power system or unnecessarily impede market development.

This chapter provides an outline of the market participants (or entities) and their roles in effecting market implementation. The operation of the various market structures is described as well as the generic mechanisms that have to be put in place to support their operation. The concept of System Marginal Price (SMP) is described and illustrated with reference to recent price history across Europe. The various forms of pricing adopted by the markets are discussed ex-ante, ex-post and pay as bid. The relationship between prices and the plant mix that is available by country is used to

Power Markets and Economics: Energy Costs, Trading, Emissions   Barrie Murray
© 2009 John Wiley & Sons, Ltd

explain how prices vary between countries. The arrangements for demand side participation in price setting are illustrated by reference to the Nordpool model.

2.2 MARKET PARTICIPANTS

Figure 2.1 shows a basic market entity diagram with all the directly active participants and key data flows. Their roles are summarised below.

The **Regulators** are responsible for regulating the monopoly sectors of the industry, which are usually transmission, distribution and system operation. This is effected through a regular (5 year) review of prices for use of system and setting targets for reductions usually in the form of the retail price index less a factor, i.e. RPI – X. As well as regulating the network monopolies, the regulator will also seek to create and sustain competition and help to protect the security of energy supplies. These duties are undertaken whilst helping to

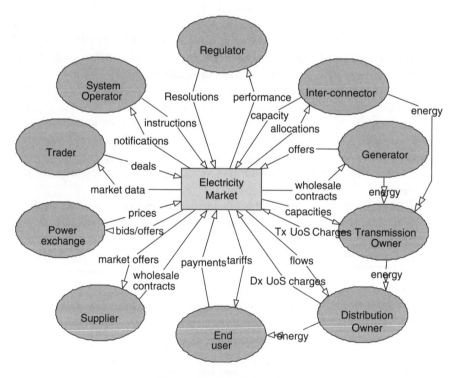

Figure 2.1   Market entities

protect the environment and tackling fuel poverty. They will also issue licences and adjudicate on any sector disputes. The regulatory duties may be combined with those of other energy sectors as in the UK where Ofgem embraces both gas and electricity. Ofgem employs some 300 staff with an annual budget of £38 m.

The **System Operator (SO)** is responsible for the real time operation of power system so as to maintain a stable, secure and safe system. This is realised by dispatching generation and demand, participating in providing contracted services to balance supply and demand at all times. The dispatch of generation is also managed so as to maintain the security of the network against credible failures and any other constraints. The quality of frequency and voltage control is maintained through the procurement of ancillary services such as reserve from generators and demand side participants.

The **Trader** operates in the market, buying and selling defined blocks of energy. They will usually operate to achieve a net zero position at the end of the day where the sales and purchases cancel each other. Traders may not participate in physical delivery unless acting to buy for a supplier or sell for a generator to make physical delivery against bilateral contracts. They expect to make money through arbitrage between different future periods and between different products such as gas and electricity.

A power **Exchange** provides a service to the market where blocks of energy can be traded anonymously. Offers to buy and sell are 'posted' to the exchange against specific prices and made visible to participants through IT systems. Deals are made and recorded by the exchange and they may also offer a clearing service to collect and make payments on behalf of participants. The exchange will also support longer term futures deals and enable forward price discovery. The exchange is funded by a small charge based pro rata on the size of deals.

Suppliers buy energy wholesale from generators either through bilateral contracts or through exchanges. They sell to end consumers either against a tariff for the particular consumer class or through a bilateral contract for larger and special consumers. They will pay the generator for the energy and also the network owners for use of their systems. They have to manage the volume risk and ensure that sufficient contracts are in place to meet demand without exposure to shortfalls in supplies or an excess that may be expensive to trade. They are also responsible for arranging metering and billing.

End Users

End users consume the energy purchased from suppliers either against a tariff or bilateral contract. They are usually categorised as industrial, commercial and domestic types based on their connection voltage, consumption and load factor/utilisation[1]. The payments usually include a fixed element based on the capacity of the demand connected and a variable proportion based on energy consumed.

Distribution Owner

The network connecting from the high voltage grid to the end user premises is described as distribution and is considered to be a monopoly. It incorporates voltage levels typically from 132 kV down to medium voltages of 415/240 V and is often radial in structure. The network users may be suppliers buying energy wholesale and transporting it through the network to their customers or generators embedded within the distribution network and selling their output to suppliers. The distribution network owner will charge network users a use of system charge that is based on the assets utilised by the user and the associated network losses. The prices charged are subject to scrutiny by the Regulator who will seek to drive them down to basic essential costs levels.

Transmission Owner

The high voltage transmission network is used for bulk power transfer and to enable the pooling of generation. It generally operates at voltages from 132 kV up to 275 kV and 400 kV and above. It is regarded as a monopoly and is subject to price regulation. Its income is derived from charges to network users based on their connected capacity and the proportional use of the transmission assets.

Generator

The generators produce energy from fuel or renewable sources and sell wholesale either through bilateral contracts or through exchanges. They will be required to pay a proportion of use of system charges to the transmission company if connected to the super-grid or to a distribution company if embedded within their network. The generators are also the principal source of ancillary services as used by the System Operator to manage system frequency, voltage and security and they receive special payments for these services. The demand side may also participate in this market particularly

---

[1] Load factor is the average load divided by the maximum capacity of an installation as a percentage.

with the provision of system reserve by shedding demand on request or automatically using low frequency relays.

Inter-connector

Special arrangements apply to the management of inter-connectors that are used to exchange energy with adjacent systems and countries. They enable external parties to participate in the local internal market. They pay for the use of the inter-connector and where congestion occurs on the route it is usual for the transmission capacity to be auctioned. In some cases energy may be 'wheeled' through an adjacent system to a third area when charges will be incurred based on the proportion of the assets used in effecting the transfer, termed the horizontal network, and the additional network losses.

Although the entities may have distinctly separate roles they may not necessarily be separate entities in the business sense. For example, a generator may also act as a supplier and becomes in effect vertically integrated. This has the advantage that the generator can better manage the volume risk through knowledge of the customer demand. Also the generator is less exposed to wholesale price risk in that tariffs are agreed with customers. Allowing vertical integration does undermine the liquidity in the market.

In some circumstances a generator may also own part of the network as in the case of RWE and Eon in Germany and Edison in Italy. Although the network parts of the business are regulated, there are inevitably concerns from independents about network access and the charges they incur for its use.

There is also the situation where the System Operator is in common ownership with the grid owner. It is argued that the System Operator should be completely independent with no interests in the market whatsoever, whereas the grid company may participate in the provision of system services like reactive energy. The preference is for the System Operator to be a separate company and not just a ring fenced business.

2.3 MARKET MECHANISMS

Irrespective of the market structure adopted in operation on a day to day basis a number of basic functions have to be performed. These are reviewed in this section to illustrate the options and how they affect the market and settlement process. The functions discussed are:

* setting market clearing prices;
* securing generation availability;

- accommodating transmission constraints;
- enabling demand side participation;
- balancing the system;
- capturing data for settlement;
- calculating payments.

Pricing

Markets generally operate on the principle of marginal pricing defined as the price of meeting the next increment of demand. The price may be determined in advance (ex-ante) of after the event (ex-post). A departure from this practice may occur where, because of some constraint, a service has to be called at a price higher than the marginal price. In these circumstances the bid price has to be paid.

a. **Marginal Pricing** Electricity markets generally work on the principle of marginal pricing where the highest price that buyers are prepared to pay is matched to the lowest price sellers are prepared to sell at. Offers from buyers and bids from sellers are matched to establish the strike price for the deal. This is the normal arrangement on stock markets. In the case of electricity markets this price represents the marginal incremental cost of production of the highest priced generator selected to meet the demand. The price is set for the half hour period consistent with the normal half hourly integrated meters used to measure energy. This result sets the price for all energy traded during that half hour. There is the option for users who do not wish to pay the price to curtail their demand. The price for each half hour will vary depending on the demand level during the period and the price and availability of generation to meet it. The concept of marginal pricing is essential to ensure that, when generation capacity is short, prices rise to encourage new entry. This contrasts with the pre-privatisation arrangements where prices were set based on average production costs. Because new generation was planned centrally it was not necessary for prices to rise to new entry prices provided the revenues covered the costs.The concepts are illustrated in the example below. Given the generation data in Table 2.1, the marginal generator at each of the half hour demand points can be found and hence the system marginal price and the average marginal price for the period. For example, at a load of 998 MW all three generators will be required and the marginal generator will be number 3 with a marginal price of £22/MWh. The marginal price can be calculated for the other

Table 2.1 Three generator system data

Generation merit order	Incremental price	Min gen MW	Max gen MW	Cum MW	Half hour demand
0	£/MWh			0	MW
1	18	200	500	500	998
2	20	150	400	900	800
3	22	100	150	1050	450
	total cap.	450	1050		average

demand levels as shown in Table 2.2 and hence the average of all periods at £20/MWh. This contrasts with the average production cost given by:

$$[(500*18 + 400*20 + 98*22) + (500*18 + 400*20)$$
$$+ (450*18)]/2156 = £19.6/MWh$$

In practice generation is subject to dynamic constraints with run up and run down rates, minimum on and off times that complicate the assessment of the marginal price bid by the generator. It is necessary to estimate the likely running periods taking account of the dynamic constraints and generator start up costs to establish an effective unit production cost.

b. **Ex-ante Pricing** This is where the marginal price is set in advance of the event and usually a day ahead, based on the results of a scheduling algorithm. In this arrangement an optimisation algorithm is used to order and select bidding generation to meet the demand during each period while minimising the costs. This should produce a least cost solution for generation but it is does not necessarily minimise the cost to consumers who pay based on marginal price. A disadvantage of this approach is

Table 2.2 Three generator dispatch

Generation merit order	Incremental price	Min gen MW	Max gen MW	Cum MW	Half hour demand	Marginal gen	Marginal gen. price
0	£/MWh			0	MW		£/MWh
1	18	200	500	500	998	3	22
2	20	150	400	900	800	2	20
3	22	100	150	1050	450	1	18
	total cap.	450	1050		average	£/MWh	20

that, since the outturn will be different from the conditions expected in the predictive schedule, a process is necessary to reconcile the differences during settlement. Bilateral deals are essentially ex-ante with prices set in advance although some contracts are related to published market prices.

c. **Ex-post Pricing** This is where the clearing price is based on the incremental price of that generator recorded as being marginal in the event. Balancing markets usually operate on this basis with the selling and buying prices based on the average prices of those generators that are bidding and used in the event to balance the system. In advance of the event, an indicative price may be provided by a market simulation to identify any shortcomings. It has the advantage that the price paid fully reflects actual conditions on the day and does not leave a requirement to settle any residual imbalances between planned and actual transferred energy.

d. **Bid Pricing** With this arrangement generators are paid at their bid price irrespective of the marginal price. This would apply to generators that are essential to run because of transmission constraints even if their price is above the marginal price of other generation. Ancillary service markets frequently operate on a 'pay as bid' basis in that the market selection process is influenced by technical issues and location and not just price comparison. The general application of a 'pay as bid' principle would tend to cause all generators to bid a little below the expected marginal price in order to secure running without loss of income. The clustering of prices around the margin would make the selection process volatile with frequent changes of units. It would also not enable a cost minimisation.

Securing Availability – LOLP

In a competitive market there is no explicit requirement for a generator to declare units available and an incentive may be necessary to ensure that sufficient capacity exists to meet demand. In the UK model this was achieved by the introduction of additional payments based on the loss of load probability (LOLP). This is the probability that shortfalls in generation availability will cause the combined capacity to be less than the expected demand for the period. This is calculated for each half hour, taking account of recently recorded statistics of the likelihood of loss of those generation units expected to be available to run and the probable range of expected demand. By attributing a value to consumer lost load (VLL) it is possible to calculate an increment to the basic marginal price designed to encourage generators to declare maximum availability, e.g. Price = SMP + (VLL − SMP) * VLL

Power purchase agreements will usually include incentives to encourage availability with specific payments geared to recorded capacity availability. These could be considered as a contribution to the capital costs of plant. In South Africa the capacity payments proposed were linked to the plant capacity margin and also varied by technology type to provide a mechanism to encourage a viable plant mix. The current thinking in developed markets is that capacity payments are not necessary and that the market prices will encourage the ideal plant margin.

Accommodating Transmission Constraints

Transmission constraints occur when the loading levels on the transmission equipment are such that loss of a component of the system would probably lead to loss of load and potentially a wider system disturbance. To avoid this situation, the operation of generation is constrained so as to contain network loading to within secure limits. It is generally not economic to design transmission networks to be constraint free and some periods will occur when the use of the cheapest generation will be restricted. This did not present a problem within an integrated utility and the constraints would be modelled and managed as part of normal operation. Within a market, however, generation expects full open access and where this would violate constraints some arrangements are necessary to manage them. The following three approaches have been proposed and applied.

1. **Post Market Settlement** The market prices are set initially ignoring transmission constraints, then the additional costs incurred in practice are added to the pool selling price and shared by all users. The transmitter may be provided with incentives to minimise the so called 'uplift costs' resulting from active transmission constraints and the use of ancillary services (UK Pool).

2. **Market Settlement** With this arrangement the constraints are modelled in the price setting algorithm resulting in different clearing prices for settlement of energy payments in the different zones of the network, i.e. zonal pricing as in Nordpool.

3. **Price Settlement** With this scheme the use of the limiting transmission route is charged for explicitly and the price is adjusted so as to balance demand to available capacity using an auction. Congestion management in

some form will be required down to the event to take account of changing circumstances.

An advantage of the first arrangement is that the market dealings are managed a day ahead and on the day the System Operator is left to manage the network and maintain security. A disadvantage is that the incentives to invest in transmission are less apparent. The use of market splitting with zonal pricing, on the other hand, points up the benefits of investment to the players directly affected by the constraints but at the cost of reducing market liquidity. The use of transmission pricing adjustments in the short term to manage congestion will add complexity in operation and may increase the risk to system security. The short term changes will undermine the ability to plan operation, which has been found to be the key to maintaining security on the day.

The ideal arrangement would be one that encourages the optimal level of investment so as to minimise the overall production cost. It is difficult to see how the above mechanisms will realise this in the absence of a joint authority. Both in the US and UK the concept of transmission user groups has been introduced but it remains to be seen if they can operate in the common interest. In practice there will be winners and losers from new investment and some generators may oppose new lines as has occurred in the UK. Privately funded development of inter-connectors can be expected when forecast market price differentials are sufficient to generate enough profit for the investor. The prospective income from traders has to be sufficient to pay for the installation and justify the ongoing costs of operation of the inter-connection.

Enabling Demand Side Participation

For a market to be fully competitive it is essential that full demand side participation is enabled through customer choice. This requires that the end users have the opportunity to bid into the market with prices at which they are prepared to buy energy or forgo supplies. This has the effect of putting a cap on the prices that generators can charge. In practice this is difficult to realise and the original attempts made in the UK were not very successful. In the Nordpool market, consumers can bid into a day-ahead market blocks of demand, together with the price at which they are prepared to reduce demand. These prices are plotted as an ascending curve and compared with the curve of generator bid prices to establish the intersection point when the price that consumers are prepared to pay matches the price at which generators are prepared to sell. If the expected system balance price exceeds their bid then their demand is not met. In practice it is only larger consumers with demand management facilities that can compete. The Nordpool model enables active demand side participation with generation and demand offers/bids matched to establish the market price for each period and each zone. All energy is then traded at that clearing price unless covered by bilateral contracts. In the multi-market model the demand side participates through bilateral contracting and exchange deals.

System Balancing

Whatever market arrangements are in place, in the event, the total system generation has to match the total demand in real time. At the close of bilateral trading or 'Gate Closure' the SO has to have the opportunity to fine tune generation and demand to ensure balance. This may be achieved by dispatching the generation of a large residual company or there may be an open Balancing Market where interested participants may bid to supply increments/decrements of generation or demand. The SO will call on these in price order as far as possible to obtain system balance at least cost.

Capturing Data for Settlement

Whatever process is in place it is necessary to capture data for retrospective settlement. This will consist of bid data, the results of price setting studies and also instructions given by the SO on target output or the use of ancillary services to control system frequency or voltage. Because of the very large sums of money involved, accuracy and an auditable process are essential requirements. It is also necessary to maintain strict data confidentiality to protect commercial interests and manage the market openly and without bias.

2.4 MARKET IMPLEMENTATION

The market preference is to trade standard products unfettered by any physical constraints so as to maximise liquidity. Whatever form the market activities and trading eventually take, it reaches the stage of becoming physical when trading risk crystallises as the outcome becomes known and deliveries have to be made. From this point the power system has to be operated in accordance with the physical laws as apply to electricity. This requires the balance of supply and demand in real time whilst observing any physical transmission constraints. At 'gate closure' the market is required to advise the SO on what contracts have been put in place and their point of entry/exit from the network. Following gate closure the SO will be responsible for buying balancing services from participants to maintain stable/secure system operation. Gate closure is typically one hour before the event when participants have to declare their physical position. Examples of how trades and prices are established and transmission constraints are managed are described below.

The Pool

This is the first step taken by many utilities to introduce competition in that it constitutes a fairly simple transition from the pre-liberalisation practice. All generation is required to bid prices into the pool at the day-ahead stage with a declared availability and a set of dynamic plant parameters. These would be fed into a unit commitment algorithm that was traditionally used to establish the optimum schedule of generation to meet the expected demand. The algorithm would take account of any dynamic plant constraints affecting the use of generation as well as transmission limitations and establish the least cost use of generation to meet the expected demand with some reserve. In the UK the algorithm used to schedule generation was called GOAL and the same algorithm was used to manage pool operation by substituting generation prices for what had previously been heat rates and fuel costs. The result of the schedule provided a list of selected generation and running periods to minimise the overall cost of production based on the prices submitted.

To manage transmission constraints, two schedules were performed at the day-ahead stage: the first, called the 'Unconstrained Schedule', ignored transmission constraints; the second, the 'Constrained Schedule', scheduled generation so as to avoid exceeding defined physical import/export limits from constrained zones of the system. The generators selected in the schedule would be paid for their energy at the System Marginal Price. Where in practice a selected generator has to be constrained off then it would be paid its lost profit. Where a generator has to be brought on out of merit then it would be paid bid price. To enable suppliers to minimise their risk they could establish 'Contracts for Differences' (CfDs) with generators whereby the payments were fixed in advance. Although all monies had to pass through the mandatory Pool the differences between these payments and the contract strike price would be exchanged outside the pool, enabling the supplier to remove the price risk.

For example, assume that a generator bids into the pool a price for the day of £27/MWh. The average pool marginal price is calculated to be £30/MWh so

How contracts for differences work

the generator is selected to run. The supplier places a CfD with the generator for a fixed 100 MW for the day at a price of 27.5/MWh. We can calculate the generator and supplier payments to the pool and those between each other. Assume that the pool buying and selling prices are equal.

The generator gets paid by the pool for $100*24$ MWh at £30/MWh, i.e. £72 000.

The supplier pays the pool for the energy it takes at £30/MWh which is also £72 000.

Outside the pool the generator has to repay the supplier the difference between the strike price and what was paid into the pool by the supplier, i.e.

$$100*24*(30-27.5) = £6000.$$

The net price paid by the supplier is then

$$£72\,000-£6000 = £66\,000.$$

This is equivalent to a unit price of $66\,000/(100*24) = £27.5/MWh$, i.e. the contract strike price.

Multi-market (Bilateral Trading/Exchange Balancing Market)

Whereas the Gross Pool was mandatory and required all energy to be traded through the pool, in this model central bidding is optional and usually enabled by trading through exchanges. The model is sometimes referred to as the 'net pool' or 'multi-market' model enabling all forms of trading. This model allows generators and suppliers to establish bilateral deals for most of their energy outside the central pool. The only requirement is that these deals are declared to the System Operator as contractual volumes with their physical location to enable overall system balancing and settlement. Balance Responsible Parties (BRPs) have to be previously registered to participate in this process. It effectively formalises the contracting that was previously enabled through CfDs. The transactions will take place at the day-ahead stage or earlier, with information passed to the System Operator (SO) to enable any constraint issues to be reviewed. Where constraints are active, either the participants will adjust their trades or the SO will make deals to shift generation/demand to offset the constraints during the daily operation. In the Nordpool, model participants can enter bilateral trade details and the generation and demand side price submissions are balanced. If the initial solution gives rise to constraint violation then the market may be split to establish a new balance point in each area that does not violate the constraint.

Following 'gate closure' no further bilateral deals can be declared and the SO will administer the central Balancing Market to effect stable system operation by buying balancing services from generators or the demand side.

Single Buyer (SB)

In this market model all the energy and services are procured by a nominated body, the Single Buyer, on behalf of end users. This will usually be realised through Power Purchase Agreements (PPAs) established between the Single Buyer and generating stations or groups of stations. These will define the generation characteristics and the payments to be made for availability and energy. In some implementations in the Middle East, fuel is provided as part of the contract based on declared heat rate characteristics or the generator may procure fuel directly and recharge the SB through the energy rates. The contracts may also include the delivery of desalinated water in conjunction with power. The single buyer sells energy on to distributors/suppliers against a Bulk Supply Tariff. Problems can occur when the predicted costs are in error and inconsistent with the previously declared BST. It is important to check the sensitivity of the predicted costs to generation availability. Simulation studies of the year ahead operation should be adjusted to test the impact of reduced availability. In Spain problems have occurred due to hydro shortfalls. In Oman reduced availability of gas fired generation forced the use of more expensive diesel. It can also be difficult to adhere correctly to the intent of the contract during real time operation where there are several different operating regimes.

Open IPP Access

An intermediate step to liberalisation is for a state utility to put in place mechanisms to encourage new entry by independents. This may take the form of a PPA or arrangements may be put in place to enable the IPP to establish bilateral deals. The IPP will not have the mixture of generation resources to balance generation with its contracted demand at all times so there is also an option to 'spill' energy to the system or buy 'makeup' against declared prices. The makeup price may be based on best new entry prices or a price profile predicted from an operational planning study. The spill energy may be paid for at the price of the fuel saved. This type of arrangement has been put in place in the Republic of Ireland and also Greece where there is a single dominant player.

2.5 PRICE ANALYSIS

This section provides an insight into those factors that affect practical price outturn and explains the differences between countries. The European Union have been promoting an open competitive market based on the multi-market model and have been striving for several years to establish a pan-European market with level prices.

Figure 2.2 shows how monthly base load prices have developed across Europe since January 2002; it can be seen that they have not converged. The general rise in prices is primarily linked to fuel price increases as shown in Figure 2.3, with increased volatility towards the end of the period linked to shortfalls in capacity. New entry prices shown as dashed are for gas fired generation with a nominal efficiency of 52%. It can be seen that prices have risen above new entry towards the end of the period but there will always be a lag before new plant comes into service. The other factor influencing the price rise is the introduction of a European Trading Scheme resulting in prices for emission credits being included in the energy price. Prices in Germany France and the UK track each other at a low level, being influenced by low priced

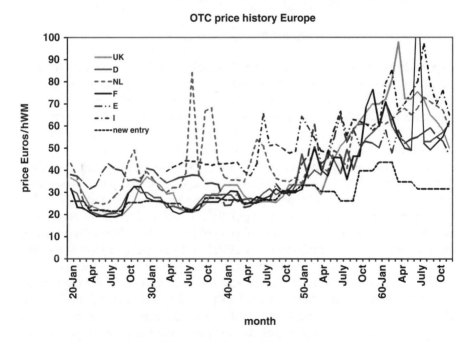

Figure 2.2   Monthly market base load price history for Europe

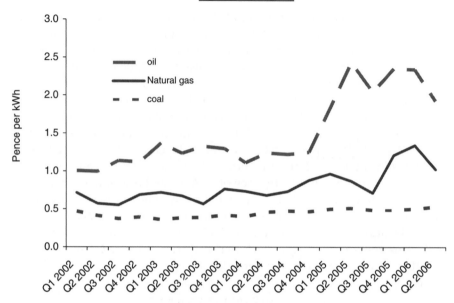

Figure 2.3   Fuel price history

exports from French nuclear stations. The high price spikes around July 2003 occurred during the Dutch holiday period when a lot of generation is taken out of service for maintenance, resulting in shortfalls. Prices in Italy are generally the highest due to the use of expensive oil fired generation at the margin. Prices in Spain were also high but have gradually reduced with the introduction of new gas fired combined cycle generation.

Figure 2.3 shows typical fuel prices across Northern Europe in equivalent pence/kWh with oil prices about twice those of coal and gas prices somewhere in between. World coal prices can be seen to be relatively stable throughout this period, based principally on supplies from Australia and South Africa. The prices delivered to particular stations will be influenced by inland transport costs and stations built close to mines will clearly benefit. Coal stocks at power stations also help to stabilise prices. More recently, world coal prices have risen due to an escalating demand for freight from China but this will not have affected locally supplied coal. In contrast, oil prices are very volatile and heavily influenced by variations in supply and demand. Perceived risks of supply interruption and the political position in supplying countries will affect short term prices. Gas prices are traditionally linked to oil prices and are therefore subject to similar levels of volatility. It has been suggested that gas prices would be better linked to a mixture of coal and oil prices, particularly as it mainly competes with coal in power generation.

The other dominant market model in Europe is that applied in Scandinavia, i.e. Nordpool. This is designed to enable full demand side participation. A typical bid structure is illustrated in Table 2.3 for a supplier with nine blocks of in-house generation available at the prices shown. The total supplier demand for each hour is shown to the right of the table together with a reserve provision of 824 MW. The block bid prices and associated MW values are shown for each hour where the price is that which the supplier is prepared to buy at or sell in increasing price order. If the market clearing price is zero, then the supplier would take all 18 660 MW from the market. If the price is 5.7/ MWh then it is cheaper to supply 220 MW from internal generator block 1 at 5.6/MWh. At a price of 9.9/MWh it is cheaper to meet all local demand using internal generation. There is now surplus generation at higher prices that can be sold at the weighted average cost of production of each block making up the bid. It can be seen through this process how the demand participates in setting the marginal price in competition.

The aggregate volumes of all bids to buy and sell energy are plotted against their price as shown in Figure 2.4. The intersection of the two aggregate curves sets the market clearing price for a particular period and also the accepted bids to buy and sell energy.

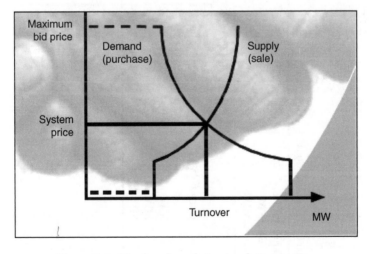

Figure 2.4 Nordpool market price determination

Table 2.3 Nordpool bid

Generator block	1	2	3	4	5	6	7	8	9	Reserve	
available MW	220	3690	250	1400	15540	3450	3510	1900	340	824	
price €/MWh	5.6	7	7.2	8.1	9.8	10.5	11.3	15.1	140		

hour	price €/MWh										local demand	total
		0	5.7	7.1	7.3	8.2	9.9	10.5	11	11.8		
1	MW	18660	18440	14750	14500	13100	0	-2440	-5890	-9400	17836	18660
2	MW	18540	18320	14630	14380	12980	0	-2560	-6010	-9520	17716	18540
3	MW	18374	18154	1464	14214	12814	0	-2726	-6176	-9686	17550	18374

2.6 SUMMARY

This chapter has described the participants in the market and outlines their roles and how they interact. It described the key market mechanisms that are common amongst the various implementations, including: setting market clearing prices, securing generation availability, accommodating transmission constraints, enabling demand side participation, balancing the system, capturing data for settlement and calculating payments. The operational stages of markets were outlined as well as how these have developed in the light of experience from the mandatory pool through to the optional multi-market model with a central balancing mechanism. It has shown that there is scope for evolution of a market rather than disruptive revolutionary change.

The last section illustrated how prices have developed and discussed some of the reasons for the differences across Europe. It is shown how the plant mix results in different generation operating at the margin and setting the price. Finally, an illustration of the Nordpool model is used to show how the demand side can participate in setting prices.

Two

The Cost Chain

This part develops the cost chain that contributes to end user prices. It covers the costs of conventional and renewable generation and the impact of emission restrictions. The basis for transmission and distribution costs is developed and it is illustrated how these contribute to the charging structures. Finally it is shown how all the cost elements combine to make up end user prices.

Chapter 3 Basic Generation Costs

This describes the calculation of basic generator costs taking account of the capital costs, fuel costs and calorific values, the efficiency of the boiler/turbine unit, and the unit auxiliary energy requirements. The impact of part loading on efficiency is explained and how the plant utilisation affects the fixed cost recovery. It describes how the plant mix and fuel availability impacts on the marginal prices across the European countries.

Chapter 4 Alternative Generation Costs

This builds up the costs of alternative and renewable generation sources including nuclear, hydro, wind, biomass, CHP and waste to energy. It describes the various incentive and subsidy arrangements employed to encourage the development of renewable sources to meet government targets.

Chapter 5 Emission Costs

This discusses the impact of restrictions on emissions on the costs of generation and how these affect the different plant types. The approach to containing emissions is discussed, including the European Trading Scheme (ETS) and the National Allocation Plans (NAPS).

Chapter 6 Transmission Costs

This outlines the approach to transmission costing and tariffs for charging for use of system based on asset costs and losses. Network security issues are discussed and the approach to planning and financing new transmission.

Chapter 7 Distribution Costs

This illustrates how tariffs for use of distribution systems are built taking account of asset costs and losses. The impact of the customer demand profile on distribution charges is shown with reference to the Eurostat definition of customer types.

Chapter 8 End User Charges and Prices

This shows how the generation, transmission and distribution charges combine to make up end user tariffs. The impact of distributed generation on the networks is discussed and how this is leading to a requirement for more active network management.

3

Basic Generation Energy Costs

3.1 INTRODUCTION

End consumer costs include charges for the production of energy at the wholesale level together with bulk transmission costs and local distribution costs. While the costs of energy receive most attention in the press, this is only a part of the end user charges. The larger consumers will be connected at higher voltages with high load factors and asset utilisation and will have rates close to the wholesale prices. However, the smaller commercial and domestic consumer connected at low voltage will employ both distribution and transmission assets and have a low load factor. The relative end user costs are illustrated in Figure 3.1. It can be seen that for the domestic consumer the network charges may exceed the basic energy charge. Although network losses are also a function of energy charges, a rise in energy charges should have only a proportional impact on end user prices. The wholesale price element is dictated by generation production costs and these are discussed in this chapter for different technologies and levels of utilisation. It is important in any comparison of the cost of different technology types to clarify the assumptions on which they are based, particularly the fuel price, the plant utilisation and project life.

Power Markets and Economics: Energy Costs, Trading, Emissions   Barrie Murray
© 2009 John Wiley & Sons, Ltd

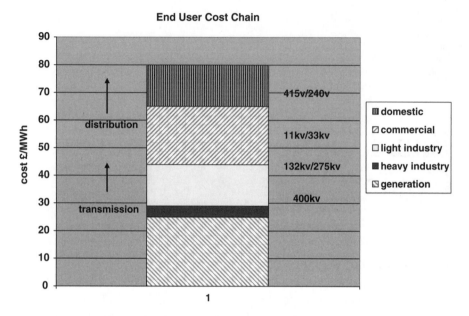

Figure 3.1   End user cost chain

3.2 COST COMPONENTS

The costs of generation that need to be recovered from the sale of energy through the life of the plant will include:

- the capital costs of the plant and interest incurred during construction expressed as an annuity or annual charge;
- the cost of fuel used in the production of energy that is exported and used internally by plant auxiliaries;
- the fixed operating costs, e.g. staff, insurance and transport, which do not vary with the plant utilisation;
- the variable operating costs, e.g. maintenance material and labour costs, which will be influenced by the plant utilisation and wear and tear.

The **output** of the plant to the grid is calculated by taking the declared unit capacity minus the energy used by the station auxiliaries. This is typically 8% for coal plant and around 4% for modern gas plant. In this example a gas generator has a gross capacity of 393 MW with a net output of 377 MW and a coal plant of 398 MW with a net output of 366 MW. The annual energy supplied will be influenced by the availability or utilisation of the station. This will never be 100% because of planned and forced outages, as well as the fact that the plant is not being selected to run in merit order[1]. This is initially assumed to be 85% in the worked example. The gas plant annual output to the grid in TWh will be given by:

$$377 \text{ MW} * 8760 \text{ h} * 0.85/100000 = 2.81 \text{ TWh}.$$

The capital costs will be dependent on: the mixture of debt and equity used to finance the plant, termed the debt/equity ratio; the life expectancy of the installation; and the expected debt and equity rates. The effective interest rate or weighted average cost of capital (WACC) is derived by averaging the rates for debt and equity in proportion to their contribution. These rates will vary from country to country and need to be established taking account of the project location. In this example, rates of 4.7% are assumed for debt and 7% for equity with a debt/equity ratio of 0.8. The WACC is then given by:

$$0.444 * 4.7 + 0.556 * 7 = 6.0.$$

The project life is used in calculating the required annual return using an annuity calculation. If the interest rate 'i' equals the WACC/100 and the project life is 'Y', then for capital cost 'C' the capital charge per year is given by:

$$\frac{c * i (1 + i)^Y}{(1 + i)^Y - 1}.$$

For example, given total investment costs of £147.65 m for a gas plant and assuming a 6%WACC and a project life 'y' = 18, then it can be shown that the capital costs would be £13.6 m/yr or £4.84/MWh.

The cost of fuel will be related to market rates, including the transport costs to the plant. The fuel prices are usually quoted in units generally used in that sector. For example coal is usually quoted in £/ton. As the calorific value[2] (CV) of coal can vary widely, this needs to be established for the particular fuel source. In the example shown in the spread sheet the cost of coal is £30/t with a calorific value of 24 GJ/t giving a price/GJ of £1.25/GJ. The efficiency for this typical coal plant is assumed to be 37.6%. The GJ are converted to MWh by

---

[1] The merit order is obtained by listing generation in order of their costs, starting with the cheapest.

[2] CV or calorific value gives the energy content of a fuel per unit of weight, e.g giga-joules/ton.

multiplying by 3600/1000, giving a price for fuel of:

Coal cost $= (1.25 * 3600/1000)/0.376 = £11.97/MWh$.

In the case of gas, the price is often referenced in p/therm with a net calorific value allowing for losses during the combustion process. Modern CCGT gas plant typically has efficiencies in excess of 50% and, in this example, 54.2% is assumed. The basic fuel cost is assumed to be 23.4 p/therm with a CV of 29.32 kWh/therm. The gas gross/net CV ratio is assumed to be 1.11. The fuel cost is then given by:

Gas cost $= 1.11 * (23.4/29.32)/0.542 = 1.63$ p/kWh or $£16.3/MWh$.

The fixed operating costs are to cover principally staff costs, transport, communication, insurance and consumables. The staff costs are calculated from the labour rate (£16.66/h) times the number of shift staff (6) for 8760 h, assuming full shift cover. The labour rate is inflated by 28% to cover other staff costs such as superannuation for pensions. For gas plant the costs are given by:

Staff costs $= 1.28 * 16.66 * 6 * 8760$ h$/1\,000\,000 = £1.12$ m/yr.

The other fixed costs for consumables are estimated at £0.562 m, equivalent to a cost of £0.2/MWh for gas giving a total fixed operating cost of:

Fixed costs $= 0.2 + 1.12/2.81 = £0.6/MWh$.

The variable costs are principally to cover maintenance material and associated labour costs. The maintenance interval and costs will vary with plant utilisation. In this example the costs are estimated at £0.81 m for materials and £1.25 m for labour for the assumed utilisation of 85%. This gives a total O&M cost of £2.06 m for a full year or £0.73/MWh and will vary in line with utilisation of the plant

The total costs for gas plant are established by adding the capital cost of £4.84/MWh, the fixed O&M costs of £0.6/MWh, the variable costs of £0.73/MWh and the fuel costs of £16.34/MWh giving a total of £22.5/MWh. The total cost calculation is shown in Table 3.1 for typical gas and coal plant.

There will be other costs incurred depending on the location of the plant and its operating regime. There will be a charge for use of the transmission system that will depend on the apportionment of costs between the generation and supply side in the particular market. These will also be start up and shut down costs dependant on the operating regime of the generator.

Table 3.1 Generation costs

		Units	Gas	Coal
Plant	capacity MW	MW	393	398
	capacity Net	MW	377	366
	load factor %	%	85	85
	annual output	TWh	2.81	2.73
	construction time yrs	yrs	2	4
	project life	yrs	18	25
Fuel	Efficiency %	%	54.2	37.6
	coal cost delivered	£/t		30
	coal calorific value	GJ/t		24
	Natural gas cost	£/mmBTU	2	
	Natural gas cost delivered	pence/therm	23.4	
	N Gas calorific value	kWh/therm	29.32	
	N Gas grossCV/netCV		1.11	
Finance	Cost of dept	%	4.7	4.7
	cost of equity	%	7	7
	inflation	%	2.4	2.4
	Debt/equity split		0.8	0.8
	WACC (D/E = 0.8)	%	6.0	6.0
Cap Costs	site &dev	£m	8.733	17.46
	EPC contract	£m	111.33	245
	Electrical conn	£m	0.533	0.533
	gas connection	£m	2.466	
	spares	£m	14.33	31.86
	interest during const.	£m	10.26	23.20
	total investment cost	£m	147.7	318.1
	capital cost	£/kW	376	799
	capital cost	£/m	13.60	24.80
O&M	consumables	pence/kWh	0.02	0.113
	labour rate	£/hr	16.66	16.66
	no of operators		6	14
	operators labour * 1.28	£M	1.12	2.62
	maintenance material	£M	0.81	2
	main & support labour	£M	1.25	2.33
Summary	capital cost	£/MWh	4.84	9.10
	fixed O&M	£/MWh	0.60	2.09
	Var O&M	£/MWh	0.73	1.59
	Fuel costs	£/MWh	16.34	11.97
	Total Generation costs	**£/MWh**	**22.52**	**24.74**

3.3 PRACTICAL OPERATING EFFICIENCIES

The efficiencies quoted by generation suppliers will usually reflect the most favourable operating conditions with units operating at a steady full load. In practice, units will operate for some time at part load and may have to regulate output to track demand. For a typical 500 MW unit the thermal output is given as 1195 MW. This is normally expressed in terms of the heat rate or kJ of energy required per kWh produced and in this case would give a gross heat rate of:

$$3600*1195/500 = 8604 \text{ kJ/kWh.}$$

The boiler efficiency will be of the order of 91%, increasing the heat rate to 8604/0.91 or 9455 kJ/kWh, equivalent to an efficiency of:

$$3600/9455 = 38\%.$$

The energy required for auxiliaries is assumed to be 4%, further increasing the heat rate to 9833 kJ/kWh. An additional 1% is added to cover the inevitable part load operation during start up and shut down giving a net heat rate of 9931 kJ/kWh or an effective efficiency of 36.2%.

For units that are required to regulate and operate at part load for longer periods the impact of part loading will be more significant. The heat requirement will have a fixed no-load element largely associated with heat losses from the installation and a variable element associated with boiler throughput.

The graph in Figure 3.2 shows the degradation of efficiency of an actual CCGT plant operating at percentages of full load. The graph can be approximated to a fixed no load heat of 9% with the rest being a function of load, i.e.

$$\text{Part load efficiency} = 100*\text{load}\%/(9 + 0.91*\text{load}\%).$$

For example the efficiency and cost of a gas fired unit when operating at 40% of full load can be calculated. Assuming a full load efficiency = 54.2% and full load cost of £22.5/MWh at 40% load, the efficiency is reduced to = 100*40/(9 + 0.91*40) = 88% of that at full load, i.e. 88% of 54.2 = 47.7%, resulting in a part load unit cost of £25.5/MWh as opposed to £22.5/MWh at full load (22.5 * 54.2/47.7).

A similar curve can be constructed for coal plant with a 625 MW unit having a no load heat cost of £696/h and an incremental cost of £12.81/MWh. In this case the no load heat is some 10% of the total heat requirement with the result shown in Figure 3.3.

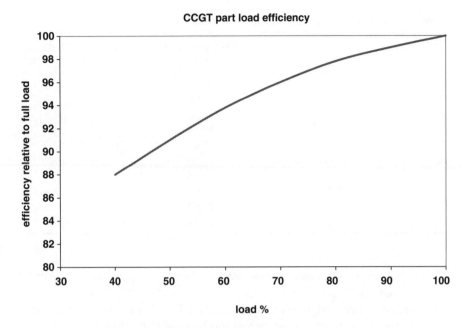

Figure 3.2 Part load efficiency

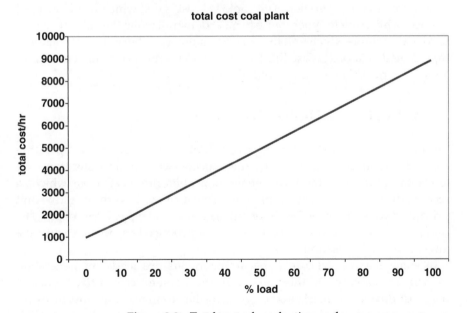

Figure 3.3 Total cost of production coal

Table 3.2 Coal plant part load variable unit costs

Load	Total cost	Effective unit cost	Effective efficiency ratio
10	1697	27.15	52.5
20	2497	19.98	71.3
30	3298	17.59	81.0
40	4099	16.39	86.9
50	4899	15.68	90.9
60	5700	15.20	93.7
70	6500	14.86	95.9
80	7301	14.60	97.5
90	8102	14.40	98.9
100	8902	14.24	100.0

Table 3.2 shows the calculations used to derive a typical generator total variable cost function.

The variable unit cost at full load of £14.24/MWh is sometimes referred to as the **Table 'A'** costs whilst the incremental cost of 12.81/MWh is referred to as the **Table 'B'** cost. These costs are used to establish the **Merit Order** of generation used in operation. The Table 'A' cost is that which would be used to select which unit to synchronise to meet demand, while the Table 'B' cost is used to determine which unit to load first. In practice, the unit cost function is represented as a piece-wise linearised function with several incremental or Table 'B' prices that are monotonically increasing.

3.4 IMPACT OF UTILISATION ON COSTS

The full generation costs including recovery of the fixed capital and operating costs are significantly affected by the expected generation utilisation. The lower the utilisation, the fewer generation units produced from which to recover the fixed costs. The graph of Figure 3.4 shows how the effective unit price increases at lower levels of utilisation for a typical gas plant. The proportion of fixed costs added to each unit produced has to increase at the lower levels of utilisation.

In some market structures specific payments are made for generation capacity availability and this makes a contribution to recover fixed costs. In the most developed markets the generator has to manage all cost recovery through unit sales. This requires a judgement as to what level of utilisation

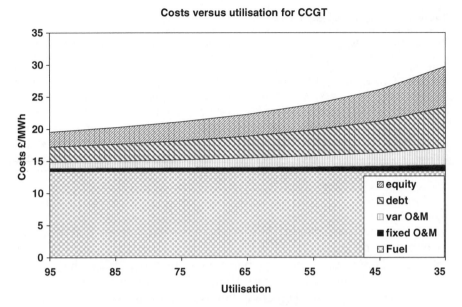

Costs versus utilisation for CCGT

Figure 3.4   Impact of utilisation on cost

might be expected from price bids into the market. To manage this risk the generators will establish contracts with suppliers against specified operating regimes. The simplest contract is termed 'base load' for continuous supply at a specified load. The second common contract is termed 'peaking' and is for supply during 12 daylight hours during week days. These contract forms help generators to establish their prices so as to recover fixed costs.

3.5 COMPARISON OF GENERATION COSTS

The analysis described in this section is sufficient to enable the costs of different types of generation to be compared. In deciding the optimum generation type factors such as cost, fuel diversity and security, and site availability will be important. The object is to establish a **'plant mix'** that will best meet the needs of the business in the longer term. The mix will include some plant designed for base load that may have high capital costs but low operating costs, such as nuclear, together with peaking plant such as open cycle gas turbines that have low capital costs but have higher operating costs. The problem can be formulated as a mixed integer linear programme and this was the practice of state utilities. In the liberalised markets the share of the

Table 3.3 Generation capital costs

Replacement costs		Belgium	France	Germany	Netherlands	UK
Nuclear	€/kW	€1769	€1525	€1771	€2028	€1783
Hydro/Geothermal	€/kW	€2059	€2045	€2138	€2598	€2149
Solid Fuel	€/kW	€1057	€1049	€1082	€1284	€1088
Gas	€/kW	€541	€537	€546	€633	€550
Oil	€/kW	€865	€859	€879	€1031	€884
Renewables	€/kW	€1433	€1423	€1477	€1774	€1484
Other	€/kW	€1433	€1423	€1477	€1774	€1484

future demand is less predictable and there is a volume risk that has to be managed to minimise the probability of over or under contracting for capacity. There is also a need to manage the fuel price risk with diversity in supplies to minimise the impact of changes in price differentials.

A market structure that is preferred in some countries, particularly where significant development is in progress, is the 'Single Buyer' model. In this structure a single organisation is responsible for purchasing energy from the generation sector on behalf of all system users. This enables the development of the plant mix to be managed while introducing competition into generation. Key parameters in making choices are the capital costs, future relative delivered fuel prices and expected generation utilisation. Table 3.3 shows some typical capital costs in Euros for the various plant types (at 2006). Since that time the costs have increased due to the rise in the price of steel, with wind power now at in excess of €2000/kW. The variation between countries is partly the result of different local labour costs associated with construction. There will also be variations in the capital costs between countries. The project life will vary between plant types with many hydro schemes still in service after sixty years while coal is typically 40–45 years before major refurbishment and gas expected to be shorter at perhaps 30–35 years.

Future fuel prices are particularly difficult to predict with increased volatility in recent years as can be seen from the graph of Figure 3.5 with prices expressed on a common pence/kWh basis. Gas prices have traditionally been linked to those of oil and are also therefore influenced by changes in the dollar exchange rate. World delivered coal prices are affected by freight charges with South Africa and Australia as key suppliers. The world demand for freight has recently increased due to the needs of China, with prices rising significantly and affecting delivered coal prices.

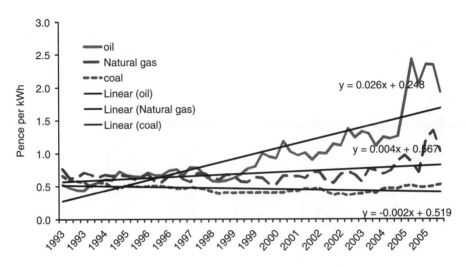

Figure 3.5 Fuel price trends

Forecasting fuel price is usually based on a mixture of long and short term trends. The difficulty is illustrated by the linear trends as shown on the graph of Figure 3.5 where the correlation is poor. The forecasting process has to be coupled with specific analysis of the future supply and demand and the production cost profile for the lead fuel suppliers. Models will usually include cross-linking between fuels. Gas delivery may be by pipeline or as LNG (Liquid Natural Gas), depending on the distances involved. An additional factor linked to fuel prices is the carbon content and CO_2 emission from its utilisation. The emission from coal plant is higher than that from gas fired generation as detailed in Chapter 5. This skews the comparison of plant types depending on the price of emission allowances in the market.

Forecasting fuel prices for a particular country involves identification of the sources of supply and their proportional contribution. This could be a mixture of local lignite with some imported international coal, as in Greece and Turkey. Whereas the international coal will incur transport costs, the lignite is mined locally, close to the power station where it is used. Gas fired generation is undergoing considerable expansion in Southern Europe in Spain, Portugal and Italy. It may be based on piped Russian or Algerian gas or imported LNG. Gas prices are currently linked to oil prices in Europe

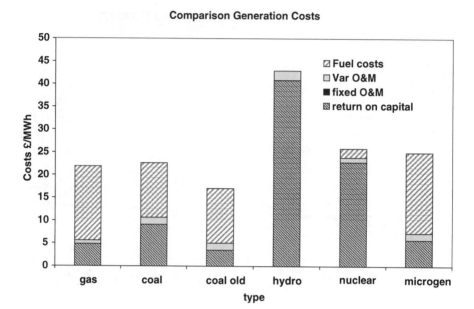

Figure 3.6   Comparative generation costs

through a 6 : 1 relationship where 1 MBtu of gas is priced at a sixth of the price of a barrel of oil. This can be explained by comparing the price per GJ.

> 1 tonne of oil contains 41.87 GJ.
> Assuming 6.6 barrels/tonne gives 6.34 GJ/barrel.
> Since 1 MmBtu is equivalent to 1.055 GJ,
> 1 MBtu is equivalent to $1.055/6.34 = 1/6$ of a barrel of oil.

In general, fuel prices are related through their energy content. When predicting prices the fuel cost/unit needs to be established as well the supply mixture and the calorific value. Locally mined lignite may appear very cheap with the price expressed in currency/ton but may have a very low calorific value.

In drawing comparisons between plant options, investors will usually assume optimistic levels of utilisation of generation even up to 100%. This is unrealistic and forced outages and planned maintenance result is typical utilisation levels of 85%. In competitive markets the utilisation will depend on market share and only a limited number of units can expect to operate base load throughout the year. To secure this role will usually necessitate a discount over the market forward price curve of perhaps 5%.

In practice there is never a new green field situation and there will be an existing stock of generation competing in the market. This generation will already have written down capital costs and can be refurbished without incurring full civil works and infrastructure costs. New entry generation has to compete, while recovering all the fixed and variable costs and entry will only occur when the market price rises sufficiently high. The histogram of Figure 3.6 shows the results of a typical analysis of costs and includes old refurbished coal plant with written off capital and new plant. It can be seen that coal refurbishment is an attractive option where capital charges are small having been partly written off with a lower expenditure to improve efficiency. The hydro costs appear high because the stations are assumed to have only a 33% load factor whereas for other stations 85% is assumed. The micro-generation costs credit the plant with a 50% efficiency to take some account of the potential to make use of waste heat. Care is required in making simple comparisons because of the large number of assumptions that have to be made including fuel price, utilisation, WACC and project life.

3.6 INTERNATIONAL COMPARISONS

The differences between power prices in each country can be explained by identifying the generation that is most expensive but needed to meet the expected demand. This will vary throughout the year and depend on the plant mix in each country. Figure 3.7 shows the type of generation that can be expected to be operating at the margin in each country through a typical year, including coal small, medium and large, open and closed cycle gas turbines,

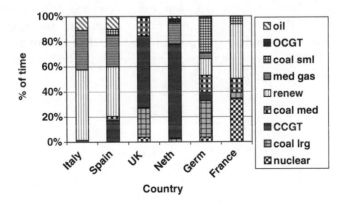

Figure 3.7   Plant at margin

renewable, and nuclear. Prices in Italy are high because expensive oil generation is operating at the margin for a significant proportion of the year. A similar situation exists in Spain, although more recently much of the oil generation has been replaced by a cheaper combined cycle gas fired generation. Prices in France are cheapest due to a high proportion of nuclear and hydro generation. Prices in Germany are also relatively low with a lot of generation based on locally mined coal. In the UK and the Netherlands marginal price is also set by gas fired generation, although some of the Dutch gas generation is older and less efficient.

Interconnections between countries have been used to export from the cheaper areas to the more expensive. France is the biggest exporter in Europe with some 6 GW continuously supplied to Italy, the UK and Germany. These transfers are not sufficient to create a pan-European market and price convergence. This is unlikely to be realised until an EHV super-grid is built linking the regions with harmonisation of access arrangements. The price differentials between countries influence the auction prices paid to reserve cross-border transmission access rights.

3.7 SUMMARY

This chapter has developed a methodology for calculating the costs of generation, including fuel, capital and other fixed and variable operating costs. It developed a practical assessment of generation operational efficiency taking account of auxiliary needs and part load operation. It has highlighted the impact of part load operation on efficiency and effective unit costs. It has also been shown how lower levels of utilisation impact on costs because of the need to spread the fixed costs over fewer units generated. A comparison is drawn between the cost of generation types to illustrate the difficulties of predicting fuel prices and making assumptions about key parameters such as utilisation. Finally, it was shown how the different generation stock in each country affects the marginal prices.

4

Alternative Energy Sources

4.1 INTRODUCTION

Concerns with global warming have accelerated, with the power sector as a focus of attention for reducing emissions. In practice this means burning less coal, gas and oil and substituting these with renewable and alternative energy sources with lower emission levels. The development of alternative and renewable sources of energy is being widely promoted across Europe and most countries have set targets for a proportion of their energy to be provided from renewable sources. The targets are generally to increase the proportion by 1% a year reaching 10% by 2010. More recently new targets have been proposed by the EU referred to as 20:20:20 and requiring a 20% reduction in CO_2 emissions (compared with 1990 levels) with 20% of energy from renewable sources by 2020. The bulk of the burden for achieving the reduction is generally placed on the power sector and this could mean that, to realise these targets, up to 40% of electrical energy may need to come from renewable sources.

The mechanisms used to create incentives vary; in the UK suppliers have to obtain a Renewable Obligation Certificate (ROC) or pay a penalty of £30/MWh (rising each year in line with inflation); Italy has 'Green Certificates' that may be traded; Germany used a default price for wind energy of €90/MWh. A related factor that will increase the prospects for wind power further is the EU commitment to reducing carbon emissions. The cost of obtaining permits to emit carbon is expected to increase electricity prices by 15–25%. This general price increase will benefit non-emitting sources like wind. It will also

Power Markets and Economics: Energy Costs, Trading, Emissions Barrie Murray
© 2009 John Wiley & Sons, Ltd

make efficiency improvements more attractive in that fuel costs and CO_2 emissions are reduced. This will encourage the development of more efficient coal and gas plant as well as CHP schemes.

This section analyses the alternative generation options that are being promoted in the interests of protecting the environment. These include renewable sources like hydro, wind, solar, wave and tidal schemes, as well as more efficient generation schemes such as Combined Heat and Power (CHP) and distributed Micro generation and nuclear. The objectives are to:

- establish the overall effective costs of alternative generation sources;
- understand and evaluate the basic arrangements for providing incentives;
- compare the costs with conventional generation.

4.2 COMPETING SOURCES

Nuclear Generation
Nuclear generation constitutes a major source of energy worldwide and currently supplies around 30% of Europe's energy. It has high capital costs and needs to be operated at a high load factor to be economic. It has the advantage that it does not emit CO_2 but there are concerns about radiation associated with failures and, politically, about nuclear technology proliferation. Waste treatment and decommissioning costs are not well established and have recently been revised upwards. Deep burial is economically attractive and may become more acceptable when compared with the potential impact of global warming. The development of the pebble bed reactor offers potentially cheaper and more modular options. If other fuel prices are sustained at high levels nuclear looks economically attractive.

Hydro Capacity
Conventional hydro capacity is already largely exploited across Europe with some 70% already developed. There are some sites in Eastern Europe capable of development as well as a larger number of micro-hydro sites. Any further increase is most likely to come from the refurbishment of existing capacity. In the UK Scottish Power and Scottish and Southern Energy have schemes that will generate a total of 1.5 TWh of qualifying output, or around 4% of the 2010 energy obligation.

Other options being considered are storage schemes, particularly when their operation can be coordinated with wind power to manage the variability.

EDP of Portugal has ambitions to realise a 50% renewable production but it will require agreement to the development of new storage sites. In the UK consideration is being given to a tidal barrier across the Severn estuary where there is a very high tidal reach. It has been estimated that the scheme could produce some 4.5% of UK energy needs or 16 TWh.

Of the still untapped potential, the small hydro plants (SHP) have a better chance of being built than large hydro with reservoirs, which face severe opposition due to their considerable environmental impact. Even the small and mini hydro run-of-the-river plants meet various obstacles. Although feed-in regulations are now in place in almost all European countries, the licensing and contract procedures are cumbersome and time consuming. Opposition from environmental groups, often based more on emotion than rational arguments, has to be countered. Requirements for maintaining a minimum water flow in the river limit the exploitable flow. Demands for the installation of fish ladders or changes in civil structures in line with the natural environment can drive up civil engineering costs to levels where the investment is not economical. An ESHA (European Small Hydro Association) study estimated that, from a purely technical viewpoint, an additional 2100 MW of SHP could be made available by upgrading the existing plants and restarting abandoned ones. Environmental concerns, however, are likely to reduce this volume to around 1.100 MW. The potential for new SHP is estimated theoretically, i.e. without any constraints, to be more than 14.000 MW, mainly made up of the large unexploited capacities in Norway and Switzerland. Taking into account environmental and economic constraints the study assumes a potential of 6.700 MW still to be exploited. Both potentials combined add up to 7.800 MW, which is 62% of present installed SHP capacity. Consequently, despite the high exploitation ratio in Europe there is still scope for further development.

On-shore Wind

It has been claimed that it is theoretically possible to obtain more than three times the UK's electricity requirements from on-shore wind. More realistically, only perhaps 5% of this is practically exploitable – around 50 TWh a year (Source: DTI). This equates to less than one-fifth of the UK's energy requirements and would require close to 20 000 MW of installed capacity or some 6000 machines. Public tolerance, planning restrictions and economics are likely to limit this quantity further. There is expected to be some 3000 MW operational in England, Wales and Scotland by the end of 2007. By 2010 it has been estimated that on-shore wind could contribute around one third of the 2010 obligation and, because of the lower cost, it is expected that the majority of early renewable build will be of this type. Load factors of around 20–25% have been recorded for on-shore sites. The machine size has gradually increased to some 3.3 MW with incurred costs of around £1000–1200/kW but these are increasing in line with steel prices. The main problem with wind power is its variability and the requirement to provide backup using conventional generation.

Off-shore Wind

Higher cost, off-shore sites benefit from higher wind speeds with load factors up to 30% and fewer planning and acceptability issues. As a result, individual turbines can be larger. The economics of off-shore wind energy encourage the development of very large wind turbines in order to justify the additional investment necessary for the more expensive support structures, grid connection and installation procedures. Machines of 3.6 MW were installed in 2007 and the Germans are considering building 5 MW turbines towards the end of the decade to make some of their deep-water sites more viable.

As tolerance to on-shore sites becomes saturated and the lower cost sites are developed, off-shore wind is expected to be the major contributor towards meeting the renewable obligation in the later years of the decade. Studies show that large quantities of off-shore wind generation are available at a competitive cost.

Co-firing Biomass

The rules for ROC accreditation say that a supplier can meet up to 25% of its obligation to purchase energy from renewable sources through co-firing with biomass – that is, burning biomass fuels, such as agricultural and forestry waste or energy crops, alongside coal in a conventional power station. The contribution from co-firing could have a big impact on the ROC market, particularly during the early years. The rules on co-firing require that, from 2006, 75% of the biomass fuel used must come from energy crops – in other words, crops grown specifically for use as a fuel – rather than incidentals arising from agriculture or forestry. The concept is that the energy source is carbon neutral in that the absorption during growing offsets that released through combustion. The eligibility of co-firing was set to end altogether in 2011. However, these restrictions are already under review by the DTI, which is under pressure from some coal generators to renew the arrangement. Co-firing could provide welcome financial relief to coal generators and could make a significant contribution to meet the renewable target.

Local CHP and Waste to Energy

Other potential sources that are expected to develop further are CHP based on local micro-generation, wave power, waste to energy and perhaps tidal schemes. Wave power still looks expensive but is being researched. Local CHP based on micro-generation can be attractive in that it potentially offers much higher efficiency than conventional generation if use can be found for the heat production. The disposal of domestic waste is an increasing problem and waste to energy schemes are an attractive option gaining in popularity.

Solar

There is increasing interest in solar energy in countries with a high number of sunshine hours such as in Southern Europe. Some local authorities are fitting solar panels to their property portfolio. Spain is expected to double its capacity in 2008 and Portugal is expected to complete the world's largest plant at Amareleja. The industry still relies on subsidies or feed in tariffs to realise 'grid parity', i.e. when its cost competes with conventional sources. However, it has been predicted that rising fuel and emission costs will enable solar to compete on equal terms within 4 to 6 years, depending on technology advances.

Polysilicon is the material used to build most solar cells, with the Fluor Corporation expected to be the lead producer. Ascent Solar Technologies are developing the application of CIGS (Copper Indium Gallenium Selenide), which is claimed to be more efficient than polysilicon. They plan to put their cells into a flexible plastic sheet that boosts connectivity and efficiency by 10% at reduced costs. Other companies such as Day 4 Energy of Vancouver are focusing on the development of the solar modules. These developments will reduce the costs of solar energy installations and, coupled with rising fuel prices, trends will accelerate the time when 'grid parity' is reached.

4.3 CURRENT PRODUCTION EUROPE

The installed capacity of the major European countries in 2008 was around 600 GW of which a little over half at 306 GW is thermal with 114 GW of nuclear, 106 GW of hydro and 68 GW of renewable sources. The expected energy production is shown in Figure 4.1, where it can be seen that the thermal production is already matched by energy from hydro, nuclear and renewable sources. The number of additional suitable hydro sites around Europe is limited and has environmental issues. It is not expected that there will be much further hydro development with some 80% already exploited. Some extra hydro output can be expected from the refurbishment of existing older installations.

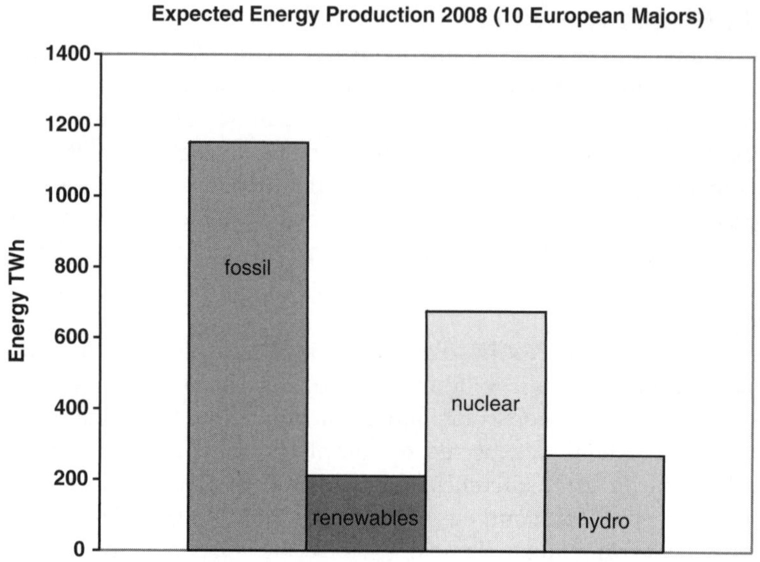

Expected Energy Production 2008 (10 European Majors)

Figure 4.1 Expected energy production 2008 Europe

There is expected to be a significant expansion of on and off-shore wind but this may be restricted due to a number of factors.

• It does not provide firm power and has to be backed up by conventional sources.
• It is environmental intrusive and some projects have been halted.
• There are system operation difficulties in managing the variable output from generation with a high proportion of wind.

Nevertheless on-going development of wind power is expected, albeit at a lower rate than has been forecast.

Given these limitations and high fuel costs, there has been a resurgence of interest in nuclear generation. The UK government has given positive signs that it would like to see the replacement of existing nuclear generation as it becomes life expired and is now even talking of expansion. Unfortunately it has taken a long time to come to this obvious decision and, given the lead time in constructing nuclear, we are likely to see a decline in production for a few years before it grows again. The existing sites are likely to be used and a number of European majors such as EdF, RWE and Eon have expressed an interest in building plant in conjunction with suppliers like AREVA and Siemens. The government have agreed with their French counterparts that they would expedite the planning process. Unfortunately a lot of the UK expertise has been dissipated over the lull years and there will be reliance on imported designs and expertise.

The economics of nuclear begin to look attractive given the prospect of continuing high fuel prices. The waste management looks less of an impediment if deep site burial is accepted and it has been suggested that this may be at an undersea location, perhaps off the cost of Cumbria. Faced with global warming and the prospect of a countryside blighted by thousands of wind farms, the public are becoming much more receptive to the nuclear option. Press reports have heralded the need for 20 000 wind turbines to begin to address the 2020 target (*The Times*, January 2008). If nuclear is allowed to decline there would need to be ten times that number to replace the European nuclear output of some 600 TWh. The other development is expected to be in combined cycle gas generation because of its high efficiency at over 50% and lower CO_2 emissions. Taking these factors into account, the forecast development of capacity is as shown in Figure 4.2. A great deal of new wind capacity is expected as well as high efficiency CHP schemes; nuclear falls a

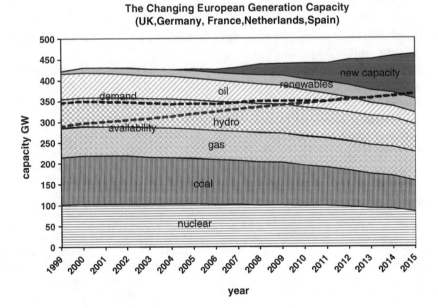

Figure 4.2   Capacity development Europe

little due to closures, then rises with new entry. Combined cycle gas increases while the fall off of coal is gradual with capacity lost due to closures being replaced by more efficient super-critical units or refurbishment.

4.4 INCENTIVE SCHEMES

These schemes are designed to provide an incentive for the development of renewable sources by providing additional revenue over and above that derived from the sale of the energy. They may take the form of a 'feed in' tariff whereby there is a guaranteed income price for a number of years. These schemes do not generally take account of the varying market energy cost but fix the rate for the contract term. Other schemes like the Green Certificate scheme used in Italy progressed from a feed in tariff to a scheme designed to support trading. In accordance with article 6 of Ministerial Decree 11/11/99, GME put in place an organised venue for the trading of Green Certificates (Green Certificates Market – MCV). The provisions governing the operation of the MCV are described in the *Integrated Text of the Electricity Market Rules,* approved by the Minister of Productive Activities on 19 December 2003. The feed in tariff was replaced by Green Certificates in January 2002 as described and illustrated in Table 4.1.

* All producers were required to have certificates for 2% of energy initially growing at 0.35%/yr.
* The MCV has been operational since March 2003 with 91 participants at the end of 2004.
* The size of the Green Certificates traded in the MCV in 2004 was equal to 100 MWh but changed in 2005 to 50 MWh.
* Certified plant includes hydro, wind, biomass, PV, tide, wave built after April 1999.

Table 4.1 Green Certificate prices

Green Certificates (CV)					
reference year	2003	2004	2005	2006	2007
weighted average price (€/MWh)	98.8	116.83	130.85	144.27	116.44
no. of Green Certificates traded	20,419	22921	8065	9801	992
Green Certificates traded (MWh)	100	50	50	50	50
value (million €)	202	134	53	71	6

- GRTN owns certificates for plant that chose the initial feed in tariff.
- There is no formal penalty but a proposal to set it at 1.5 * maximum price paid.
- GRTN sets reference price based on the difference between the average cost of the outputs purchased by GRTN under CIPs and price of electricity.
- Price was €81.1/MWh in 2002; GRTN acts as a reserve and regulates price to encourage new entry.

The mechanisms of the incentive scheme used in the UK can be used to illustrate how the premium associated with the 'green' element of the energy can be valued. The requirement laid down by government in the 2000 Utilities Act is that suppliers have to provide evidence that a percentage of the energy supplied is derived from accredited 'green' renewable sources. This is currently set to rise at roughly one percent each year to 10.4% by 2010 and 15.8% by 2015. Failure to comply with this requirement incurs a penalty payment originally set at £30/MWh. Eligible renewable generators receive Renewable Obligation Certificates (ROCs) for each MWh of electricity generated. These certificates can then be sold to suppliers, in order to fulfil their obligation. Suppliers can either present enough certificates to cover the required percentage of their output, or they can pay a 'buyout' price for any shortfall. The buyout price is set each year by Ofgem, and in 2007/08 stands at £34.30/MWh, with ROC trading administered by the Non-fossil Purchase Agency.

The owner of a wind generator can therefore sell the electricity as well as the ROC certificate. In addition, if the overall government requirement is not met, then the money derived in the form of penalties from those failing to meet their commitment is redistributed amongst qualifying ROC holders. This means that the effective value of the ROC is greater than the avoided cost of £30/MWh. If, for example, only 66% of the target percentage 'green' energy is met, then in effect the total payments are divided amongst 2/3 of the participants, i.e. (30/0.66), giving a ROC value of £45.5/MWh.

The current value of the ROC will depend on the extent to which the target proportion of 'green' energy is being met and was £39.84/MWh at the end of 2006. The overall relationship is as shown below in Figure 4.3, based on a default price of £31.39/MWh as applied during 2005.

The future value of the ROC will depend on the build up of competing renewable sources and equilibrium will be reached when the ROC value together with the electricity price equates with the renewable energy cost.

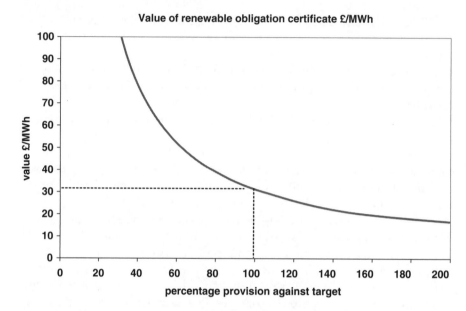

Figure 4.3   ROC mechanism

The UK also has a Climate Change Levy (CCL) of £4.3/MWh on energy supplied from non-renewable sources to commercial customers. This is effectively a tax that renewable and some other accredited sources do not have to pay and they receive a Levy Exemption Certificate (LEC) that may be worth some 80% of the £4.3/MWh (£3.5/MWh) to good quality CHPs that provide energy efficiency.

4.5 MARKET PRICING

The price for the energy from renewable or alternative sources will be influenced by what the market is prepared to pay. In the case of nuclear, because of the high capital costs and low operating costs it is generally preferable to operate it base load. It is also not generally considered to be very flexible and added costs can be introduced due to 'poisoning out' at low load when it takes a long period to restore load. Nuclear output will then preferably be sold against a base load contract. The capacity of a system to accommodate base load will depend on the load duration curve and new nuclear will inevitably displace other plant operating base load that will influence the price.

4.6 THE ECONOMICS OF ALTERNATIVE SOURCES

Nuclear

The capital costs of nuclear, based on recent contracts, is established at around £1750/kW (2008) and a life expectancy of 35 years or more can be expected. This can be seen in Table 4.2 to make up 83% of the total unit costs with low fuel costs. The decommissioning costs are less well established but this is a one-off cost at the end of the period and any provisions made at inception will have accumulated significantly. It should also be noted that a charge of £1/MWh generated will accumulate some £260 k/MW

Table 4.2 Hydro and nuclear costs

		Units	Hydro	Nuclear
Plant	capacity MW	MW	31	400
	capacity Net	MW	30.07	355
	load factor %	%	33	85
	annual output	TWh	0.09	2.64
	construction time yrs	yrs	5	8
	project life	yrs	70	35
	Efficiency %	%		36
Finance	Cost of dept	%	4.7	6
	cost of equity	%	7	10
	inflation	%	2.4	2.4
	Debt/equity split		0.8	0.8
	WACC (D/E = 0.8)	%	6.0	8.2
Cap Costs	site & dev	£m	47.12	12.5
	EPC contract	£m		450
	Electrical conn	£m		0.6
	gas connection	£m		
	spares	£m		12
	interest during const.	£m	11.07	216.00
	total investment cost	£m	58.2	691.1
	capital cost	£/kW	1877	1728
	capital cost pa	£/m	3.53	60.51
Summary	capital cost	£/MWh	40.64	22.89
	fixed O&M	£/MWh	3.2	2.75
	Var O&M	£/MWh	2.06	1
	Fuel costs	£/MWh	0	5.4
	Total Generation costs	**£/MWh**	**45.90**	**32.04**

of capacity over the life of the plant or about 15% of the original capital cost of £1750 k/MW. It is likely that the existing nuclear sites will be retained and new plant built by a large utility able to bear the associated risks. The cost of debt and equity shown in the table is assumed higher to take some account of higher risks. Even so at gas prices above £3/GJ nuclear begins to look competitive. However, the economics of nuclear can be seriously impaired if high levels of utilisation are not maintained due to plant failures. This reduces the contribution to the fixed capital cost, which makes up the bulk of the costs.

Hydro

Hydro is expensive to construct and can have high associated environmental costs. The capital costs at some £1800/kW are not so much higher than other plant but the availability of hydro energy is usually low at 25 to 35%. This leads to much higher costs/MWh as the capital has to be recovered from fewer units generated. Table 4.2 shows that these costs at £40/MWh are about twice those of nuclear. A life expectancy of 75 years for the civil installation is typical, although several phases of plant refurbishment will be required through the lifetime. Because of the effect of discounting future cash flows assuming a project life of 45 years only adds costs of £2.5/MWh. The main problem with further hydro development is establishing finance and overcoming environmental objections.

Wind

The prospects for on-shore and off-shore wind power needs to be evaluated to take account of:

* the value of the energy produced;
* the value attributed to the 'green' element of the energy in the form of a traded ROC or 'Green Certificate';
* the basic cost of building and operating the generator installation;
* analysis of the competing sources for the provision of renewable energy as affects the value of incentives.

Most of the existing installations have been based on shore or in shallow water but there is increasing interest in the development of off-shore wind in deeper waters.

Off-shore Wind

Off-shore projects initially require higher investments than on-shore due to turbine support structures and grid connection. The cost of **grid connection**

Off-shore wind costs

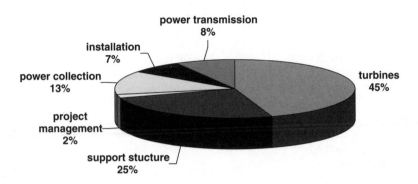

Figure 4.4   Off-shore cost makeup

to the shore is typically around 25% of the total cost, a much higher fraction than for connection of on-shore projects. Other sources of additional cost include foundations (up to 30%), grid connections and adapting the turbines for marine use. In practice, operation and maintenance is proving more expensive with access difficulties reducing the realised availability. One advantage of off-shore location is the higher consistent wind speed resulting in expected load factors of 30%.

The pie chart of Figure 4.4 shows a typical distribution of the capital investment costs, however the water depth and distance to shore can have a significant impact on the distribution of the costs. The similar magnitudes of cost for several different components (wind-turbine, support structure, power collection and transmission, and operation and maintenance (O&M)) emphasises the importance of an integrated approach to the design of the whole wind-farm development.

Investment costs reduced from about 2200 €/kW for the first Danish off-shore wind farms to an estimated cost of 1650 €/kW for Horns Rev (£1137/kW) (equivalent to £49/MWh). However, costs are dependent on the cost of steel and, as this has increased, prices during 2008 have returned to the higher values. Together with the other costs shown in Table 4.3, the unit price rises to £54.8/MWh. In practice maintaining off-shore installations has proved difficult, leading to reduced availability and utilisation. If the load factor realised was only 25% then costs would be €65.5/MWh. At the higher capital cost of £1692/kW the unit cost is £78.7/MWh.

The capital costs for on-shore wind are 25% lower, at £850/kW, with less cost associated with support, installation and grid connection. However the

Table 4.3 Wind power costs

Typical wind data	Off shore	On shore
Unit size MW	3	3
Average load factor	30	25
Annual output MWh	7884	6570
Capital cost £m	3.4	2.6
Capital cost £/kW	1137	852
WACC	7.5	7.5
Project life	15	15
Capital charge £m/yr	0.4	0.3
Capital charge £/MWh	49.0	44.1
Fixed O&M (35 k/yr)	4.4	5.3
Variable O&M £/MWh	1.33	1.2
Total £/MWh	54.8	50.6

load factor is likely to be less at 25% and this gives unit costs of £50.6/MWh for on-shore wind or, at the higher capital cost of £1270/kW, the unit cost is £72.2/MWh.

Micro-generation CHP

By locating generation local to industrial and commercial complexes there is more opportunity to provide a use for heat in the form of hot water or air resulting in very high overall efficiencies. The installation analysed below is based on a 100 kW unit that also produces 167 kW of hot water and 20 kW of hot air. If all this energy can be usefully used the overall effective efficiency rises above 80%.

The left-hand side of Table 4.4 shows the basic data assumptions and the right-hand side the calculations. The calculated results are as follows.

- The running hours are the operating hours times the availability (6200 * 0.95).
- The electrical production is the capacity times the running hours (100 * 5890).
- The hot water production is the boiler output times its operating hours (167 * 6200/1000).
- The hot air production is given by the hot air output time the running hours (20 * 5890/1000).
- The avoided fuel in the boiler is the fuel that would have to be used to produce the hot water at the rated boiler efficiency (1035.4/0.850).

Table 4.4 Micro-generation costs.

			Micro		
T 100 installed (low)	euro, 000	115	Running hours	hrs/y	5890.0
T 100 installed (high)	euro, 000	140	electrical production	MWh	589.0
power production	kW	100	hot water production	MWh	1035.4
T 100 electrical effic.	%	30	hot air recov. prod.	MWh	117.8
Hot water	kW	167	avoided fuel in boiler	MWh	1218.1
Hot air (recovered)	kW	20	MT fuel consumption	MWh	1963.3
Boiler efficiency	%	85			
			income with avoided elec.	euro, 000	51.2
Electricity price	€/MWh	87	income with hot water	euro, 000	30.5
Boiler gas price	€/MWh	25	income with hot air	euro, 000	2.4
CHP gas price	€/MWh	25	MT gas consumption	euro, 000	−49.1
value of hot air	€/MWh	20	MT maintenance	euro, 000	−8.8
MT maintenance	€/MWh	15	**total income/yr**	euro, 000	**26.1**
Operating hours	hrs/yr	6200			
Availabilit	%	95	Payback range from	5.4	4.4

- The machine fuel consumption is given by the electrical output divided by the electrical efficiency (589/0.3).
- The income from the electricity is calculated from the electricity production times the assumed price (589 * 87/1000).
- The income from hot water is based on the production and price that would be paid for production from the boiler at its normal efficiency using gas (1035.4 * 25/0.85).
- The hot air income is given by the production times the assumed value (117.8 * 20/1000).
- The gas consumption cost is given by the fuel used times the gas price (1963.3 * 25).
- The maintenance cost is given by the electricity production times the cost per unit (589 * 15/1000).

The electricity price includes the distribution and transmission charge that would be included in the local distribution charges for electricity and represents the avoided cost. It also includes some 80% of the CCL that together with the basic energy price results in a per unit revenue of €87/MWh as shown in Table 4.5. The hot water is priced on the avoidable cost of the alternative of using gas to heat the boiler directly with an efficiency of 85%.

Table 4.5 Micro-generation unit costs

Electricity price			Production	MWh	Costs	Euros
avoided energy	E/MWh	31.5	electricity	589	capital	14415
CCL tax on energy	E/MWh	3.5	water	1035.4	fuel	49083
Dx charge	E/MWh	42	air	117.8	maintenance	8835
Tx charge	E/MWh	10	total	1742.2	total	72333
total	E/MWh	87	cost E/MWh			41.5

The electricity price includes the distribution(Dx) and transmission (Tx) charge; the table also shows the effective unit cost based on capital, fuel and O&M costs, divided by the total MWh produced and equals €41.5/MWh, assuming that all the water energy is used.

In practice it is often difficult to find a use for all the hot water, particularly through the summer period, without investing in expensive refrigeration installations. For example, if only 50% of the water energy could usefully be used then:

$$\text{Effective energy price} = 73406/(589 + 0.5 * 1035.4 + 117.8)$$
$$= €59.9/\text{MWh}.$$

Waste to Energy

Rising fuel prices have made it more attractive to convert waste to energy. The energy content is assumed in this example to be 10 GJ/t with a conversion efficiency of 27%, giving: $27/100 * 10/3.6 = 0.75$ MWh/t. The operating costs are principally to cover staff and maintenance with additional costs for firing fuel and handling the raw materials and residual waste. Including capital the total costs are £41.2/te[1] (£55/MWh) against revenues of £26.3/te for electricity and £29/te for the ROC and £6/te from recycled materials i.e. £61.2/te or £81.6/MWh. The costs and revenues are itemised in Table 4.6.

4.7 COMPARISONS

The above analysis illustrates the number of key assumptions that can affect the comparison of the alternative generation sources. In the case of wind,

---

[1] te represents a metric ton or 1000 kg and 1 t = 2240 lb, 1 t = 1.016 te.

Table 4.6 Waste to energy costs

Based on Tonnes per annum plant			
Capital cost £ million at April 2006			51
Depreciation period (Years):			15
size k tons/yr			240
GJ/t			10
efficiency			27
MWh/t			0.75
price/MWhr			35
revenue/ton			26.25
ROC/MWh			38.6
ROC/t			29.0
Operating costs £/te		Revenues (£/te)	
Capital: £	20.23	Materials	6
Staff: £	6.97	Nutrients	0
Raw Materials: £	0.65	Electricity	26.3
Maintenance: £	8.49	Heat	0
Utilities: £	0.54	ROC £/t	29.0
Fuel: £	0.38		
Waste disposal: £	3.93		
Total cost/te	**41.19**	**Total/Te**	**61.2**
Input	net rev £/t	**Input 20.0**	

the capital costs and assumed load factor were critical. On-shore wind costs varied from £50.6/MWh, when the utilisation was assumed to have a 25% load factor, up to £57.3/MWh with a 22% load factor (as recorded for a particular site). For off-shore, the figures are £54.8/MWh with a 30% load factor and £65.5/MWh with a 25% load factor. With this level of costs, the generation is only made viable by the sale of the ROC certificate. If higher steel prices and capital costs are assumed, then unit costs range from £72.2/MWh on-shore up to £78.7/MWh for off-shore.

In the case of micro-generation, the overall effective costs are very dependent on the extent to which the hot water can be utilised. If all the water is utilised the effective cost is £42.1/MWh, while if only 50% is utilised the costs are £59.9/MWh.

In the case of waste to energy schemes, the costs are estimated at £41.2/te or £54.9/MWh based on waste with an energy content of 10 GJ/te. If the energy content of the waste is less at 8 GJ/te, then the energy cost rises to £68.7/MWh.

Table 4.7 Distributed generation comparative costs

Technology	Scenario	Cost/MWh	Scenario	Cost/MWh
On-shore wind	L.F. 25%	50.6	L.F. 22%	57.3
Off-shore wind	L.F. 30%	54.8	L.F. 25%	65.5
Micro-gen	80% water	47.1	50% water	59.1
Waste	10 GJ/t	54.9	8 GJ/t	68.7

Table 4.7 illustrates how the variation of key parameters within a credible range shifts the price by typically £7–15/MWh or £25/MWh if higher capital costs are assumed. The average energy price from these alternative sources is £57/MWh, taking all scenarios. This compares closely with the German feed-in tariff of £62/MWh (€90/MWh) for wind power. This makes wind power a viable option if lower capital costs are assumed but not for the higher capital costs currently being experienced, which result in unit costs in excess of £70/MWh.

The UK ROC mechanism provides additional revenue, rather than a feed in tariff, as an incentive. Certificate prices in 2008 were around £39/MWh. This enables this alternative generation to compete in a market with prices set by conventional coal/gas generation with costs around £23–30/MWh (depending on fuel prices). The cost minus the ROC income is then £(70 − 39)/MW, i.e. £31/MWh. If full pass through of the costs of emission allocations is included at £12.9/t CO_2 (€17/t), then coal/gas costs rise to £32–34/MWh. It is only by virtue of this mechanism and the similar arrangements in other countries that wind farms can compete and are being built. It also helps that marginal electricity prices are currently high and in excess of £45/MWh (€60/MWh).

4.8 SUMMARY

This section has described the various types of renewable and sustainable energy sources and the incentive schemes designed to encourage their application. Typical costs have been developed for nuclear and hydro, on-shore and off-shore wind farms, CHP based on micro generation and waste to energy schemes. It has illustrated the dependence on incentives to make renewable schemes viable and the impact on costs of different assumptions on load factor. In the case of CHP, the importance of finding uses for the heat produced is illustrated. The summary table of costs shows that from these sources, with the assumptions made, costs are typically twice those for energy from conventional generation sources such as gas and coal. It is only by virtue of the subsidy arrangements that wind power is being built.

The **Centre for Policy Studies** report in 2008 launched an Exocet at wind generation that has been summarised as:

- Britain faces an energy gap of up 32 GW by 2015 as older coal and nuclear power stations are paid off.
- At the same time, Britain has made a binding commitment to deliver 15% of all its energy consumption from renewable energy sources by 2020.
- Government policy is based on using wind power both to help close the energy gap and to meet its renewable energy targets.
- If the Government is to meet its renewable target, **then the amount of electricity to be generated by wind farms will have to increase by more than 20 times**.
- This will be very expensive. Electricity generated by wind turbines already enjoys huge subsidies and tax breaks through the Renewable Obligation scheme.
- The Government has now accepted that the total costs of meeting the 2020 target will be **£100 billion**. This is equivalent to £4000 for every household in the country.
- The Royal Academy of Engineering has calculated that **wind energy is two and a half times more expensive** than other forms of electricity generation in the UK.
- Wind generation does not provide a reliable supply of power. It must be backed up by other base-load sources.
- Greater reliance on wind power could lead to electricity supply disruptions if the wind does not blow, blows too hard or does not blow where wind farms are located.
- The experience of Denmark – often hailed for its pioneering development of wind farms – is that **wind energy is expensive, inefficient and not even particularly 'green'**. There are signs that other countries are losing some of their enthusiasm for wind power.
- There is no evidence that people are prepared to pay for wind power. **Only 15% of people say that they are 'fairly' or 'very willing' to pay higher electricity bills if the extra money funds renewable power sources such as wind.** The figures for 'very unwilling' and 'fairly unwilling' are 37% and 24% respectively.
- This over-reliance on expensive wind energy, coupled with rising gas prices, will drive six million households into fuel poverty.

- Present wind farm planning applications do not take into consideration the economic viability of the project or whether the topography and meteorological conditions are suitable.
- The planning system already favours wind farm developers. But if the Government is to meet its renewable target by 2020, then current planning regulations will have to be weighted even further in favour of wind farm suppliers.
- The Ministry of Defence has recently lodged last minute objections to at least four on-shore wind farms, claiming the turbines will interfere with their national air defence radar.
- **The energy gap must be filled with equivalent base-load capacity as quickly as possible.**
- The UK should therefore now develop its nuclear, clean coal (including coal gasification) and other renewable supplies of energy (particularly tidal).
- **Wind energy, in contrast, should only play a negligible role in plugging Britain's looming energy gap.**

5

Emissions

5.1 INTRODUCTION

Carbon emissions and carbon footprints have become part of every-day language with everyone aware of the impact on global warming. It is also becoming an economic reality in terms of its impact with prices/ton expected to average between €20/t and €25/t CO_2 through to 2012. This will have a significant impact on power prices and it will be shown in this chapter that this will add around €7/MWh to gas fired prices and €15/MWh to coal production prices where allowances have to be purchased in the market to match output in excess of free allowances. Free allowances are likely to be discontinued in phase 3 and prices are expected to almost double by 2020 to €40/t CO_2. This will have a dramatic impact on the relative merits of different types of generation and tips the balance in favour of energy sources with little or no CO_2 emissions such as hydro, wind and nuclear.

The purpose of this chapter is to analyse the impact of emission restrictions on the economics of power generation. The arrangements for monitoring and managing emissions are also discussed, together with the associated trading schemes applied in the UK and across Europe. The ultimate objective of the United Nations Framework Convention on Climate change, which was approved by Council Decision 94/69/EC of 15 December 1993, is to achieve stabilisation of greenhouse gas concentrations in the atmosphere at a level that prevents dangerous anthropogenic interference with the climate system. As a result, mechanisms have been introduced to reduce CO_2 emissions progressively to mitigate the impact on the environment.

Power Markets and Economics: Energy Costs, Trading, Emissions   Barrie Murray
© 2009 John Wiley & Sons, Ltd

5.2 EMISSION TRADING SCHEMES (ETS)

Market arrangements were considered the best mechanism to realise the least cost approach to abatement of greenhouse gas emissions and Emission Trading Schemes (ETS) have been introduced to facilitate this. The mechanisms provide producers of CO_2 with allowances that are related to their normal annual emission levels. These allowances are issued free but are set to be less than the producer's historical requirement, thereby encouraging abatement or incurring penalty payments. There is also the option to trade and purchase allowances from other producers with a surplus realised through the early application of abatement. This process is designed to encourage the abatement to take place where the cost is least, with the allowances being progressively reduced through subsequent periods of the scheme.

The initial UK-ETS was introduced for four years ending in December 2006. An auction of unallocated allowances was organised to establish a price. Participants were asked to bid to provide reductions with payment from a pot of £215m that was initially provided by the government. The term was for three years and the auction resulted in prices of £54.3/t CO_2 or £18/t/yr. The total reduction over the three-year period realised from the expenditure of £215 m was 3.95 mt CO_2. The on-going arrangement proposed was that the market would set the price that participants would have to pay if they exceeded their allocation. The payments would be to buy allowances from those participants that had succeeded in reducing emissions below their target or from the government, in this initial implementation. The market was dominated by three large players with 50% of the allocation. Some 3500 trades were effected for volumes ranging from 100 mt to 100 000 mt carried out mostly around the time when compliance was checked. Trading took place between direct participants and non-direct participants who were included on the Emissions Trading Register. The monitoring, reporting and verification was conducted annually by accredited third parties. Participants had three months to prepare their verification report and to trade to meet their targets. This market met with limited success because of the domination of three large players and the initial over provision of allowances.

Directive 2003/87/EC laid the foundation for the European Trading Scheme and required each member to translate the requirements into their national legislation. The first phase of the scheme came into force in January 2005 running to the end of 2007 and covered CO_2 only. The second phase from 2008 to 2012 covers all the greenhouse gases. For each period referred to in the Article, each Member State is required to develop a national plan stating the total quantity of allowances that it intended to allocate for that period and how it proposes to allocate them. The distribution is established by industrial sector and subsequently for particular installations. Some 93.7% of the expected emissions were allocated in the UK with 6.3% reserved for new entrants. The amount reserved varied from country to country depending on the likely level of new entry. For the five-year period beginning 1 January 2008, and for each subsequent five-year period, each Member State has to decide upon the total quantity of allowances that it will allocate for that period and initiate the process for the allocation of those allowances to the operator of each installation.

The EU scheme covers all installations with an output greater than 20 MWthermal, which involved 1000 sites in the UK. There are requirements that stipulate arrangements for registration and verification with any failure to meet targets penalised at a cost of €40/t CO_2. Under the burden sharing agreement, the UK was allocated a total of 736.3 mt, which was some 8% or 65 mt CO_2 below the expected output. The target was to reduce this by a further 12.5% from the base year to 653 mt CO_2 by the end of the first period. The power sector, as a major contributor to emissions, was targeted to provide a large proportion of the required reduction.

The Clean Development Mechanism (CDM) set up through the 1997 Kyoto Protocol enables credits to be gained by sponsoring the development of clean solutions in fast developing countries such as China. The board regulating the CDM strictly defines which types of project are allowed and what they need to demonstrate compliance. The credits are usually created through 'smokestack' solutions that can prove a reduction in emissions or efficiency improvements. There is also non-regulated activity where companies are voluntarily seeking to improve their image through the pursuit of a green policy. This, in turn, is supported by carbon offset retailers who trade in the provision of carbon reductions without regulation. Many projects in this sector have not been audited to confirm that reductions are truly being realised.

5.3 LARGE COMBUSTION PLANT DIRECTIVE (LCPD)

The EU's LCPD requires that all new plants with a thermal capacity above 50 MW and operational before 1987 must meet Emission Limit Values (ELVs). This defines limits on the emission of SO_2, NOx and dust to be realised by 2008. For a typical coal plant the limits amount to 400 mg/m^3 of SO_2, 500 mg/m^3 NOx and 50 mg/m^3 of dust. There is an option to opt out of the scheme and take a limited life derogation. This limits the plant to 20 000 operating hours starting in 2008 and ending in 2015 when the plant must close. Implementation is either through a system of ELV for individual plants or by establishing a National Emission Reduction Plan (NERP). The NERP defines the total emission limit for the country with allocation effected through a trading system.

Older coal plant that does not meet the target maximum emission levels can either:

- fit emission reduction equipment;
- take the derogation and close by 2015;
- purchase any credits needed and use low sulphur coal.

The directive is designed to limit the use of older less efficient coal plant with relatively high emission levels. Whereas a number of plants had intended to take the derogation option, spurred by coal becoming more competitive, some are now choosing to refit and stay in operation for longer.

5.4 GENERATION CO_2 EMISSIONS

The level of CO_2 emission varies with the fuel used in the generation plant. The higher the efficiency, the lower the emission per unit of energy generated. Coal has the highest carbon content followed by oil and then gas as shown in Table 5.1.

The table shows the typical carbon content of fuel for each giga-joule of energy. Given the specific weights of carbon and oxygen as 12 and 16, the amount of CO_2 can be calculated, i.e. 1 ton CO_2 contains $1 * 12/44$ ton carbon. The price for CO_2 allowances will depend on the demand/supply balance in the ETS market. The price of CO_2 in the above example is assumed to be

Table 5.1 Emissions by fuel type

Fuel	gC/GJ	tC/mtoe	tCO₂/GJ	Price/GJ	Efficiency	Price/MWh
Lignite/Brown coal	25 200	1.169	0.0924	0.277	33	3.02
Bituminous coal	23 700	1.100	0.0869	0.261	38	2.47
Oil	19 900	0.923	0.0730	0.219	40	1.97
Natural gas	13 500	0.626	0.0495	0.149	52	1.03

£3/t (€4.35/t) enabling the price per giga-joule of energy to be calculated. By assuming typical plant efficiency values as shown, the price for the CO_2 allowance per MWh generated can be calculated. It should be noted that the natural gas emission cost is low both because of the lower carbon content per GJ and the higher efficiency. Equally, if the efficiency of the bituminous coal plant were to be raised to 48% then the additional cost would be less and given by:

$$\text{New added cost} = 0.261 * 3.6/0.48 = £1.96/\text{MWh},$$

as opposed to the £2.47/MWh shown in Table 5.1.

5.5 PRODUCTION COSTS

Whilst a large number of the allowances have been issued free, the plant operating at the margin, which sets the market price, will generally not have spare free allowances. Its production price will therefore need to cover the cost of purchasing extra allowances through the market. These additional costs will be more in the case of coal than gas generation and this can be expected to alter the competitive position of coal/gas. This is illustrated in the graph of Figure 5.1, where the price of coal at £1.5/GJ is half that of gas at £3/GJ. However, this competitive advantage is reduced by the difference

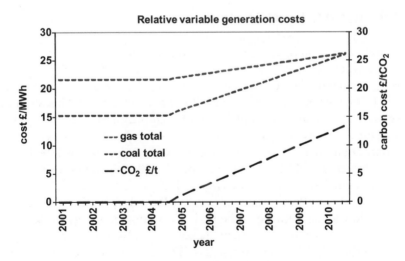

Figure 5.1 Gas versus coal prices with CO_2

in plant efficiencies and almost eliminated by the costs of the additional CO_2 allowances.

The CO_2 price that will result in the cost/MWh of generation between coal and gas being equal can be calculated in this example, if it is assumed that the gas price is £3/GJ with other variable costs of £1.11/MWh and that the coal price is £1.5/GJ with other variable costs of £1.46/MWh. Also assume a gas efficiency of 52.6% and coal of 39% then:

Gas production cost $= £3*3.6/0.526 + 1.11 = £21.6/MWh.$

Coal production cost $= £1.5*3.6/0.39 + 1.46 = £15.3/MWh.$

CO_2 production for gas $= 3.6*0.0495/0.526 = 0.338t/MWh.$

CO_2 production for coal $= 3.6*0.0869/0.39 = 0.802t/MWh.$

Costs are equal when$(0.802-0.338)*CO_2cost = 21.6-15.3.$

i.e. the costs are equal when CO_2 costs $= £13.5/t$ CO2 as shown in Figure 5.1.

5.6 NATIONAL ALLOCATION PLANS

The European Union (EU) signed up to an emissions reduction target under the Kyoto Protocol from the base-year level of 1990. Through the Burden Sharing agreement, the EU target was distributed between the Member States of the EU-15. Each member is required to establish National Allocation Plan (NAP) that lays down the overall CAP for the country and the allowances that each sector and individual installation, covered by the Directive, will receive. The chart of Figure 5.2 shows the base case CO_2 emissions for 1990 for each country, together with the target reduction by 2008–2012 in mt CO_2.

It can be seen that Germany, the UK and Italy have both the highest level of emissions and are required to make the largest reductions. France has relatively low levels because of the high proportion of energy derived from nuclear generation and hydro plant and, accordingly, has a neutral target. In the case of the UK, the base case figure is 747.2 mt CO_2 and the requirement is to reduce this by 93.4 (12.5%) to 653.8 mt CO_2 by 2010. The full range of

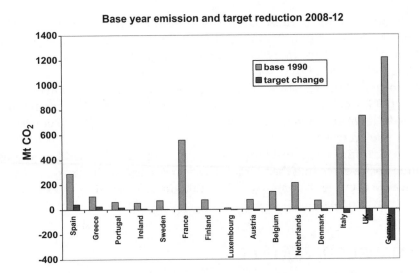

Figure 5.2 Base year emissions and target reductions

percentage targets are shown in Figure 5.3 for each member state and range from +27% for Portugal to −28% for Luxembourg, where the negative target is to allow for expected economic growth. These national targets are further broken down in the allocation plans of each country. Internal UK targets are

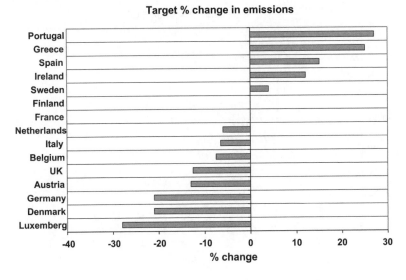

Figure 5.3 Target percentage change in emission

for the power sector to realise a large proportion of the reduction, around 50%. From a base year value of 247 mt CO_2 a reduction to 171 mt CO_2 was originally planned by 2010. This was in large measure reached by 2003 with levels of 174 falling to 152.5 mt CO_2 by 2004 with a further planned reduction of 23.5 mt CO_2 to give 129 mt CO_2 by 2010. This represents an overall fall of in excess of 100 mt CO_2 from the 1990 levels. This is largely due to the 'dash for gas' that shifted a lot of power generation from coal to gas following the liberalisation of the market in 1990.

The performance against target is regularly reported by the EU and most countries are exceeding their target. This is consistent with a market surplus with most countries having spare allocations for sale, resulting in a surplus of supply over demand.

5.7 MARKET OPERATION

The ETS market price has been very volatile and prices have fallen from above €20/EAU (1 European Allowance Unit = 1 t CO_2) at the beginning of 2006 to below 5€/EAU in April 2007 as shown in Figure 5.4. This reflects the fact that the free allowances for the phase 1 period were too generous, leading to a surplus of supply. This situation was corrected when the allowances for the

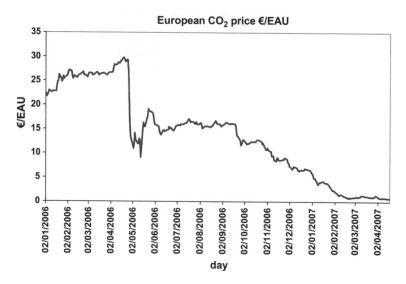

Figure 5.4 European CO_2 price history

phase 2 period came into effect and forward prices are rising again to €22/MWh during 2008. The latest market prices can be found on the website of the European Energy Exchange.

There are a number of reasons why the ETS market has been described as not working effectively including:

- the uncertainty over the NAP allocations and the regulatory policy;
- lack of transparency in the supply and demand of EAUs;
- the volatility in the prices seen in the market;
- poor supply of information on actual utilisation;
- a lack of standardisation on the rules for allocation.

All these factors are a prerequisite to enabling market participants to analyse the market and make predictions. This situation in turn does not create a good environment in which investments can be appraised. There is concern that if the EU unilaterally pursues the penalisation of industry that are making emissions, the industries could be exported to less stringent environments.

5.8 IMPACT OF CAPACITY MIX

The total emissions from power generation can be calculated from records of annual energy production from each plant. Given the efficiency of the generation, the number of GJ of fuel consumed can be calculated for each MWh of energy produced. Given the CV of the fuel or type, the amount of CO_2 released can be calculated. This is summated for all plants to give the total emission.

For example, for the UK we can assume that the total energy production is 350 TWh with 37% from coal generation and 40% from gas fired generation and 5% from oil, with the remainder met by nuclear generation. If it is also assumed that the average efficiency of coal plant is 38%, with gas plant at 52% and oil at 40%, then the total emission can be calculated as shown in Table 5.2.

Table 5.2 Total emissions from generation

	tons/TWH	% gen.	TWh/yr	Mt CO_2/yr
nuclear	0	18	63	0
bituminous coal	825575	37	129.5	107
oil	658544	5	17.5	12
natural gas	343655	40	140	48
totals		100	350	167

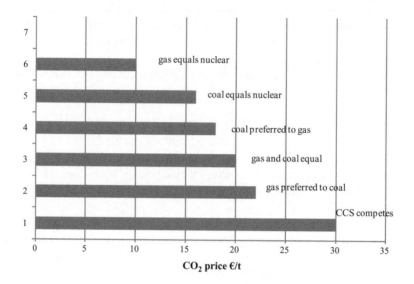

Figure 5.5 Impact of CO_2 on plant competitiveness

This illustrates the benefit of gas fired generation with its lower emission levels. The coal emission could be reduced from 107 to 85 mt CO_2 by an efficiency improvement from 38% to $38 * 107/85 = 47.8\%$. Carbon capture and storage is another option that can enable coal to compete with wind; it is discussed further in Chapter 15.

Some idea of the general impact of carbon prices on the relative competitiveness of the different technologies can be established by comparing when prices converge. Figure 5.5 shows six CO_2 price scenarios where one technology looks profitable in relation to a competing technology. It can be seen that at prices above €10/t nuclear looks attractive in relation to gas and above €17/t it competes with coal. Above €20/t gas is preferred to coal and at €30/t CCS (Carbon Capture and Storage) looks attractive. This result will change as fuel prices change.

5.9 INTERNATIONAL APPROACH

In **New Zealand** a more radical approach has been taken to supporting renewable sources by ban on all new thermal plants, unless needed for security. The legislation required for this policy was introduced to parliament in 2008 and if passed most new capacity will need to come from renewable sources, i.e. hydro, geothermal and wind.

There is considerable capacity in NZ for new large-scale hydro schemes. However, much of this capacity is in national parks. Capacity for new geothermal plants is limited. Therefore it is likely that most new capacity requirements will be met by wind.

The Electricity Commission in New Zealand has modelled five scenarios for future development of the electricity market. This modelling work was done before the government announced its policy of banning new thermal plants. The expected cost of incremental production is shown in Figure 5.6. As the expected demand increases so the options for development change with costs increases. Initially hydro, geothermal and wind dominate but as the best sites are exploited, biomass and solar begin to compete.

In **Australia,** the main support for renewables is the Mandatory Renewable Energy Target, which requires the generation of 9500 GWh of extra renewable electricity a year by 2010. The MRET operates by imposing a legal liability to support renewable energy generation on large wholesale purchasers of electricity.

The liable parties are directly responsible for supporting an increase in the amount of electricity generated from renewable energy sources. This is implemented through the surrender of Renewable Energy Certificates (RECs) in proportion to their acquisitions of electricity. Each REC represents one

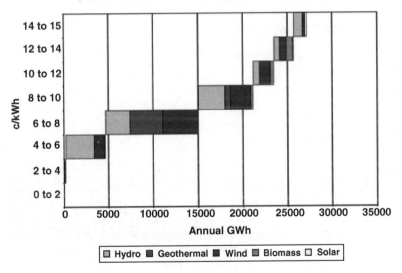

Figure 5.6 New Zealand generation cost comparisons

megawatt hour (MWh) of eligible renewable electricity. Each state may also set targets and New South Wales requires that 10% of energy should be produced by from renewable sources by 2010 and 15% by 2020. The graph in Figure 5.7 shows a continuing increase in validated RECs.

In **Canada** the provinces retain responsibility for electricity matters within their respective jurisdictions and make decisions to restructure their markets based on their own assessment of their needs. Wind capacity continued to show strong growth in Canada in 2006, more than doubling from 680 MW in 2005, to around 1460 MW in 2006. Most of this growth was seen in the province of Ontario, although others are also moving forwards with their own wind generation. Although hydropower is a plentiful source of renewable power, providing 60% of energy, interest in wind capacity has increased markedly now that Canada is looking to limit its aggregate CO_2 emissions from other sources. For the foreseeable future, however, sources such as natural gas will continue to see strong growth, driven in part by growth in the oil sands industry.

In the **USA** non-carbon-emitting renewable sources such as wind, solar, biomass and geothermal power, although growing, still supplies only a fraction of US energy needs. Several states, most notably California, have required that power utilities implement renewable portfolio standards mandating that alternatives and renewable sources account for a certain percentage of total power supply by a given date. Unfortunately, these efforts

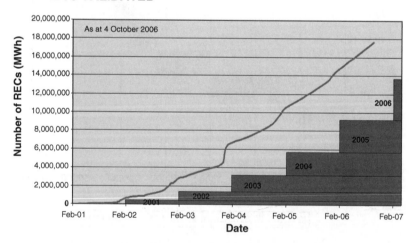

Figure 5.7   RECs in Australia

are in response to the refusal of the federal government to introduce mandates itself. The result is a veritable jumble of state-level policies aimed at boosting the sector, with no overall guiding hand. Despite this, the renewable energy sector is expanding and, in 2006, the United States experienced the largest growth in wind-powered generation of any country in the world, with an increase of 27%. There is also renewed interest in nuclear and solar band on CSP (Concentrating Solar Power) as a means of reducing emissions.

5.10 SUMMARY

This chapter has described the approach being adopted to reduce emissions from power plants by progressively tightening the levels allowed with penalties of €40/t CO_2 applied to any excess. Market arrangements have been put in place to allow allowances to be traded to encourage the technique of abatement at least cost to be applied. In the UK the initial scheme ran from 2002 to December 2006. Unallocated allowances were auctioned to establish a price basis for subsequent trading. In January 2005 the European ETS (Emission Trading Scheme) came into force enabling cross-border trading. Under the scheme rules each country is given an allowance that they have to dispense amongst their user base. This is realised by the National Allocation Plan (NAP) that apportions allowances to all units with an annual output greater than 20 MWh. The different country allocations and the progress towards meeting them are shown. The method of calculating typical levels of emissions from power generation based on different fuels is described together with the impact on wholesale market prices and relative competitiveness. It shows how coal plant will be adversely affected because basic emission levels/GJ are around twice those of natural gas with the impact on prices/MWh being three times higher due to the lower efficiency of coal plant. It also shows how this improves the competitiveness of nuclear generation, which is making a comeback.

The full costs of meeting government targets on emission reductions are yet to be impressed on the economy but are now becoming apparent with CO_2 prices around €22/t and expected to rise to around €40/t. At these prices power costs could be doubled and this will have an adverse impact on the competitiveness of UK industry that may not be acceptable to government. It remains to be seen how well the ETS scheme meets the requirements of the future and how future phases of the scheme will be managed. During a period of recession it seems unlikely that the full impact of the ETS will be passed through to consumers.

6

Transmission

6.1 INTRODUCTION

Transmission facilitates operation of the market in enabling wholesale trade between generators and suppliers largely independent of their location. This maximises the liquidity in the market and promotes competition. In general, the larger the consumption in the interconnected market, the greater the liquidity and competition. It enables traders for the most part to regard the grid as infinite. To ensure fair open access to all system users there is a requirement to demonstrate independence from any participant involved in trading energy. This was not realised where transmission ownership was coupled with generation so the initial step was for transmission to be unbundled from generation.

In the organisation of state industries it was usual for the operation of the power system to be integral with the wires business with common ownership. During 2007/8 the EU have been pressing for ownership to be unbundled to establish truly independent TSOs that are able to manage operation of the system without any prejudice.

In a statement in 2008 the European Regulators reiterated their support for the Parliament's position on 'ownership unbundling' of transmission system operators.

'The key is to deliver effective solutions as soon as possible. Fair and equal access to the networks and appropriate investment incentives on transmission system operators are essential to Europe-wide security of supply. Ownership unbundling is

Power Markets and Economics: Energy Costs, Trading, Emissions   Barrie Murray
© 2009 John Wiley & Sons, Ltd

the most effective means of avoiding discrimination. Moreover, the greater the degree of unbundling the less additional, intrusive regulation is needed. In its advice to the European Commission, ERGEG advocated that the model required in the 3rd package is in principle ownership unbundling and that there is no justification for less unbundling in gas than in electricity, as the potential for discrimination does not differ.'

The ISO (Independent System Operator) is also responsible in most market models for identifying the need for development of the network based on operational experience. Similar initiatives have taken place in the US where the FERC (Federal Energy Regulatory Council) order 2000 required utilities to hand control of their networks to an independent entity. This led to the establishment of Regional Transmission Organisations (RTO) exercising coordinating control over several transmission networks. The PJM RTO, for example, coordinates energy transfers across some 15 US states. As well as managing the network assets, they also continuously schedule and dispatch generation to keep the system in balance.

This chapter explains the role played by transmission systems in facilitating electricity markets. The costs incurred by the owners and operators in managing the network and the mechanisms adopted to recover these through tariffs for use of system are discussed. The chapter describes:

• the impact of transmission in market operation;
• how costs are recovered through use of system charging tariffs;
• the impact of inter-connector congestion on market prices.

Transmission is generally considered to be a natural monopoly and as such is subject to regulation. The objectives of the Regulator are to limit prices close to costs and drive them down through efficiency improvements.

6.2 IMPACT OF TRANSMISSION CONSTRAINTS IN MARKETS

For the most part bilateral deals across networks can proceed without inhibition. However, in some circumstances constraints on the network may become active when the difference between the generation and demand in an area of the system exceeds the interconnecting transmission capacity with the rest of the system (having allowed for security requirements). Several approaches are used to deal with this situation, as described

- Split the market and let zonal prices separate until transfers match capacity available (the Nordpool trading area is designed to split when constrained).
  - o Establish optimal unconstrained flow (equal Lambda) for supplier.
- Ignore constraints in market operation – let the TSO resolve constraints in real time and share costs through uplift – ex-post.
  - o Establish constrained optimal solution to maintain security for TSO.
- Explicitly charge for use of the inter-connector to manage transfer through a bilateral contract, auction (as in Europe) or rationing.
  - o Establish optimal use of system charge for inter-connector owner.

In the first option, when it becomes apparent that interconnecting flows would exceed capacity the market is split by the Market Operator. This has the advantage that those customers within a constrained zone bear the additional costs as opposed to the cost being spread amongst all users through uplift. The diagram in Figure 6.1 shows the Italian high voltage network with the thick lines indicating where market splitting may be necessary. This will occur when the secure capacity of the transmission lines across the boundary is less than the required transfer resulting from an optimal market solution. The inset shows the resulting prices in €/MWh for each zone for a time when the constraints were active. In this case the transfers from North to South are limited resulting in rising prices moving South as a result of having to use more expensive generation within the importing zones. The Nordpool market operates by balancing generation prices against demand side bids. If the total market solution results in excessive transfers, then the market is split across the overload boundary and separate prices are established for each area. The import to a constrained zone will be limited to the secure capacity with supply and demand balanced internally.

Another option for dealing with internal network constraints is to establish the total market solution and then in the event let the grid operator instruct generation so as to manage constraints. This will require generation to be operated out of merit and incur additional costs. If a generator is deselected, although in merit, it may receive 'constrained off' payments related to lost profit. Alternatively if a generator has to be used even though not in merit it would receive 'constrained on' payments based on the generators bid into the market rather than the marginal price that will be lower.

Figure 6.1   Market split Italy

In the case of inter-connectors between systems as, for example, between Germany, Belgium and the Netherlands, then if the demand for transmission by traders across the route exceeds the capacity auctions may be held as illustrated below. Traders will bid to reserve capacity a year, or perhaps month, ahead of the event. Prices are established competitively and have to be recovered from the proceeds of the trade.

The auctions are usually managed by the respective TSOs, these being Tennet for the Netherlands, Elia for Belgium and RWE and E.ON Netz for Germany. The high premium for export from Germany to the Netherlands can be seen in Table 6.1. This occurs because the Netherlands relies for some 15% of its supply requirements on imports. As prices are relatively

Table 6.1 Auction NW Europe

From	To	Available (MW)	Obtained (MW)	Price (€/MW)
ELIA	TenneT	338	328	4.70
TenneT	ELIA	328	327	0.11
RWE Transport-netz Strom	TenneT	356	356	7.14
TeeneT	RWE Transport-netz Strom	356	356	0.07
E.ON Netz	TenneT	216	216	7.02
TeeneT	E.ON Netz	216	216	0.01

higher than in Germany there is competition to export, driving up the cost of reserving transmission.

6.3 TRANSMISSION CHARGING

Charges for use of the transmission network are usually based on the assets utilised and the losses incurred in energy transfers across the network. They will therefore include a charge related to the capacity of the user's installation. This will affect the proportion of the transmission assets that has to in place to meet the user needs at peak times. There will also be a charge related to the energy transfer as this will affect the losses incurred on the network that have to be paid for. Typical transmission tariffs are shown in Table 6.2 for Germany and the Netherlands for a large consumer having a capacity of 10 MW with energy of 70 000 MWh/yr.

It can be seen that the tariffs include a capacity payment and what's called a commodity payment for the energy. There are also other charges principally for metering either on a monthly or annual basis. Although the charges are very differently structured overall, they are about the same and relatively small for this user with a high utilisation. Eurostat define a set of standard consumer characteristics that enable tariffs to be compared, shown in Table 6.3. The tariff calculation above is for the largest consumer category with the highest load factor with an effective full load utilisation of 7000 h. Because the charges are related to the installed capacity or peak demand the charges for consumers with lower levels of utilisation are higher in that the fixed capital cost recovery has to be shared between fewer units of energy.

Table 6.2 Transmission tariffs

RWE			Netherlands		
tariffs			**tariffs**		
capacity tariff	€/kW/yr	23.28	capacity tariff	€/kW/yr	10.27
commodity	€c/kWh	0.19	commodity	€/kWh	0.004
metering	€/month	377	monthly/kW	€/kW/mon	1.03
			standing + meters	€/yr	7,800.00
			maintenance	€/yr	
			system service	€/kWh	
Assumed load			**Assumed load**		
capacity	MW	10	capacity	MW	10
energy	MWh	70000	energy	MWh	70000
utilisation hrs	hours	7000	monthly peak	MW	1.6
Charges			**Charges**		
			monthly capacity	€/yr	19776
capacity	€/yr	232800	annual capacity	€/yr	102700
commodity	€/yr	133000	commodity	€/yr	280000
total	€/yr	365800	total	€/yr	402476
Other fixed charges	€/yr	4524	**Other fixed charges**	€/yr	7800
total charges	€/yr	370324	total charges	€/yr	410276
charges	€/MWh	5.3	charges	€/MWh	5.9

Table 6.3 Eurostat definitions

Category	MW	MWh	Utilisation (h/yr)
Domestic			
Da	0.003	0.6	200
Db	0.0035	1.2	343
Dc	0.0065	3.5	538
Dd	0.0075	7.5	1000
De	0.009	20	2222
Commercial and Small Industry			
Ia	0.03	30	1000
Ib	0.05	50	1000
Ic	0.1	160	1600
Id	0.5	1250	2500
Medium-Size Industry			
Ie	0.5	2000	4000
If	2.5	10 000	4000
Ig	4	24 000	6000
Large Industry			
Ih	10	50 000	5000
Ii	10	70 000	7000

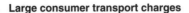

Large consumer transport charges

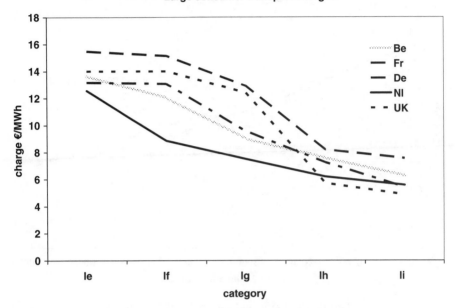

Figure 6.2 Transmission charges in NW Europe

This is illustrated by the graph of Figure 6.2 that shows how the transmission charge per unit increases for the lower utilisation customers.

The higher capacity consumers will be fed from higher system voltage levels and will therefore use less of the network with fewer transformation levels giving lower system losses. It can be seen from the graph that charges reduce with utilisation. The charges also vary between the countries of NW Europe, sometimes leading to complaints from industrialists who are in competition. A trend line of the average charges may be established based on the MWh consumption as shown in Figure 6.3 where the charge is given by 13.64–MWh/10 000.

6.4 DERIVATION OF USE OF SYSTEM CHARGES

The approach generally adopted for calculating charges aims to identify the proportion of the network utilised by injections or extractions at each node of the system by generators or suppliers. This may be estimated using a DC load flow model (DCLF). The methodology is sometimes called Investment Cost Related Pricing (ICRP).

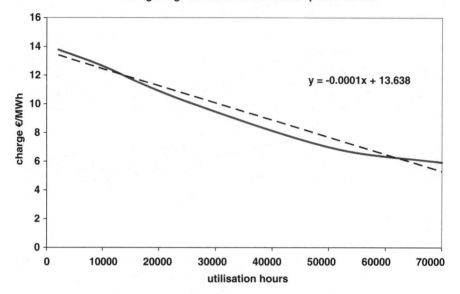

Figure 6.3   Large end user transmission prices

- A network model is used to assess the changes in flow on all lines resulting from an injection of 1 MW at each node.
- The results are expressed in terms of the increment of MW-km required to accommodate the injection.
- The studies are usually based on winter peak loading conditions.
- Added factors are used to take account for the higher costs of cables.
- The zonal marginal MW-km figures are converted to costs by multiplying by the standard cost for transmission equipment (e.g. 400 kV around £10/MW-km).
- This is multiplied by a factor to take account of security requirements, e.g. 1.8 to provide backup for maintenance and forced outages.
- A constant may be added to distribute the costs between generation and demand (50%–50%) as in the UK, generators pay 27% and demand 73%.
- Zonal values are calculated from the capacity weighted average nodal prices.
- The network losses may be embodied in the trading arrangements or managed by the TSO.

In most countries nearly all the charge is levied on the load side rather than generation. The exceptions are countries such as Great Britain, Norway and Romania, where a proportion of the charge is levied on the generators. The generators no doubt pass this cost through but it enables the application of discriminatory zonal charges.

The derivation of use of system charges as described above leads to different charges at each node of the system that in practice would be complex to administer. It is usual for nodes with a similar price and impact on the network to be grouped into defined areas or zones. This enables prices to be geographically differentiated and used as a mechanism to encourage new generation to be sited in zones with a capacity shortfall. The tariff is based on the assessment of the costs with a proportion related to the installed capacity and a proportion based on the energy transfer. In most countries the tariffs also include provision to cover network losses and system services.

6.5 INTERNATIONAL TARIFF COMPARISONS

The tariffs structures adopted vary considerably in the proportion of the charge that relates to the energy transferred as opposed to that based on the registered capacity or power. Table 6.4 shows the mixture applied across

Table 6.4 European tariff makeup (source ETSO)

	Power part	Energy part			Power part	Energy part
Austria	25%	75%	Ireland		34%	66%
Belgium	48%	52%	Italy		0%	100%
Czech Republiuc	11%	89%	Lithuania		72%	28%
Denmark	0%	100%	Netherlands		67%	33%
Estonia	77%	23%	Norway		22%	78%
Finland	0%	100%	Poland		25%	75%
France	37%	63%	Portugal		2%	98%
Germany	87%	13%	Romania		0%	100%
Great Britain	60%	40%	Slovak Republic		9%	91%
Greece	59%	41%	Slovenia		49%	51%
Hungary	0%	100%	Spain		31%	69%
			Sweden		56%	44%

Euro per MWh

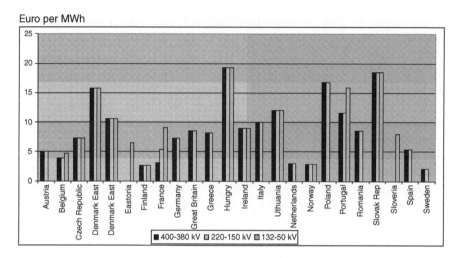

Figure 6.4   Comparison of total transmission charges (Source ETSO)

Europe varying from 100% energy relating in Hungary to 77% capacity relating in Estonia. It may be appropriate for a network with high losses to include more of the charge in the energy part whereas, if accommodating the capacity includes most of the cost, then charges would be biased towards the power part.

The tariffs applied across Europe can be compared for a load with 5000 h utilisation by adding together the generation and demand side charges on a charge per MWh basis. The results of a survey carried out by ETSO are shown in Figure 6.4, where it can be seen that there appears to be a wide variation. Some of the very high charges are the results of added regulatory charges not related to TSO activities and for items such as stranded assets, public interest and renewable subsidies. When these are removed most countries fall in the range €5–10/MWh. The charges are similar for the different voltage levels, with the exception of France, which has a special feature reflecting the costs associated with connection at different voltages.

6.6 TRANSMISSION INVESTMENT

A key question with transmission is who determines the need for investment and who pays. Usually the sector is regarded as a monopoly and regulated by a regulator. In these circumstances the owner will be subject to a regulatory review, typically every five years. This process involves a review of the proposed capital spend including the following.

- A review of how this category moves with the growth forecasts for demand – there will be notable overlap with the reinforcement category.
- Non-load related Capex – this includes refurbishment and reinforcement and is a major component of overall Capex. Provisions for the latter half of the regulatory period are significant and require analysis.
- Entry and Exit Capex – this will reflect and perhaps be linked to assumptions on entry (generation) and exit (demand connections) provisions.
- Continuity of supply – evidence of trends may reveal that the level of customer disturbances is low and we might question the level of security against routine outages, especially given the investment in line refurbishment and protection upgrades. The major risks of failure relate to strategic system planning and operational awareness, and will probably not reflect into the next regulatory period.
- Unit costs – these might be calculated as a benchmark figure, but care is needed in comparing like with like. Unit cost information is not readily available otherwise. The cost section will look at the unit costs for the network assets. There will be some benchmarking involved, if possible focusing on the effective use of contractors.
- Non-network related Capex, including IT spend. This will cover each of the major projects planned and whether they are justified, properly costed and capable of being delivered with the resources available. This will cover both the network operation's more general business systems – based on what we would expect a best practice utility to deploy
- The treatment of customer contributions is material to the net allowance and should also be considered, although this is not primarily a technical issue.

Having established agreement on the Capex and proposed charging arrangements the network owner would be able to recover costs with a small margin.

The benefits of pooling generation lead most countries to establish a national super-grid. There is growing interest in increasing interconnection capacity between countries to realise similar benefits. In Southern Africa 13 countries are cooperating under the auspices of SAPP (Southern African Power Pool) to establish competitive trading between countries. This requires agreement on the use of system changing arrangements and compensating utilities for wheeling through their systems. The European Union are actively promoting the rationalisation of the management of networks leading to the establishment of a pan-European market. In Central America the SIEPAC Project (Electrical Interconnection System of the Central America Countries) has two fundamental purposes:

1. the establishment of a Regional Electricity Market (REM) becoming more progressively competitive, and
2. the development of a regional transmission line (1800 km, 230 kV, single circuit), to be interconnected with the national electrical systems.

The basic mechanism used to create the REM is the Treaty of the Regional Electricity Market of Central America, subscribed to by the Presidents of the six countries in December of 1996, and ratified by the six National Congresses. Also, the company owning the SIEPAC line (EPL), initially formed by the state electricity companies, has been legally constituted.

As the networks become more closely coupled, so there are opportunities to rationalise the arrangements for trading as markets become more closely coupled. This can be seen in Europe with the emergence of the Benelux, the Iberian and all Ireland markets.

6.7 INTERCONNECTION INVESTMENT APPRAISAL

New investment in interconnection may be sponsored by the interconnected TSOs. In the case of major interconnection development this could be established as a commercial venture with costs recovered through charges for use of the asset. This involves predicting the potential use and earning potential of a new link. A simple example of the evaluation of an inter-connector between two systems with different cost functions is described below. The optimal global solution occurs when the link enables free use of generation so that marginal costs in each part of the system are the same, sometimes called the 'Equal Lambda Criteria'. In the simple system shown in Figure 6.5 this would occur when the combined system marginal price is €25.4/MWh with a transfer of 3.3 GW across the link.

In practice the available capacity may be less than the ideal 3.3 GW. The standard approach to deriving the available capacity is to determine the total transmission capacity (TTC). From this there may be some Already Allocated Capacity (AAC) against long term contractual arrangements that is subtracted. A provision is then made called the Transmission Reserve Margin

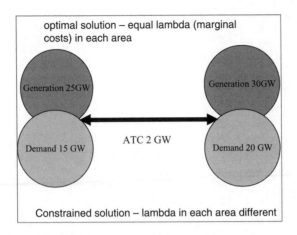

Figure 6.5   Model inter-connection

(TRM) for emergency transfers for things like reserve support. The Available Transmission Capacity (ATC) is then given by:

$$ATC = TTC - AAC - TRM.$$

In this example the ATC is 2 GW.

The two system incremental price functions are shown in the graph of Figure 6.6 plotted against their demand. Using the Microsoft Solver function the optimal solution to meet the total system demand of 35 GW at minimum cost is found to occur when the incremental price in each sub-system is the same at €25.4/MWh. This is generally the case and is often referred to as the 'Equal Lambda Criteria'. The two system price functions in this example are assumed to be represented by the polynomials with the factors shown in Table 6.5.

The corresponding generation in each sub-system, at the optimum, is then 16.7 GW (G1) and 18.3 GW (G2). When offset against the demand (D1 and D2) in each sub-system, it results in a transfer between the two systems of 3.3 GW. Given the generation levels in each system the marginal prices can be calculated based on the assumed price functions. It can be seen in Table 6.6 that these are equal, in line with the Equal Lambda Criteria. The table also shows the total production costs (€637.7) that can calculated from the integral of the cost function at the optimal demand levels and these add to equal the solution found using solver. This solution, however, makes no provision for revenue for use of the inter-connector.

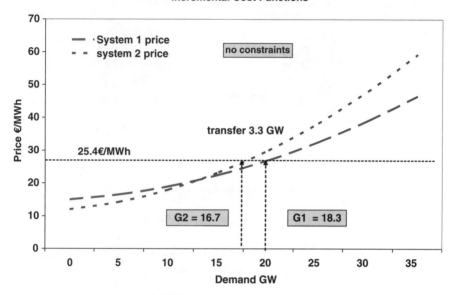

Figure 6.6 Interconnected system cost functions

If we now assume that the ATC is 2 GW, then the optimal transfer above would exceed the capacity and be unacceptable. A new solution can be found that obeys the constraint limit of two 2 GW as shown in Table 6.7. It can be seen that the incremental prices in the two systems are now different as would result from market splitting. The difference of around €3/MWH (€27.2 – €24.2) is equivalent to the charge for use of the network link that would cause the flow to be restricted to 2 GW in an optimal solution.

There are a range of other solutions with different link capacity charges that give different results for overall cost minimisation as shown in Figure 6.7. The dashed line shows how the transfer for the least cost solution (including the charge for use of the link) varies as the charge is varied. A very low charge

Table 6.5 Merit order function

Price function	System 1	System 2
constant	15	12
first order	0.2	0.3
second ord.	0.02	0.03

Table 6.6 Optimum transfer

Establishes minimum cost with no constraints using LP solver				No constraints	
		Marginal price	Integrated cost		
price functions €/MWh	P1=	25.4	349.1		
	P2=	25.4	288.6		
total cost	f(P1*G1) + f(P2*G2)€		637.7		
	Generation			demand	transfer
	G1 =	18.3	D1 =	15	3.30846
	G2 =	16.7	D2 =	20	−3.30846
	Totals=	35		35	

would give the same result as the optimum unconstrained solution with the transfer of 3.3 GW as shown on the right-hand scale. Conversely a high charge results in a low transfer. The solid line shows the resulting revenue to the inter-connector owner from charges for use of the inter-connector. It can be seen that a charge of around €4/MWh results in maximum income with a flow of 1.5 GW. A lower price of around €3/GWh results in a flow equal to

Table 6.7 Constrained solution

Establishes minimum cost with constraint added using solver				Constraints 2 GW	
		Marginal price €/MWh	Integrated cost		
price functions €/MWh	P1 =	24.2	315.9	constraint GW	2
	P2 =	27.2	323.7	UoS €/MWh	0
Cost=	f(P1*G1) + f(P2*G2)€ + const.cos		639.7	Tx income	0
	Generation			demand	transfer
System 1	G1 =	17	D1 =	15	2
System 2	G2 =	18	D2 =	20	−2
	Totals =	35		35	

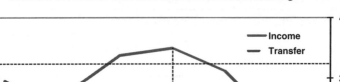

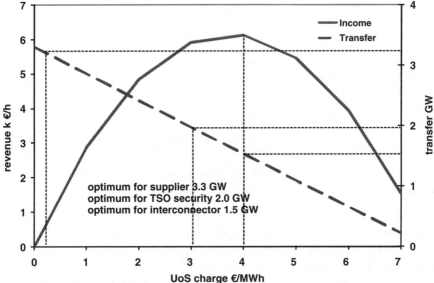

Figure 6.7 Optimal link size and revenue

a constraint limit of 2 GW. With high charges the system price differential is offset by the charge for use of the inter-connector reducing the flow for the least cost solution. Low charges increase the flow but not necessarily the revenue. In this example a link capacity of 2 GW would enable the optimal revenue earning transfer of 1.5 GW with some margin for emergency reserve transmission. In practice it would be necessary to evaluate a range of system operating conditions with price predictions for some 15 years ahead to evaluate an investment opportunity fully. It is important to note that the operating point on the cumulative merit order curve will change because of the transfer.

6.8 INTERNATIONAL PRACTICE

Practice around the world varies with the choice often being influenced by the distances involved and state of market development. A vertically inte-grated utility may grant open access to its transmission network to specific entities, e.g. non-utility generators and large users. In a more developed market with separate transmission, access is implicit in the competitive electricity market rules and is thus granted automatically to all the market agents. The access mechanism is regulated through the establishment of procedures for the connection of new assets to the transmission system. These will typically cover site details and capacity to be installed and the control and monitoring arrangements. With new generation as well as size, type and location there will be a requirement for technical details of the automatic voltage control and frequency control aspects. In a vertically integrated utility the network owner/operator will advance plans for endorsement by the regulator whereas in a fully competitive market the Independent System Operator will identify the need for developments. Whatever the arrangements, the process of regulation will aim to ensure open access and equitable charging and also that network development takes place consistent with all user needs on an equitable basis. This will include ensuring that the network owner establishes an optimum network without excess expenditure. It is not generally economic to develop a constraint-free network and mechanisms are required to deal with constraints when they become active.

Different approaches are often used to deal with what are termed internal and external constraints:

- PJM internal costs based on postage stamp charging with a standard rate expressed in $/kW/yr irrespective of location. RTO manages interconnection with LMP (Location Market Prices) based on local generation and loss costs; FTRs (Financial Transmission Rights) are used for hedging.
- The EU calculates a compensation fund ITC for Inter TSO transfers. The horizontal network is identified and costs are apportioned using transit keys that compare the wheeling with total asset utilisation; costs are recovered through a charge on import/export and an entry charge at the perimeter of €1/MWh.
- The UK establishes nodal use of system charges using DCLF (Direct Current Load Flow) model to establish asset utilisation and then groups nodes into zones; losses are managed using a loss adjustment through the market; interconnection is managed by auction.
- In Nordpool internal constraints are managed by counter trade and incur a cost whereas inter-connector congestion is managed by market splitting and generates a bottleneck income. Internal charges are not differentiated by location.
- Merchant transmission may be built to exploit short term price differentials between separate markets with all revenue accruing to owners.

• Australia manages congestion by splitting regions, allowing different marginal prices, but there is a common marginal price within each region; the surplus revenue is auctioned to enable risk to be managed.

In general, the mechanisms adopted are designed to minimise their impact on the functioning of the market. The charges are designed to cover capital costs and losses incurred as a result of the transfer. In the specific case of wheeling power through a network there is a need to identify those assets used by the transfer (the horizontal network) and their costs. These are then apportioned in the ratio of energy that is wheeled to the total energy transported on the network. A particular difficulty with wheeling is that the physical path of the flow will not necessarily be consistent with the contracted flow. To avoid complicating the market operation it may be left for TSOs to manage the distribution of income to cover their costs based on detailed network analysis studies.

6.9 SUMMARY

This section has described how transmission constraints affect the energy markets and the techniques used to manage them, including market splitting, and the consequent reduction of liquidity. The methods used to develop the use of system charges and typical tariffs are described for a range of Eurostat customer types. It is shown how these are closely linked to the network utilisation with lower charges when the load factor if high. Examples of tariffs applied across Europe are compared, showing the different allocations to the generation and demand side; the proportion of energy and capacity charges applied; and comparison of overall totals is given. An example is used to illustrate how constraints on an interconnection affect market prices in the coupled zones and how charges for use restrict economic flow and affect the interconnector owner's revenue. Finally, some of the international practices used to manage networks and internal and external constraints are outlined.

7

Distribution

7.1 INTRODUCTION

Distribution creates the final link in the chain to the smaller end user commercial or domestic consumer. The load factor of this type of consumer is very low and as a result charges have to be high to recover the costs involved in providing and maintaining the connection and metering assets utilised. In the original industry structure each distribution company would have a franchise to supply customers within its geographic area. The same organisation owned and maintained the equipment and managed the customer supply, metering and billing. Supplies would be made against a publicly declared tariff. Following restructuring it was proposed that:

- the ownership of the network could be split from the business of consumer supply;
- the franchise to supply consumers within an area would be progressively removed.

The EU mandated the programme for removal of the franchise by gradually lowering the size of consumer eligible to swap suppliers. Initially this was set at MW levels consistent with the large industrial users and reduced to include all non-domestic consumers by July 2004. Subsequently from July 2007 the scope was extended so that all domestic consumers could choose their supplier. The network owner recovers operating and capital charges through the use of system tariffs that are in place with suppliers and different consumer

Power Markets and Economics: Energy Costs, Trading, Emissions   Barrie Murray
© 2009 John Wiley & Sons, Ltd

groups. The suppliers buy energy wholesale and in turn will have tariffs to supply their end users, including energy and use of system charges. Larger consumers may have negotiated bilateral arrangements with suppliers.

This chapter explains the financial aspects of managing a distribution system in a market environment. The costs incurred by the owners and operators in managing the network and the mechanisms adopted to recover these through tariffs for use of system are discussed. It includes:

- observations on the market status;
- a discussion of the financial arrangements of a distribution system;
- a description of how costs are recovered through the use of system tariffs;
- the approach to benchmarking costs for the purposes of regulation.

Distribution, like transmission, is generally considered to be a natural monopoly and as such is subject to regulation. This includes mechanisms to limit prices close to costs and to drive through efficiency improvements.

7.2 MARKET STATUS

Following a series of reviews, the Commission expressed concern about the development of competition in the market and put forward its third energy package in September 2007. This called for the separation of network ownership from supply though two options:

1. an obligation to unbundle network ownership from generation and supply – a move that is likely to be resisted by the French and Germans;
2. the establishment of an independent TSO to manage access to and the utilisation of network assets, coupled with a requirement on the network owners to concede control to the TSO.

The Commission also saw the need to harmonise and strengthen the role of national regulators calling for their formal cooperation. It was also suggested that the voluntary TSO cooperation would benefit from being formalised.

The Commission have made it clear that unbundling is likely to be their preferred option and would solve the conflict of interest that inevitably occurs when incumbents are asked to grant network access to their competitors. Their self-interest is to impede access to protect their market share. France and Germany have so far rejected the Commissions call, stating that unbundling is only one measure for promoting competition and not a cure-all. In opposition the UK, Denmark and The Netherlands are all active promoters of unbundling.

7.3 COMMERCIAL ARRANGEMENTS

The original industry structure adopted by most countries was that each distribution company would have an obligation to supply customers within its geographically defined area. Energy was procured against a BST (Bulk Supply Tariff) and sold on to consumers against a retail tariff designed to cover the energy costs and system costs. Where supply has been made fully competitive, then consumers can choose their supplier. The suppliers will buy energy wholesale and pay use of system costs to the local network owners, recovering costs and margins through the tariffs applied to their customers. There are practical complications with the operation of full supply side competition including:

- managing the administration of customers changing suppliers;
- arranging metering data capture and administration for suppliers;
- arranging responsibility for balancing supply and demand in the event.

These complications add a considerable cost to the process of supply and it is not surprising that some countries have chosen not to pursue this option. Most of the benefit from a market can be derived from enabling competition in generation and there is not much added benefit from enabling competition in supply when the costs are considered. Several different arrangements have been adopted:

- Retain the **geographically defined distribution** companies supplied by a single buyer as in parts of the Middle East such as Oman and Abu Dhabi and in Africa. This has the advantage that the government is in a position to bias tariffs, perhaps to foster electrification or encourage industrial investment. Efficiency is maintained through the process of regulation.
- Retain geographically defined franchise areas for small retail customers but **enable competitive supply for large consumers**. This arrangement fixes responsibility for supply but enables innovative competition, enabling joint ventures with generators and consumers. These sometimes take the form of efficient combined heat and power schemes. Countries in Africa and the East have adopted this approach to enable rural electrification whilst encouraging industrial development.

• Enable **full supply competition,** as originally in the UK and across Europe. This gives customer choice and there has been a considerable amount of what is described as customer churn (changing supplier). This has been coupled with some hard intrusive doorstep selling. This arrangement has also enabled generators to establish a degree of vertical integration through their supply arms. This has created less dependence on wholesale prices as these are passed through, and hence reduces market liquidity and opens the way for market manipulation.

It is claimed that real cost savings accrue from supply competition, particularly where there are synergies between, say, gas and electricity supply. It is doubtful that these offset the ongoing costs of maintaining a selling force and administrating customer changes and metering. It also detracts from the visibility of distribution charges and encouraging efficiency in an area where costs and opportunities are higher than for the supply process.

7.4 METERING AND BALANCING

A key component of distribution and supply is metering and its costs are usually itemised on tariffs and may be open to competition. The usual arrangement is for BSP (bulk Supply Metering) to be located on the LV side of the bulk supply transformers that supply the distribution network from the super-grid. Consumers are then metered at their premises. The losses occurring in between are recovered through an energy related charge embodied within the distribution use of system tariff.

In a fully liberalised market that enable bilateral trades there is a system requirement to declare expected transfers to the System Operator to enable management of overall supply and demand. Where there is a single user such as a distribution company then the BSP points (Bulk Supply Points) can be conveniently defined as balance metering points. The distribution company will then be responsible for declaring the expected transfers prior to 'gate closure', which is typically an hour before the event. The parties responsible for making submissions are registered and called variously Balance Responsible Parties (BRPs) in Germany or Programme Responsible Officers in the Netherlands.

Where supply is competitive the metering arrangements are more complex with different suppliers operating within the same metered zone. There is a requirement for secondary metering of consumers within the distribution area who are not supplied by the main supplier or local distribution company.

These either have to be netted off the BSP metering or, alternatively, the supplier may choose to let the principal supplier make returns on their behalf. In this event, agreements need to be established as to how any costs resulting from being out of balance are shared.

The metering data is used in the settlement process and is usually collected daily through a dial up system collecting data from on-site transducers and feeding it to a central computer. The data has to be verified and aggregated and then used to establish preliminary settlement results. The main BSP metering and that to large consumers will be time of day metering to support half hour or hourly settlement. Domestic metering is cumulative without any period resolution and it is necessary in processing to assume standard customer type demand profiles to reconcile the hourly or half hourly data.

7.5 COST OF DISTRIBUTION

Table 7.1 shows a typical cost makeup for a large distribution company or the summated costs of several utilities for a small country. The major cost component at €716 m (42% of total) is for operation and maintenance of the network assets. The second highest cost is for servicing the capital Regulated Asset Base (RAB of €8028 m). Assuming a weighted average cost of capital of 6% the RAB incurs an annual cost of €481.7 m (28% of total). Depreciation on the asset base adds a cost of €231 m (14% of total). Tax and public service costs add €66.2 m with the rest made up of losses at €215 m, which are higher on distribution networks than for transmission. The total costs €1710.9 m have to be recovered through the tariffs for use of system.

The O&M costs include other ongoing costs and can be broken down further as shown in Figure 7.1 into the following:

• new capital investment related costs (31%);
• existing plant operation and maintenance (20%);
• supporting commercial operation, settlement, accounting etc. (15%);
• metering installation, testing, reading etc. (13%);
• customer service, liaison, agreements, billing etc. (12%);
• the management of the asset base including outage planning (7%);
• provision of information, to customers, regulators, investors etc. (2%).

A large proportion of the O&M costs (80%) will be payroll related for salaries and pension provisions. These will be analysed by the regulator, together

Distribution O&M

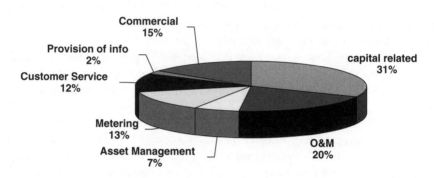

Figure 7.1   Distribution cost makeup

with the planned development of staff numbers as part of the general periodic price review

7.6 DISTRIBUTION TARIFFS

A typical distribution tariff is shown in Table 7.2 for NW Europe; it is designed to recover the cost of the equipment used and is based on the declared capacity of the installation and operating costs and losses that reflect the energy delivered. The calculations shown are for a medium sized commercial or industrial Eurostat type 'la' customer (0.03 MW peak demand and energy requirement of 30 MWh/yr). All the charges are reduced to a price per kWh to establish an effective charge per unit. It includes a capacity charge of €1207/yr calculated from the product of the capacity tariff and the capacity (41.47 * 30 * 0.97) scaled by the 'E1' factor. The 'Y' factor is multiplied by the annual energy to calculate the proportional charge (0.003186 * 30 * 1000 = 95.58). The 'Other Charges' includes a 'system service charge' covering the overall operation of the system and specifically identifies the cost of losses and pensions provisions all multiplied by the energy supplied and added to the annual metering charge of €728/yr to total €788.5/yr. A transmission charge of €324/yr is added to the capacity and other charges based on 10.8 times the energy transferred (10.8 × 30 = 328). This is to cover the transmission use of system charge. These total costs per year are divided by the energy supplied to give an effective charge per MWh of €80.5/MWh. Similar calculations can be undertaken for the other distributors and other Eurostat consumer types to establish an overall pattern as shown in Figure 7.2.

Table 7.1 Distribution overall costs

Distribution costs €m	1710.9	%
O&M	716.6	42
WACC*RAB	481.7	28
Depreciation	231.2	14
Tax	21.7	1
Public service obligations	44.5	3
Cost of network losses	215.2	13
Corporate tax	0.1	0

It can be seen how the charges reduce for the larger customers with higher load factors. Type 'la' with a load factor of 11.4% pay around €68.6/MWh while type 'le' with a load factor of 45.6% pay some €19.7/MWh Table 7.3 shows the utilisation of the different Eurostat customer types. The costs for type 'le' users are around a quarter of those of 'la' and consistent with the network fixed costs being distributed amongst four times as many units. The

Table 7.2 Distribution use of system tariff

Tariffs		
capacity tariff	€/kW/yr	41.47
Y factor	€/kW	0.003186
system service tariff	€/kWh	0.00024
metering tariff	€/yr	728
losses tariff	€/kWh	0.00074
pensions	€/kWh	0.0010368
Assumed load		
capacity	MW	0.03
energy	MWh	30
load factor	%	11
Capacity charges		
E1 factor		0.97
Capacity charges	€/yr	1207
proportional charge	€/yr	95.58
total capacity charge	€/yr	1302.97
total capacity charge	€/kWh	0.04
max allowed by CREG	€/kWh	0.07
price used	€/kWh	0.04
Other charges	€/yr	788.50
total charges + Tx	€/yr	2415.47
charges	€/MWh	80.5

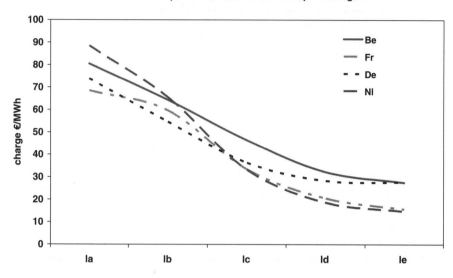

Figure 7.2   Distribution charges by customer type

network owner is responsible for proposing a set of tariffs for review by the regulator who will compare the absolute level and the distribution of charges amongst customer types. It can be seen that similar charges apply across the countries in NW Europe in this example.

Table 7.4 shows how the costs are constructed for a 'Id' consumer with a capacity of 0.5 MW and an annual energy of 1250 MWh. The tariff elements are shown followed by the assumed load details and finally the calculated charges for this customer type.

The monthly capacity charge is calculated as the product of the monthly charge times the monthly peak times 12 in this example. It enables the capacity charge to be varied according to a monthly declared peak. The annual capacity charge is the product of the capacity tariff and the annual peak capacity. The commodity charge is calculated from the sum of the commodity and system service tariff times the annual energy. Other fixed charges are for metering and maintenance. These charges are added and divided by the energy to give an effective unit charge.

Having established a set of tariffs for each customer type, the total revenue of the distribution company for use of its network can be estimated. If the customers are categorised by Eurostat types then the annual energy of each is known and the charge/MWh. Table 7.5 shows a typical mix of customer types

Table 7.3 Eurostat customer types

Category	MW	MWh	Utilisation (h/yr)
Domestic			
Da	0.003	0.6	200
Db	0.0035	1.2	343
Dc	0.0065	3.5	538
Dd	0.0075	7.5	1000
De	0.009	20	2222
Commercial and Small Industry			
la	0.03	30	1000
lb	0.05	50	1000
lc	0.1	160	1600
ld	0.5	1250	2500
Medium-Size Industry			
le	0.5	2000	4000
lf	2.5	10 000	4000
lg	4	24 000	6000
Large Industry			
lh	10	50 000	5000
li	10	70 000	7000

and their annual total energy. There are a large number of small domestic class users with a reducing number of larger customers. Using typical network unit charges, the total revenue can be estimated as the product of the two and comes to €1710 m as shown. This can be seen to match the total cost figure shown in the Table 7.1 and illustrates how the distribution company costs could be recovered.

7.7 OPEX REGULATION

The regulatory process aims to reduce the distribution charges to those of the most efficient utility. The process will involve a review of historic costs, as well as those predicted for the next five years. A target reduction in total charges will be proposed, often based on the change in the retail price index (RPI) together with a target reduction percentage termed 'X', the so called RPI–X formula. From Section 7.3 it can be seen that the largest cost element is

Table 7.4 Use of system charges for type ld

tariffs		
capacity tariff	€/kW/yr	9.87
commodity	€/kWh	0.0072
monthly/kW	€/kW/mon	1.06
standing + meters	€/yr	1142
maintenance	€/yr	588
system service	€/kWh	0.0011
Assumed load		
capacity	MW	0.5
energy	MWh	1250
monthly peak	MW	0.50
Charges		
monthly capacity	€/yr	6360
annual capacity	€/yr	4935
commodity	€/yr	10375
total	€/yr	21670
Other fixed chai	€/yr	1730
total charges	€/yr	23400
effective charges	€/MWh	18.7

for operation and maintenance, the so called OPEX (Operating Expenditure). This is the most controllable cost, with the others more influenced by external factors.

The regulators will draw comparisons of OPEX costs with other utilities but the difficulty is in finding one with similar characteristics against which to benchmark. The number of customers supplied is the key parameter but also of particular importance is the load density or average load per customer and the line lengths or average transmission distances involved per customer. The usual practice is to introduce factors to adjust the basic customer number to account for these other factors and establish an adjusted number. Data is collected for a number of utilities, including the number of consumers 'N', the total line length utilised and the load supplied. These are used to establish the average load/consumer 'U' and the average line length/consumer 'L' for all the utilities. Then the adjusted customer number Na is given by:

$$Na = N * (1 + \beta \, \delta U/U + \gamma \, \delta L/L).$$

Table 7.5 Total revenue estimate

Type	Capacity MW	Energy MWh	Consumers	Tariff €/MWh	Revenue €m	Revenue %
Da	0.003	0.6	1666000	92.6	93	5
Db	0.0035	1.2	1428000	73.3	126	7
Dc	0.0065	3.5	768923	56.0	151	9
Dd	0.0075	7.5	666400	50.5	252	15
De	0.009	20	555333	45.0	500	29
la	0.03	30	55533	68.6	114	7
lb	0.05	50	33320	55.1	92	5
lc	0.1	160	18300	34.3	101	6
ld	0.5	1250	4970	23.3	145	8
le	0.5	2000	3490	19.7	138	8
totals				revenue €m	1710	100

The values of beta and gamma that create the best fit to the results have been found in practice to be 0.25. Figure 7.3 shows a typical result for a benchmarking exercise using these factors and comparing the OPEX with the adjusted customer number of a number of small utilities.

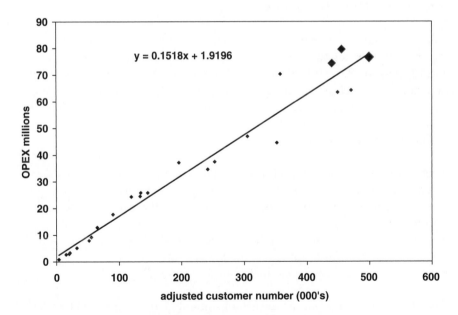

$y = 0.1518x + 1.9196$

Figure 7.3 Benchmarking distribution OPEX

It can be seen that the results do follow a trend line and, although not providing a definitive comparison, they are indicative of how a utility compares on average with others in the same area. The regulators may also be subject to complaints, particularly from industrial users, who are in competition with industries in other countries or may have plants in other countries. This will be dealt with by a detailed review of their specific characteristics and charges. Staffing and salary levels will be compared with other utilities whilst allowing for natural turnover and the age profile. Allowances for future rises in staff costs will be critically appraised and compared with out-sourcing options as these represent an on-going cost.

A factor that often distorts the comparisons is the amount of development that the organisation has to digest. As the services are required to be available on a 24/7 basis the introduction of any new functions or processes has to be staffed over and above the staff necessary to support normal operation. This is particularly relevant when introducing changes to accommodate market operation where inadequate provision may jeopardise successful implementation. In these circumstances the use of contract staff may be a better option than increasing the normal staff headcount.

7.8 CAPEX REGULATION

The other major component of distribution expenditure is for new capital equipment to meet the needs of new loads or embedded generation; reinforcement of the network; refurbishment and other non-network infrastructure costs such as system control facilities. A typical breakdown is shown in Table 7.6, a large proportion of the expenditure relates to new business and load growth necessitating reinforcement of the existing system.

The regulatory process will examine:

- new business entry and exit Capex, which will reflect assumptions on entry (embedded generation) and exit (demand connections) provisions;
- reinforcement expenditure will increase with the growth forecasts for demand;
- non-load related Capex – this includes refurbishment and is a major component of overall Capex for the DSO;
- non-network related Capex, including IT spend.

The objective is to encourage the establishment of an optimum network that meets customer requirements for security at minimum cost. The plans for the

Table 7.6 Distribution Capex

Capex component	€ ('m)	%
New business	847	32%
Reinforcements	611	23%
Network Non-Load related	1011	38%
Non-Network	192	7%
Total capex	2,661	100%

major projects would be reviewed for their justification, costing and whether they are capable of being delivered with the resources the utility has available. Continuity of supply trend data may reveal that the level of customer disturbances is low and the level of security against routine outages may be questioned. It is difficult to determine what constitutes the optimum network, taking account of security and costs. The costs should include network losses, given the increasing costs of energy. This question may be addressed in part by critically appraising the network planning standards.

Of particular importance in appraising costs will be a review of the processes put in place to manage assets, including the asset register and project management techniques. Data on the age of plant will provide a guide to the likely need for programmes of replacement or refurbishment.

7.9 BUSINESS RISK

Considering the main costs that are not directly controllable that affect the business, the cost of capital and wage costs constitute the major part. The data of Table 7.1 show the capital costs at £481.7 m with a WACC of 6%. If the WACC increases to 8% then this adds a cost of:

Increase in capital costs $= 0.02*8028$ m $=$ €160.5 m.

If it is assumed that the O&M cost of 716.6 m are made up of 80% labour costs then if these rise by 8% then:

Increase in O&M $= 0.08*0.8*716.6$ m $=$ €45.8 m.

These two credible factors give a total increase of:

Total cost increase $=$ €206.3 m.

This represents an increase of 12% on the original total cost of £1710.9 m and these two aspects will be the subject of debate with the regulator and may lead to indexed prices agreements.

On the revenue side, the business is subject to loss of revenue from customer migration to other areas as industries decline. This may be addressed by a selective pricing policy aimed at retaining industrial users. Based on the data in Table 7.5 the overall tariff increase to cover the addition cost discussed above would need to be 12%. If all the costs were levied on the larger industrial/commercial users (type 'le' to 'la') then costs would need to increase by:

$$100 * (206.3)/588.6 = 35\%.$$

If, however, the industrial tariff remained unaltered then the tariff to smaller users would have to increase by:

$$100 * 206.3/1122 = 18.4\%.$$

This form of discrimination may not be acceptable to regulators in a developed country but may be acceptable in a developing country seeking to attract new industry.

7.10 DISTRIBUTED GENERATION

With the advent of large scale efficient generation and the super-grid, the distribution networks became largely passive radial networks. This is as opposed to active networks with embedded generation affecting the flows through the network. More recently there has been an increase in the proportion of embedded generation. This may take the form of local small wind-farms or a small scale combined heat and power scheme, a waste to energy scheme or micro-generation scheme as described in Chapter 4.

These active sources of energy can have a significant effect on the local distribution network causing changes in flows and deviations in voltages. Research and development programmes have been established to develop control and management schemes for these networks similar to those applied to the interconnected transmission system. When combined with active control and possibly storage there is an opportunity to create a virtual power plant that can be operated harmoniously along with super-grid connected generation. Some local municipalities have actively pursued these local options and successfully contained the energy bills for their property portfolios.

It has been shown in Figure 7.2 that the distribution element of end user charges ranges from around €30/MWh (€c3/kWh) rising to €90/MWh (€c9/kWh) for the small domestic user. The avoidance of this charge makes a significant difference to the viability of local schemes. Recognising this, some municipalities have established direct wire connections between their premises to fully exploit their embedded generation schemes. Overall it does not seem a viable long term arrangement to bypass the existing distribution network and it raises questions about network charges for embedded generation. This is highlighted where the local installation has surplus energy to supply to the distribution network. Energy injected at the extremity of the network can have the effect of reducing flows and overall losses. Against this embedded generation, supplies require active management to avoid interference with the quality of supply to other consumers. If rates are set just based on the avoided energy cost then it is likely to promote more incidences of direct wiring from generators to other local consumers. Regulators have tended to react to encourage new entry, particularly where high efficiency schemes are promoted. Some form of partnership arrangement needs to be established that fully recognises the costs and benefits and leads to full exploitation of the local distribution network assets.

7.11 SUMMARY

This chapter has discussed the unbundling of distribution into wires ownership and supply and the various implementations that have been adopted. It illustrates the makeup of a distribution companies total cost principally including asset related capital charges, operation and maintenance and system losses. The structure of typical tariffs is shown and how these compare between countries and for different customer types. A representative customer base is used to show how the total tariff revenue lines up against the total operating costs. The process of regulation is outlined for reviewing OPEX and an approach to benchmarking utilities against each other taking account of the number of customers and relative loading and line lengths is described. Finally the process for reviewing Capex in terms of new business, reinforcement, non-load-related and the non-network costs are discussed. This chapter has provided an overview of the overall financial arrangements underpinning a distribution business and how this is regulated. It has also raised questions about the impact of a growth in distributed generation and their use of system network charges.

8

End User Charges and Prices

8.1 INTRODUCTION

The concept behind restructuring of the power sector was to introduce competition, which economists believed would lead to lower prices for end users. The theory is that given a choice of supplier then customers are able to exercise options to get the best deal to meet their needs. It is difficult to judge how successful this strategy has been, given the changes that have also occurred in fuel prices, generation technology and demand levels. One measure of success of this concept is judged by how many consumers have changed supplier or customer 'churn' as it is sometimes called. A high proportion of consumers have changed but there is also recognised to be a category of consumer that is resistant to change. This has led to some aggressive doorstep selling as a customer capture has been estimated to be worth several hundred pounds to a supplier.

The regulatory function also takes an interest in end user prices through its role in regulating the transmission and distribution sectors. For example Ofgem reported that in the UK 50% of consumers had moved to a new supplier over a six year period. On average, standard credit customers switching for the first time saved between £79 and £126 by switching to dual fuel, £92 by switching gas supplier and between £20 and £47 by switching electricity supplier, providing they shop around and switch to the cheapest supplier in

Power Markets and Economics: Energy Costs, Trading, Emissions   Barrie Murray
© 2009 John Wiley & Sons, Ltd

their area. The two-tier pattern of prices that had prevailed since the beginning of competition, where incumbents maintained their prices to existing customers whilst offering lower prices to attract new customers, was beginning to break down.

With companies becoming more multinational they will have the opportunity to compare energy prices across borders. A typical project may be to review current and prospective energy costs for an industrialist seeking to identify where to locate a new energy intensive plant. This will involve a review of the cost chain and comparison with other candidate countries.

In the previous chapters the costs incurred in generation, transmission and distribution have been analysed. In this chapter it is explained how these come together to make up the cost chain leading to end user prices. This includes the cost of energy from generation, and the transmission and distribution costs involved in delivering that energy to the consumer supply point. The chapter:

- discusses the costs making up the charges to end users;
- explains how tariffs are structured by suppliers; and
- compares charges to different customer types.

The data used in this chapter are typical but will vary significantly with time, particularly the energy costs that will be influenced by the prevailing fuel prices. The chapter illustrates how a price review can be undertaken by breaking down the charges into their constituent parts and analysing these against costs and those of similar utilities.

8.2 PRICE COMPARISONS

The prices for large consumers are based on the wholesale energy price, plus a charge for network access and use of system, and any local tax. A typical set of prices are shown in Figure 8.1, which illustrates the range of variation in wholesale energy prices and the additional network and supply costs. The dotted line shows a new entry cost, with Spain and Italy showing a large premium to wholesale prices. This is because of older oil plant setting high marginal prices. End user prices in Italy are correspondingly much higher than the average in Europe, reflecting the high wholesale price. The high transmission cost seen in Germany highlights why network access charges have been the subject of investigation by the German Federal Cartel Office. The wide variations in system-related charges are not always explained by major network or tax differences and should be the subject of more visibility

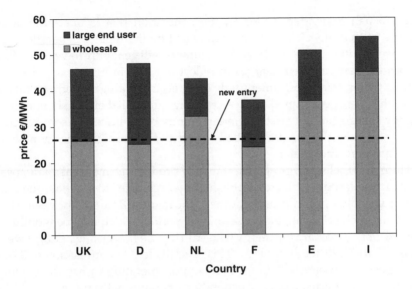

Figure 8.1 End user price comparisons NW Europe

given the monopoly status of the network operators and their impact on end user charges.

The plant mix in each country will be an important determinant of the energy price component. As oil is currently very expensive, any country burning oil at the margin will have very high prices. As gas prices are linked to oil, gas fired generation operating at the margin will also drive up prices. The advantage of cheap wholesale prices is that they enable a country to export surplus energy and maximise the contribution to fixed costs, helping to keep internal costs low. This is particularly important with nuclear stations that are less flexible and have high capital costs, as in France the biggest exporter in Europe. Larger consumers have the opportunity to service their energy needs by contracting across borders using the service of exchanges. Alternatively if an indigenous player wishes to restrict foreign entry, this can be contained by high network charges. This has been evident in some instances where vertically integrated companies operate and it can be construed as a form of protectionism.

8.3 END USER ENERGY PRICES

The estimation of basic generation energy prices was described in Chapter 3. The energy cost appropriate to a specific consumer class will depend on the profile of its demand. The system marginal cost of energy will vary from half hour to half hour, depending on the generation that is operating at the margin at that time. This will be influenced by the type of generation, fuel and overall utilisation. The largest consumers will generally have time of day metering, enabling their charges to reflect the system marginal price accurately. Other small consumers will have accumulating metering that just gives the energy consumed between readings and will therefore have a single energy charge, possibly with different energy block prices. In some circumstances different tariffs are applied for off-peak overnight energy metered through a separate meter.

The market sells energy against standard products termed 'base' and 'peak' load. These 'products' were established by exchanges to facilitate the maximum amount of liquidity and trading in the market. Base load prices are for a fixed energy level throughout the contract period, which may be monthly or annual. Peak prices are for energy taken during the 12 working hours of weekdays, i.e. for 3120 hours per year. This is equivalent to a utilisation of 35.6%, as opposed to typically 80% for a generator operating in base load mode. Assuming that the fixed costs of generation operating at the margin are 20% of the total costs, then this has to be recovered from the units generated and will give rise to higher charges at lower utilisations. For example if we assume that the variable costs make up 80% of the total costs with 20% fixed costs the percentage difference between base load and peak generation prices to achieve full cost recovery can be calculated.

$$\text{Base load price} = \text{Variable } (V) + \text{Fixed } (F),$$

where $V = 0.8$ and $F = 0.2$ per unit for a unit base load price of 1.0.

For a peaking generator, F has to be recovered from 3120 units generated as opposed to 7008 hours for an 80% utilised base load generator.

The fixed cost/unit generated has to increase in the ratio $7008/3120 = 2.24$, i.e. a fixed proportion per unit of $0.2 * 2.24 = 0.448$.

Per unit peak price $= 0.8 + 0.448 = 1.24$, i.e. the peak price is 24% higher than the base load price and is typical of that occurring in developed markets.

These costs can be used to illustrate how energy prices are structured for consumers based on their utilisation. For example, for a customer with a utilisation of 6500 hours, the energy supplied is equivalent to full load for 6500 h of the year equalling 6500 MWh for a maximum load of 1 MW. Therefore:

$$8760 * B + 3120 * P = 6500 \text{ MWh},$$

where B is the base load proportion and P the additional peaking proportion of the load.

Also the maximum load is given by P superimposed on B, i.e.

$$B + P = 1\,MW.$$

Substituting

$$8760 * B + 3120 * (1-B) = 6500$$

$$5640 * B = 3380, \text{ i.e. } B = 0.6 \text{ or } 60\%.$$

This means that, for a consumer with a utilisation of 6500 h, the energy charge will be made up of 60% base load and 40% peak with a per unit price given by:

$$0.6 * 1.0\,pu + 0.4 * 1.24\,pu = 1.096\,pu \text{ (times base load price).}$$

Similarly for a utilisation of 4000 hours:

$$5640 * B = 4000 - 3120 = 880$$

$$\text{i.e. } B = (\text{util. h} - 3120)/5640 = 16\%$$

$$\text{Price} = 0.16 * 1.0\,pu +).84 * 1.24 = 1.2\,pu \text{ (times base load).}$$

This assumes peak prices are 1.24 time base load prices as described above.
If the utilisation is less than 3120 hours then all the energy is deemed to be peaking energy. If the utilisation is less than 1000 h, then a super-peak price may apply to reflect the highest price seen during the day.

A super peak per unit price can be calculated assuming that the variable costs are the same but that the fixed costs have been reduced to 0.15 per unit due to the lower inherent capital cost of peaking plant or some of the capital older plant operating in peaking mode having been written off.

$$\text{Super-peak price} = 0.7 + (7008/1000) * 0.15 = 1.75 * \text{base load price.}$$

The Dutch used to sell wholesale electricity against a tariff called the SEP Protocol. This identified four categories of utilisation making up the demand profile. Table 8.1 shows the capacity and energy charges in Guilders up to the breakpoint utilisation levels.

Table 8.1 SEP Protocol

	BASE1	MID1	PEAK1	SPEAK
Energy Cost capacity utilisation	43.3	51.2	91.2	1250
	260000	205000	125000	0
	1	0.75	0.035	0.008

The implicit assumption in this simplified assessment is that consumer high load periods occur during weekdays when peak prices will apply. Also, the low load periods, which reduce the overall utilisation, will always occur out of the normal working week period when base load prices will apply. In practice, tariffs may be set based on actual customer declared load profiles or standard profiles. In the case of some domestic customers, special off peak tariffs may apply for 1200 kWh of their total 3500 kWh and all this energy may be met using peaking contracts.

8.4 TOTAL END USER PRICES

Using the analysis above, together with the cost of distribution and transmission derived in Chapters 6 and 7, the total end user costs can be estimated as shown in Table 8.2.

A graph of the total end user prices and the price of the energy component is shown in Figure 8.2. It can be seen that a large proportion of the small user costs are associated with the transmission and distribution of energy.

It can be seen how the end result compares with actual prices recorded by Eurostat in €c/kWh for a similar time period shown in Figure 8.3 (€c15/kWh = €150/MWh). Both the actual and synthesised curve show an apparent discontinuity where the unit price rises. This occurs because of changes in the Eurostat consumer type utilisation hours. They also coincide with the points where the tariff structures change, embracing different connection voltage levels. The tariff used will depend on the specific connection arrangements and voltage for each consumer. The level of charge is smaller in those markets where competition between suppliers is fully competitive as in the UK. The logarithmic trend in the graph of prices versus utilisation hours in Figure 8.4 shows a more consistent trend. It illustrates the profound effect that utilisation has on the end user prices. This results in both higher energy charges and higher transmission and distribution prices.

Table 8.2 Cost comparisons by customer type

	MW	MWh	Util (hrs/yr)	Base %	Peak %	Super peak	Per unit price	Energy €/MWh	Tx/Dx cost €/MWh	End user €/MWh
Domestic										
Da	0.003	0.6	200	0.0	0.0	100.0	1.75	70.0	92.6	162.6
Db	0.0035	1.2	343	0.0	0.0	100.0	1.75	70.0	73.3	143.3
Dc	0.0065	3.5	538	0.0	0.0	100.0	1.75	70.0	56.0	126.0
Dd	0.0075	7.5	1000	0.0	0.0	100.0	1.75	70.0	50.5	120.5
De	0.009	20	2222	0.0	100.0	0.0	1.24	49.6	45.0	94.6
Commercial & Small Industry										
la	0.03	30	1000	0.0	0.0	100.0	1.75	70.0	68.6	138.6
lb	0.05	50	1000	0.0	0.0	100.0	1.75	70.0	55.1	125.1
lc	0.1	160	1600	0.0	100.0	0.0	1.24	49.6	34.3	83.9
ld	0.5	1250	2500	0.0	100.0	0.0	1.24	49.6	23.3	72.9
Medium-Size Industry										
le	0.5	2000	4000	15.6	84.4	0.0	1.20	48.1	13.4	61.5
lf	2.5	10000	4000	15.6	84.4	0.0	1.20	48.1	12.6	60.7
lg	4	24000	6000	51.1	48.9	0.0	1.12	44.7	11.2	55.9
Large Industry										
lh	10	50000	5000	33.3	66.7	0.0	1.16	46.4	8.6	55.0
li	10	70000	7000	68.8	31.2	0.0	1.07	43.0	6.6	49.6

End user prices by Eurostat category

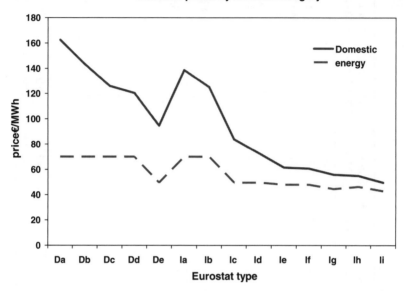

Figure 8.2   End user price profiles

8.5 TARIFF DEVELOPMENT

The end user will have an agreement in place with a supplier responsible for administering the supply, including maintaining the service, metering and billing. The supplier will in turn procure energy and transmission/distribution services to meet the needs of its customer base. In most European countries the franchise to supply in a distribution area has been progressively removed and customers may choose their supplier. The supplier may be a separate business, part of a distribution business, a municipality, a generator with an associated supply business or any business with an existing customer base. The bulk of the energy needs are likely to be procured against longer term base and peak load contracts with the rest from shorter term contracts through a market. The supplier will need to establish sufficient contracts for energy to maintain some level of security of supply to its customer base. The contracts to suppliers are usually termed Bulk Supply Tariffs (BSTs) and

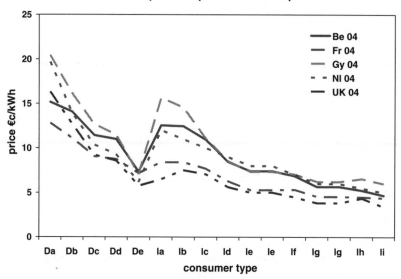

Figure 8.3 NW European tariffs

may be with the state generation company or a mixture of private companies with some generation ownership by the supplier. Whatever the arrangements, the supplier will have a profile of contracted energy prices varying with time of day/year.

The tariff for selling on to end users will need to reflect the suppliers energy cost profile. This is easier where time of day metering is available as for larger users. However, for the smaller users with accumulating meters assumptions have to be made about the demand profile in setting the energy component of the tariff. The ideal tariff will be one where the energy price (P) for the period is the average of the marginal prices in each half hour (M) weighted according to the energy consumed in the half hour (Q), i.e.

$$P = (M_1Q_1 + M_2Q_2 \ldots M_nQ_n)/(Q_1 + Q_2 \ldots + Q_n).$$

The supplier will seek to establish a customer base with a mixture of loads that results in an overall profile that is relatively flat and can be largely met from the cheaper base load contracts.

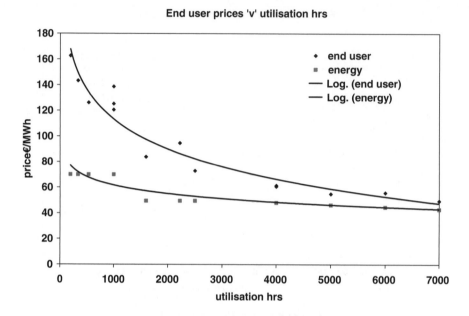

Figure 8.4 End user prices versus utilisation

The energy tariff may also include a specific capacity payment related to the maximum demand expected or this may be embraced within the energy charges. It has been shown how capacity is included in transmission and distribution tariffs and it may also be explicitly referenced in energy supply contracts. The objective will be to ensure that sufficient generation capacity is retained in service to meet demand. A typical arrangement is that included in the original UK pool where an increment to the system marginal price (SMP) was based on an estimate of the loss of load probability (LOLP) and the value attributed to loss of consumer load (VLL). The LOLP was based on the probability of reduced generation availability coinciding with the probability of a higher demand level. The VLL was based on an estimate of the value to consumers of averting a supply interruption. The Pool Selling Price (PSP) is then given by:

$$PSP = SMP + LOLP * (VLL - SMP).$$

This would apply for most of the time with additional charges added during peak periods to cover other operating costs. In some market implementations a simple capacity charge may be levied. The end user tariff may in turn include a maximum demand charge to cover the energy related capacity charge and some meter installations are equipped with maximum demand metering to enable this.

Using the data on Tx/Dx prices shown in the Table 8.2 a suitable time of day tariff quote can be calculated to recover costs from a prospective medium sized customer. The demand profile is assumed to be made up of a stable demand of 0.15 MW, a demand of 0.3 MW during weekdays and a further demand of 0.1 MW during the weekday peak hour. Assuming a base load energy price of €40/MWh with a 12 h peak rate 25% higher and an hourly super-peak rate 75% higher then:

Maximum demand $= 0.15 + 0.3 + 0.1 = 0.55$ MW.

Annual energy $= 0.15 * 8760 + 0.3 * 3120 + 0.1 * 260 = 2276$ MWh.

Nearest class of customer = 'le' with a transmission/distribution charge of €13.4/MWh.

The **off-peak** overnight and weekend tariff would need to be €53.4/MWh, made up of an energy charge of €40/MWh with a network charge of €13.4/MWh.

The tariff for **week day** energy would need to be covered at peak rates at 1.24 * base rates i.e. €49.6/MWh for energy with a network charge of €13.4/MWh, i.e. a total rate of €63/MWh.

The **peak rate** for energy taken during the peak hour of weekdays would be charged at 1.75 times the base rate, i.e. €70/MWh plus a network charge of €13.4/MWh, i.e. a total of €83.4/MWh.

8.6 CUSTOMER SWITCHING

One criteria of the benefit of creating supply competition is the number of consumers that have seen benefit in switching suppliers. The graph of Figure 8.5 shows the proportion of customers switching supply in the first years following liberalisation in the UK. Since this period, developments in the more widespread use of the internet have led to websites being established to make it easier for customers to compare prices. Where the regulatory function enables the process, then competition in supply can become a reality. It requires the opportunity to discover and compare prices and a simple switching process to be put in place. In the UK several websites have been established to support the process.

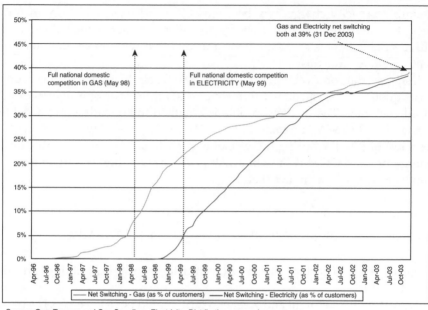

Source: Gas: Transco and Gas Suppliers, Electricity: Distribution companies

Figure 8.5 Customer net switching

8.7 SUMMARY

This chapter has developed the relationship between base load, peak and super-peak prices. These are used to estimate energy charges to different customer types based on their utilisation and likely demand profile. These energy costs are combined with transmission and distribution charges to establish the total end user costs. These are shown to compare with the prices applied in the countries of NW Europe and exhibit a fit to an algorithmic trend when compared with utilisation. It illustrates the profound effect of load factor or utilisation on end user prices. The development of optimal energy tariffs is discussed. Larger users will have time of day metering with charges defined for each half hour period. For smaller users the ideal tariff will be when the price equates to the average volume weighted system marginal price. This will usually be based on an assumed demand profile for the customer type where only integrated metering is available. Finally, some indication of the success of the introduction of supply competition is indicated by the number of customers switching supplier.

This chapter completes the explanation and make up of end user pricing structures and the rationale behind them as seen in liberalised markets.

Three

Market Operation

This part focuses on the operation of markets and covers the trading arrangements and price forecasting. It introduces the mechanisms used to trade ancillary services and illustrates their costing. The process for cross-border trading and the auctioning of inter-connector capacity is described. The final chapter deals with the process of investment appraisal and risk assessment.

Chapter 9 Trading Arrangements

This describes the arrangements that have been put in place and the exchanges that have been established across Europe to support trading. It identifies the perceived shortcomings in performance and market power issues. It describes the use of bilateral contracting, exchange trading and the balancing market, the products that are traded and how risk is managed.

Chapter 10 Power Price Forecasting

This explains the approaches adopted to forecast prices including predicting energy and demand levels and generation availability and statistical forecasting. Market simulation based on the dispatch process is discussed and the derivation of marginal prices is illustrated.

Chapter 11 Importance of Ancillary Services

This discusses the need for ancillary services and their role in supporting system operation. It describes the arrangements that have been adopted to manage their procurement on a competitive basis and how the costs and prices can be assessed.

Chapter 12 Role of Interconnection

This discusses the role of interconnection in coupling markets and supporting cross-border trading. It describes how capacity is reserved and discusses the use of auctions to manage over subscription. It outlines an approach to assessing charges for wheeling across intermediate networks.

Chapter 13 Investment Appraisal

This describes an approach to appraising development proposals in new generation. It includes prediction of fuel prices and availability to enable costs to be established. These are used to estimate utilisation and future revenues within a market environment. Finally the analysis of risks and other political/social issues is discussed.

9

Market Trading

9.1 INTRODUCTION

The facility to trade is an essential component in realising a competitive market. In practice this requires:

- a sufficient number of trading partners to enable choice;
- a mechanism whereby current and future prices can be discovered;
- a degree of market liquidity that realises price interaction;
- the absence of dominant market power.

In practice these requirements are less easily met. Attempts at restructuring have usually required the state generating companies to be split into three to five blocks. This was the case in countries such as Italy and the UK, whereas in New Zealand no company could own more than 5% of capacity. In practice, mergers and acquisitions have depleted the number of competing players with organisations such as EdF, E.ON, and RWE dominating across Europe. Other countries have chosen to retain national champions such as ENEL in Italy, Iberdrola in Spain, and Electrabel in Belgium, on the grounds of national security.

The mechanism for price discovery relies on exchanges publishing data based on actual transactions through a period. Reporting agencies also canvas data on prices and provide regular bulletins of typical contract prices. Economic forecasting houses will also publish their views on future prices. It is not always clear what information is being reported and there are often significant discrepancies between reporting sources. This may be because the

Power Markets and Economics: Energy Costs, Trading, Emissions   Barrie Murray
© 2009 John Wiley & Sons, Ltd

period covered with some exchanges does not include weekends or reporting volume weighted as opposed to time weighted data is used.

Liquidity can take several years to establish and in the UK it took from 1990 to 2002 to realise gas market liquidity. It does take time, but the process can also be impeded by blocking, market power and ineffective regulation. A restricted number of trading hubs clearly benefits good levels of liquidity. In Europe only the UK National Balancing Point has meaningful liquidity for gas trading.

New entry will be inhibited if a large indigenous player is able to exercise market power. It can often happen that a single player controls much of the plant operating at the margin and setting prices. A vertically integrated player is less sensitive to wholesale prices as sales are internal from generation to the supply division against a transfer price so the wholesale price does not affect the company's bottom line.

In the previous chapters it has been shown how end user costs are built up of generation, transmission and distribution. This chapter explains how the energy component of costs is procured by suppliers through trading. It discusses:

- how suppliers trade energy to meet their demand profile;
- the role of power exchanges and brokers;
- the approach to managing the volume and price risk.

The data used in this section are typical but will vary significantly with time, in particular, the energy costs, which will be influenced by the prevailing fuel prices.

9.2 EUROPEAN MARKETS

The EU identified four serious shortcomings in the operation of the European gas and power markets:

1. excessive market concentration in most countries;
2. a lack of liquidity preventing successful new entry;
3. limited integration between markets;
4. the absence of data transparency undermining price discovery.

The EU plan to use its full powers under competition rules to improve the situation and encourage the development of interconnection. This process starts with the formation of closely coupled regions and is expected to develop as a result of their coupling as interconnection is extended. In the liberalised world funding new interconnection has to be shown to be economic, based on expected revenues from leasing capacity on the link. This requires a sustained price differential through the project life. A fundamental difficulty is that this differential may be undermined by another market participant choosing to build generation in the high cost country, offsetting the price differential. This is a feature of uncoordinated development that necessitates adding in a risk element that weakens the economic case and delays new build.

Not all countries are in favour of open market based competition and have undermined its development. The French have always advocated the Single Buyer market model and introduced something called TARTAM in 2007 (Tarif Réglementé Transitoire d'Ajustement du Marché). This mechanism allowed eligible users to opt for a regulated tariff as opposed to a market based tariff. This was prompted by clients complaining that they were paying 70% above the regulated tariff on a market based tariff. The prices for the regulated tariff were pegged at a percentage above a base, depending on customer size, but were all below market wholesale prices. The option to take the tariff had to be exercised for at least two years and provided some certainty to consumers on future energy prices affecting their business. The revenue shortfall was to be made up by contribution from a levy on all end users through the Electricity Public Service Contribution (CSPE) and from EdF to recompense suppliers offering the regulated tariff. Clearly this type of development will undermine market operation and liquidity and reverts back to a centrally administered tariff system.

9.3 DEVELOPING MARKETS – CHINA

In contrast to the situation in Europe, China is still very much in the throes of restructuring and its history can be reviewed. The industry is massive and during the 1990s was growing at 9% a year with some 290 GW of capacity by 2000 and is expected to reach 550 GW by 2010 with 150 000 km of HV transmission making it comparable to Europe. Reform began in 1985 when grants for new power plants were abolished and utilities were ordered to set costs on a cost plus basis. In 1997 a semi-autonomous State Power Corporation (SP) was established to manage and plan the development of the system. Subsequently pilot generation bidding systems were established in several provinces; this became nationwide by 2005. It was planned that by 2010, following completion of the Three Gorges project, a fully interconnected system would be established leading to a more liquid and competitive market in generation. The restructuring plan included (see *Power System Restructuring and Deregulation*, 2002):

- establish the state power corporation;
- separate government from enterprise functions;
- establish a fully interconnected system through 2010 to 2020 according to economic criteria;
- open up the distribution and supply side to competition with unified pricing.

In essence the market is operated on a Single Buyer basis with a mixture of mechanisms to finance generation. Some new generation was contracted on a cost plus basis with interest, while others were selected to operate against bid prices. Some generation involved in the supply of heat was excluded from the process.

The development strategy for the industry gave priority to hydro and renewable generation sources coupled with the application of large scale 600 MW efficient units. The policy took into account the retro fit of older coal and hydro plants to improve efficiency.

In practice pricing has been controlled by the state and has been distorted. In some instances the state did not allow fixed cost recovery, with prices below marginal production costs leading to financial loss. The government sees the need to maintain control over the industry, recognising its strategic importance to the overall economy, and this will impede restructuring. At the same time there is a need to encourage inward investment and this has led to a multiplicity of different contracted price arrangements with each new power plant. Some PPAs that included a guarantee to buy a defined proportion of energy are not being honoured. There has also been reluctance for provinces to trade across interconnectors, even at times of power shortages, with each province seeking to maintain autonomy. This situation undermines the realisation of the development and operation of an optimum system. Given the pace of development of the industry and its strategic importance it is understandable that the Chinese government have chosen to exercise control through a single buyer model where they audit all contracts. This has to be managed against a contract structural framework that provides the flexibility needed for optimum integrated operation.

9.4 MARKET POWER

Privatisation in the UK was followed by the sale of successor companies to foreign interests while other countries have seen the benefit in retaining national champions. On the generation side, we see EdF as the leader in the European market with 40 million customers of which 28 million are in France.

They operate as a vertically integrated business with generation, transmission and distribution assets. The market opening in France is largely theoretical with only 5% of eligible consumers having a supplier other than EdF in 2006. A survey indicated that some 50% of customers did not realise that they could change supplier and competition is inhibited by selective tariffs that are below normal market prices. RWE and EOn are the national champions in Germany and it has been claimed that network access has proved difficult for new entrants. In Italy ENEL remain a dominant force and the planning approval process has delayed new entry. In Spain Iberdrola and Endesa remain the dominant market forces. The advantage of these larger entities is that they are better able to manage risk and the security of supply. This is contrary to the realisation of a competitive liquid market, which benefits from having a level playing field with many competing buyers and sellers.

On the customer side there is developing interest in the establishment of end user consortia that are able to negotiate the best terms with the large generators/suppliers. For example Exceltium is a French limited company founded by seven industrial groups, including Air Liquide, Alcan, Arkema, Arcelor Mittal, Rhodia, Solvay and UPM-KYmmene, and representing 60 companies across France. Its objective is to provide some price stability by establishing long term 15 year supply contracts based on production costs. They established a memorandum of understanding with EdF to manage volume and price risk through a commercial partnership.

The Exceltium plan was to establish the supply agreement in 2007, given that approval is obtained from the European competition authorities. Other organisations such as Blue Sky and Fortia are pursuing a similar approach and, with their combined demand representing up to 20% of some countries capacity, they will have a profound effect on market operation. The international response to the increasing consolidation of the industry has been limited, even though EU Directives have been translated into national legislation.

9.5 TRADING ARRANGEMENTS

There are several market mechanisms available to affect trades that operate through the various timescales up to the event including:

- a bid process or auction;
- bilateral contracts that may be established through a broker;
- buying blocks of energy through an exchange;
- spot trading through an exchange
- the Balancing Market.

Contracts for larger blocks of energy making up a large proportion of the requirement for the period ahead may be established though a tendering process. The volumes involved and the lead time make it worthwhile and practical to invite tenders to get the best price. This process may typically take place at six monthly intervals. Adjustments for the months ahead may be made using monthly contracts that are often managed through a broker when anonymity is preferred.

Exchange trading tends to be for shorter periods where suppliers and generators are fine tuning their positions at the week/day ahead or within day stage. Exchanges have been established at several strategic locations around Europe. The key ones are as shown in Figure 9.1, marked by asterisks, and include Nordpool covering the Nordic area; the Amsterdam Power Exchange (APX) covering the Netherlands and the North West and the European Energy Exchange (EEX) covering the central area. An exchange has been established in Paris called Powernext. The UK Power Exchange has been absorbed by the APX, and the Leipzig exchange by the EEX. Local pools also exist in Spain and, more recently, in Italy and Greece.

Cross-border trades are enabled if transmission capacity is available. This may involve the management of congestion and associated auctions of transmission capacity by the Transmission System Operators (TSO) managing the area. Figure 9.1 shows the control areas that are responsible for maintaining stable secure operation in their region. At some point called 'gate closure' trading is suspended and the responsible parties have to submit their

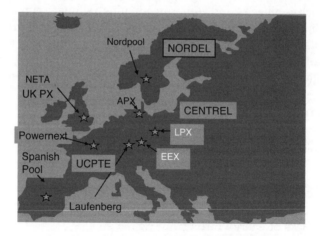

Figure 9.1 European exchanges

contracted position to the TSO. From then up to the event the TSO uses bids into a Balancing Market to maintain system balance.

9.6 BILATERAL TRADING

These are deals directly between suppliers and generators usually for large blocks of base load and peak generation or to meet a specific demand profile. The supplier will need to establish the profile for its total customer base for the year ahead on a half hour by half hour basis. The larger industrial users will be able to supply a profile based on their production cycles. For smaller and domestic users it will be necessary to assume a set of typical profiles. The aggregated demand may be expressed as a demand duration curve as shown in Figure 9.2. This shows the proportion of the year that the demand is at different levels.

There will inevitably be some risk in the assessment of the demand level termed the 'volume' risk. This will result from basic forecasting errors that may occur when the weather is different from the average for the period as well as customer 'churn', where users change their supplier. The supplier will have to estimate the range of possible outturns in order to formulate a trading strategy. As the event approaches the estimation, error will reduce and there will be possibilities to fine tune the contracted position.

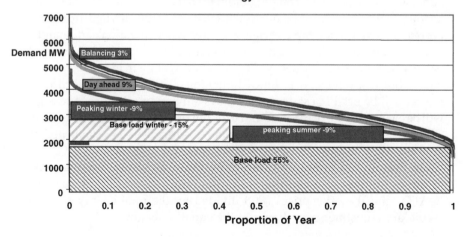

Figure 9.2 Traded volumes under load duration curve

The load duration curve can be broken down into a number of blocks as shown in the graph of Figure 9.2. There will be a basic continuous load that may be met from a competitively priced annual base load contract; there will be a shorter high load period during winter that can be met using a six-monthly base load contract. The demand profile may be more closely tracked using monthly base load contracts. There will also be a requirement for peaking contracts to cover the higher weekday demand levels. In each case there will be an estimated energy requirement shown as a percentage of the total. The contracted amount will allow for error and will generally be less than the predicted demand. Further trading will take place at the day ahead and within day to fine tune the contracted generation contracts to meet the latest expected outturn demand. The volumes of energy traded progressively reduce as the event is approached.

9.7 BALANCING MARKET

At the point of gate closure the supplier and generator will have to declare their contracted volumes to the TSO. This is usually an hour before the event when registered parties qualified to make returns to the TSO have to make their submissions. They are commonly known as Balance Responsible Parties (BRPs) and return Programmes of Generation/Demand to the TSOs for the period ahead (in the UK called Final Physical Notifications (FPNs)). There will inevitably be some errors in the submitted predictions that the TSO will need to address. This is realised through a voluntary Balancing Market that operates to keep the system in balance up to the event. Bids are invited from market participants to provide rapid increase/decrease of generation or demand. The TSO will buy these increments and decrements of power to effect system balance and manage frequency. The selection will be made on an economic basis while respecting any technical limitations. Those bids called within each period will be used in establishing the system buy or sell price. These prices will be charged to participants found to be out of balance, having taken more or less energy than they declared at 'gate closure'. This is established from metering data collected by the Central Data Collection Agent (CDCA).

The **System Buy Price** (SBP) for each period is calculated from the total cost of energy from the accepted offers calculated from the product of the volumes (QAPO) and the offer prices (PO) divided by the total energy with some secondary adjustments as shown in the equation below:

$$SBPj = \{\Sigma i \Sigma n \{QAPOn\ ij * POn\ ij * TLMij\}\}/$$
$$\{\Sigma i \Sigma n \{QAPOn\ ij * TLMij\}\} + \{BPAj\},$$

where Σi represents the sum over all BM Units and Σn represents the sum over those accepted offers QAPO with prices PO giving the weighted energy cost. (The term TLM is an adjustment to take account of losses.) This is divided by the energy (QAPO) to give a price per MWh. The term BPA is the transmission company's buying price adjustment (BPA).

Similarly the **System Sell Price** (SSP) is determined from the sum of the product of volume (QAPB) and bid prices (PB) of accepted bids divided by the total energy as shown in the equation below to give a price in £/MWh:

$$SSPj = \{\{\Sigma i \Sigma n \{QAPBn\ ij * PBn\ ij * TLMij\}\} /$$
$$\{\Sigma i \Sigma n \{QAPBn\ ij * TLMij\} + UESVAj\}\} + \{SPAj\},$$

where Σi represents the sum over all BM Units and Σn represents the sum over those accepted Bids with the term SPA the transmission selling price adjustment. The system sell and buy prices are effectively the average price of bids and offers as used. These data are used to calculate the imbalance cash flow and the System Operator BM cash flow and require the following additional data to enable settlement:

- from the TSO: FPNs, bid/offer data, acceptance data, Balancing Service volumes and any adjustments;
- from the CDCA: the BM unit metered volumes, the inter-connector metered volumes and GSP metered volumes;
- Transmission Loss Multipliers (TLMs) as used to allocate losses.

The data from the TSO consists of dispatch instructions with 'from' and 'to' times and these are recorded as spot times and associated MW values. This applies to FPNs as well as the bid/offer and acceptance data. This spot data is translated into settlement period half hour integrated values based on linear interpolation between the spot values.

9.8 EXCHANGE TRADING

Power exchanges have been established that operate in a similar manner to stock exchanges. They use IT systems to display current bid and offer volumes and prices and enable clients to establish deals for physical delivery on an anonymous basis. The products are usually defined as base load or peak and may cover days or blocks of power for 4 hours down to individual half hours.

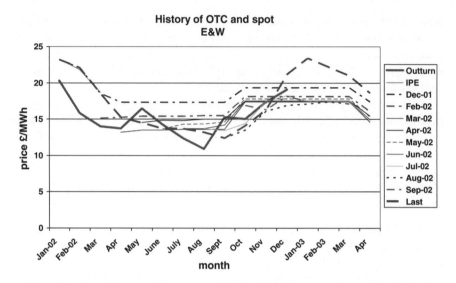

Figure 9.3   Market price development

The exchanges support price discovery and will publish forward prices to enable users to judge their positions. These prices are not a forecast but reflect what has been offered to the exchange by buyers and sellers. These will vary depending on market sentiment and the graph of Figure 9.3 shows the range of variation in traded prices over successive months, together with the outturn on the day.

The solid bold line shows the outturn derived from the prices contracted on the daily spot market. The bold dash line shows the last monthly forecast derived from the data for the month before the event; the other fainter lines show the prices published in earlier months. It can be seen that these show a significant range of variation. The trader will take account of these as well as his or her own forecast in making judgements about deals and their timing. To be an effective mechanism the market needs a lot of participants to ensure liquidity and support price discovery. This in turn requires that the market is structured around standard products such as base load and peak load.

9.9 SUPPLIER RISK

The **supplier** will have to agree contract prices with consumers and set tariff prices for smaller users in advance and will be exposed to a **risk of prices** for wholesale energy being higher. The risk is minimised by contracting ahead for energy from generators for the period for which the customer prices are fixed. This approach may not be optimum if prices are falling when there would be advantage in delaying dealing until close to the beginning of the supply period. Equally, if prices are expected to rise then the supplier may choose to contract further forward for blocks of energy. In a competitive supply market, failure to maintain competitive prices will result in loss of customers. The supplier will determine strategy, making use of any published forward curves and independent estimates.

The other source of risk to the supplier is the **volume risk** resulting from not having an accurate estimate of the final demand of the customer base. This has to be declared to the TSO at 'gate closure' and if the outturn is different from the declared volumes then the supplier is exposed to pay for 'make up' or 'spill' at the balancing market prices. These will not be known in advance and may be very high at times of shortfall. The supplier is better able to minimise this exposure if it has generation assets or demand management facilities that can be used to adjust the grid demand. The supplier may also prefer to take a long position by declaring a slightly higher demand than expected to avoid high makeup prices. The other option is to contract with a demand aggregator to take the responsibility for managing the risk in the Balancing Market.

The supplier will use IT based facilities to support the management of the process. These will enable contracts with end users to be evaluated by setting the demand profile against a profile of existing contracted energy supply prices. The package will also support demand aggregation as deals are established.

There is also a counter-party **credit risk** related to direct sales contracts with wholesale customers. This is usually managed by assigning an internal credit limit to each major customer. This will be backed with insurance to minimise the losses from a failure of customers to pay their debts. This may cover typically 70% of the amounts receivable from the larger customers.

9.10 GENERATION RISK

The **generators** are also exposed to **price risk** and have to decide what and when to contract for their expected output. They have similar decisions in how far ahead to contract depending on whether they expect prices to rise or fall. They are also exposed to balancing market prices as they may have plant problems that prevent them from meeting their contracted commitment. They will also have to manage their **fuel price risk**. They will need to contract forward for fuel supplies to meet their contracted energy requirement. Similar decisions have to be made depending on expected fuel price movement. The generator may have several fuel price contracts in place for the year or so ahead to back up contracts with suppliers or include fuel price indexing in contracts. Sometimes the fuel contracts are structured on a 'take or pay' basis when the generator is obliged to pay irrespective of whether the fuel is used. This applies particularly to gas contracts where, unlike coal, local storage may not be available. This can give rise to some very low prices when the market is oversupplied.

The generator also has to manage **volume risk** and decide on how much output would be contracted long term as opposed to trading on the spot market at the day-ahead stage or bidding into a balancing market where prices may be higher. A problem with operation in a spot market is that the utilisation will not be know ahead to enable fuel supplies to be contracted. The other risk in the short term is predicting the number of hours of operation over which start up costs have to be recovered.

The generators will have packages that model the costs of operation of their portfolio to support bid development. They will also need to model the dynamic characteristics of the plant such as run up and run down rates and minimum on and off times, as these will affect their flexibility to deliver.

For example consider a 300 MW peaking generator bidding into a day-ahead market. Assume that it has a variable running cost of £15/MWh with a no load heat requirement of £300/h and a start up cost of £2250. It has a minimum stable generation of 100 MW when starting. It has a minimum on time of 3 hours, a run up rate of 10 MW/min and run down rate of 30 MW/min. The cost of a 4 hour block bid in £/MWh that could be made into the market is calculated as shown below.

- Run up from MSG of 100 MW takes $200/10 = 20$ minutes at an average load of $(300 - 100)/2 = 200$ MW and MWh $= 200*10/60 = 66.6$ MWh.
- Run down takes $300/30 = 10$ minutes at average load of 150 MW $= 25$ MWh.
- The generator operates at full load of 300 MW for 3.5 h, generating 1050 MWh.
- Total production $= 66.6 + 25 + 1050 = 1141.6$ MWh.
- Total costs to include start up, variable running and no load heat costs $= 2250 + 1141.6*15 + 4*300 = £20\,574$, equivalent to a price of 20574/1141.6 $= £18$/MWh.

The output profile is shown in Figure 9.4.

If the generator bids this 4 h price into the market expecting to get at least 4 hours running but is only selected to run for two hours and sets the marginal

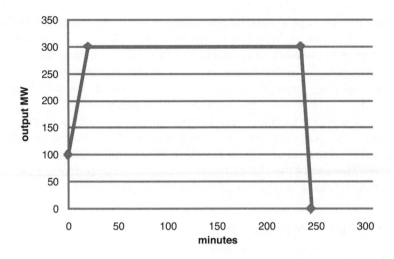

Figure 9.4 Peaking generator output profile

price for those hours then the money that would be lost can be calculated as follows:

The start up and run down produce 66.6 + 25 MWh and takes 30 minutes.

The full load running time is 1.5 h at 300 MW producing 450 MWh.

Total production = 66.6 + 25 + 450 = 541.6 MWh

Total costs to include start up, variable running and no load heat costs

$$= 2250 + 541.6 * 15 + 4 * 300 = £11\,574.$$

Total revenue = 541.6 * 18 = £9748.8.

Loss = 11574 − 9748.8 = £1825.

As well as the basic price risk, the generator also has to manage the impact of the plant dynamics on the costs that would be incurred. This risk inevitably has to be factored into the prices submitted into the Balancing market and results in premiums of typically £5–10/MWh or more at times of shortage.

The generator is also exposed to the **balancing risk** with potential differences between the actual metered generation and the notified contracted position. The error has to be settled through the balancing mechanism at generally unfavourable prices. This risk may be managed by maintaining a portfolio of generation including some flexible plant. In the UK, for example, British Energy also own Eggborough, a mid-merit coal power station that can be used to manage the risk associated with non-availability of nuclear plant.

There is also a **capital and liquidity risk** to the business due to its reliance on generation availability to maintain an income stream. This is critical to ensuring the availability of sufficient liquid funds to operate the business. This can be partly offset by the use of business interruption insurance but this will generally not cover all eventualities. Customers may also require that cash is deposited as collateral against the generator failing to deliver the contracted energy. In a volatile market this requirement may present a risk to liquidity. The generator will seek to minimise this risk by establishing collateral-free contract arrangements and maintaining standby letter of credit facilities. There may also be exposure to interest rates or foreign exchange rates that will need to be managed by the treasury function.

9.11 MARKET INTERACTION

The mechanism of short term interaction with the market can be illustrated by considering the position of a peaking generator bidding into an exchange. Assume a generator with capacity of 300 MW with a start up cost of £2250 and a required cost recovery of £20.76/MWh operating into a market. The market has an expected marginal price for the day ahead as shown in Table 9.1. The objective is to find the price bid for the day that will result in the generator being selected to run and maximise the net revenue from the market.

It can be seen in Table 9.1 that the system marginal price exceeds the generation cost of £20.76 from hour 18 to 27 where the average is £24/MWh for the 10 half hours. The return is then given by:

$$300 \text{ MW} * (£24/\text{MWh} - £20.76/\text{MWh}) * 10/2\text{h} = £4860.$$

A start up cost of £2250 has to be subtracted, giving a net return of £2610.

It would not be economic to bid to run the generator through hours 33 to 35 because the extra revenue would not cover the additional start up cost and this would be precluded by declaring the generator unavailable through these hours. The system price profile and running period of the generator are shown in Figure 9.5.

9.12 ARBITRAGE SPARK SPREAD

With the extended use of gas fired generation and gas markets there are opportunities to arbitrage between gas and electricity markets. A gas fired generator with a take or pay gas contract has the option either to use the gas

Table 9.1 Market day-ahead price prediction

	Marginal price £/MWh		
half hour		half hour	
HH050902-01	18.7	HH050902-25	24.0
HH050902-02	17.7	HH050902-26	24.4
HH050902-03	17.3	HH050902-27	25.7
HH050902-04	16.0	HH050902-28	20.7
HH050902-05	14.0	HH050902-29	20.7
HH050902-06	13.3	HH050902-30	20.7
HH050902-07	14.0	HH050902-31	20.0
HH050902-08	14.0	HH050902-32	20.0
HH050902-09	14.0	HH050902-33	22.0
HH050902-10	13.3	HH050902-34	22.0
HH050902-11	17.3	HH050902-35	22.0
HH050902-12	16.2	HH050902-36	20.7
HH050902-13	16.7	HH050902-37	20.0
HH050902-14	18.6	HH050902-38	19.7
HH050902-15	20.6	HH050902-39	18.0
HH050902-16	20.3	HH050902-40	17.8
HH050902-17	20.7	HH050902-41	17.7
HH050902-18	21.8	HH050902-42	17.0
HH050902-19	24.5	HH050902-43	17.0
HH050902-20	22.9	HH050902-44	17.7
HH050902-21	25.8	HH050902-45	17.4
HH050902-22	23.3	HH050902-46	18.3
HH050902-23	25.0	HH050902-47	19.3
HH050902-24	22.7	HH050902-48	19.3

to generate electricity or sell the gas back to the market. The decision will be based on the relative worth of the electricity given the prevailing market price versus the spot gas price. This has led to the concept of spark spread to indicate the difference between the gas price expressed in units per MWh based on an assumed efficiency and the actual power price.

An example is shown in Figure 9.6 where it can be seen that the power price is above the converted gas price and the spark spread is positive, indicating that it would be preferable to use the gas to produce electricity. There may be other periods when power prices are driven low during low load periods when it is preferable to sell the gas. This form of trading is essentially short term and seeks to exploit market imperfections. The

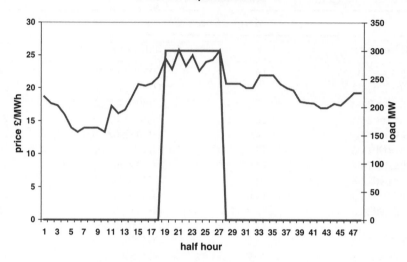

Figure 9.5 Spot market bidding

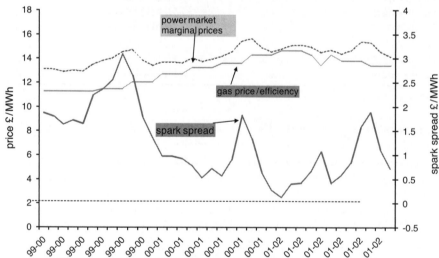

Figure 9.6 Spark spread

participating generation needs to be sufficiently flexible to take advantage of premium pricing in the spot electricity market and will usually be a peaking plant.

The option to exercise arbitrage can create problems with the operation of power systems. If gas prices are driven high due to shortages in winter it can cause a lot of gas-fired generation to choose to sell gas and be withdrawn from service, creating a power shortfall. This may occur during winter when both gas and power demands are high.

Some of the gas contracts are established with an interruptible clause, meaning that supplies can be withdrawn for a period to alleviate meeting a peak gas demand. A similar practice is applied to some contracts with larger electricity consumers. The interruptions are usually limited to a number of hours each year. This can also lead to power system problems if gas shortages lead to the interruption clause being invoked on a number of generators at the same time.

9.13 SUMMARY

This chapter has discussed the state of development of the pan-European markets for gas and electricity and the perceived shortcomings arising from too much concentration in a few players, the lack of liquidity and transparency and poor integration. It has described the way suppliers have to develop a profile of their future demand requirement and then contract for supplies from generators to meet it using commonly traded products. The supplier has to determine what and when to trade. They have to manage the volume risk resulting from not having an accurate estimate of customer demand and the price risk resulting from adverse variation. The supplier will manage the risks by progressively increasing the contracted volumes as the event approaches. The best prices may be established through auctions for large blocks of energy or through competitive exchanges for smaller volumes.

The generator has to secure contracts for their expected available output at the best price. There will be a risk of adverse price movement if contracts are placed prematurely on a rising market. They will also have a 'volume risk' that results from plant failure restricting the ability to meet their contracted demand. The generators also have a fuel volume and price risk. They may be uncertain of their expected utilisation and hence fuel requirement if they trade in the shorter term markets. They also have fuel price movement to manage. In the day-ahead spot market they also have to estimate the likely running hours over which they need to recover start up costs and this has been illustrated with examples.

Finally the 'spark spread' and option to arbitrage between gas and electricity markets is discussed. The potential power system problems that can occur as a result of generators choosing to sell gas rather than generate and gas suppliers exercising interruption clauses are described.

10

Market Analysis

10.1 INTRODUCTION

Participants in the market will need to take a view of expected developments in prices. This could be to support decision making in a number of different circumstances including:

- an investor seeking to identify the potential revenue from a new plant over the project life of typically 15 years;
- a supplier contracting for wholesale energy for the period ahead, which may be typically from a few months to two years;
- a generator trading the available output capacity into the wholesale market over the months to years ahead;
- a trader operating in the short term spot market;
- a player with flexible generation or demand trading in the balancing and ancillary services market.

Generally the requirements can be grouped into short term/spot to medium term market and the longer term contract market. In the short term the current conditions on plant availability and weather and demand will have a significant impact and need to be modelled. In the longer term contract market, the rate of demand growth and generation new entry will be important parameters. The participants will wish to understand the development of base load and peak prices. In the short term this may need to be resolved down to hourly values up to monthly, whereas the longer term will focus on

Power Markets and Economics: Energy Costs, Trading, Emissions   Barrie Murray
© 2009 John Wiley & Sons, Ltd

quarterly to annual values. The participants will also wish to track the basic assumptions underlying the prediction in terms of demand growth, new entry and plant margin as well as fuel prices and plant efficiencies.

In the previous chapter the mechanisms for trading in the market were reviewed. In this chapter we explore models for analysing the market to support trading and investment appraisal. The objectives are to:

- illustrate the prediction of system demand;
- show how marginal costs and prices can be predicted;
- develop a prediction based on the level of competition expected in market operation.

The data used in this chapter are typical but will vary significantly with time, particularly the energy costs that will be influenced by the prevailing fuel prices.

10.2 MODELLING OVERVIEW

There are various approaches that have been adopted to market forecasting with varying degrees of success. These include:

- a simulation based on a chronological demand profile with generation dispatched to meet demand whilst recognising plant dynamic characteristics;
- a simulation of market operation based on a load duration curve with generation dispatched using a merit order;
- a simulation that explicitly takes account of transmission constraints in the solution;
- price tracking where the forecast is based on previous history and volatility using statistical techniques.

The simpler models generally employ heuristic techniques whereas the more complex models are based on linear and dynamic programming and Lagrangian relaxation techniques. Energy markets do not behave like conventional equity markets. It has been proposed (D. Pilipović 1997) that they exhibit a mean reverting behaviour. This is characterised by the price movement in reaction to an event being followed by one in the opposite direction but over-shooting the mean trend. This process continues, with damping, eventually settling on a new value. Events tend to be corrected either through the dissipation of what caused them or though the response of the supply side. Unlike equity markets, energy markets are heavily influenced by the physical processes necessary to support their operation and the requirement to keep generation and demand in balance at all times. The prevailing weather will affect demand and hence price; the loss of generation or new generation coming into service will affect the price profile, constraints on plant and transmission will affect what generation can be used to meet demand.

A typical market price profile is shown in Figure 10.1 and includes the market base and peak prices derived from a market simulation. The modelling can be designed to follow the normal weather trends and patterns of generation availability but will never replicate the actual weather changes. In a typical simulation it can be expected that a good modelling price prediction would move around the actual outturn values as shown but generally reverting to it rather than exhibiting bias.

The approach adopted for modelling needs to take account of the expected use and the likely degree of accuracy of the input data. There is little point in sophisticated detailed modelling when the fuel price prediction is known to be of limited accuracy. The level of detail needs to take account of the relative impact of the variable on the result. Given the range of error in potential inputs it is usual to model a set of plausible scenarios that provide a backcloth to the base case result.

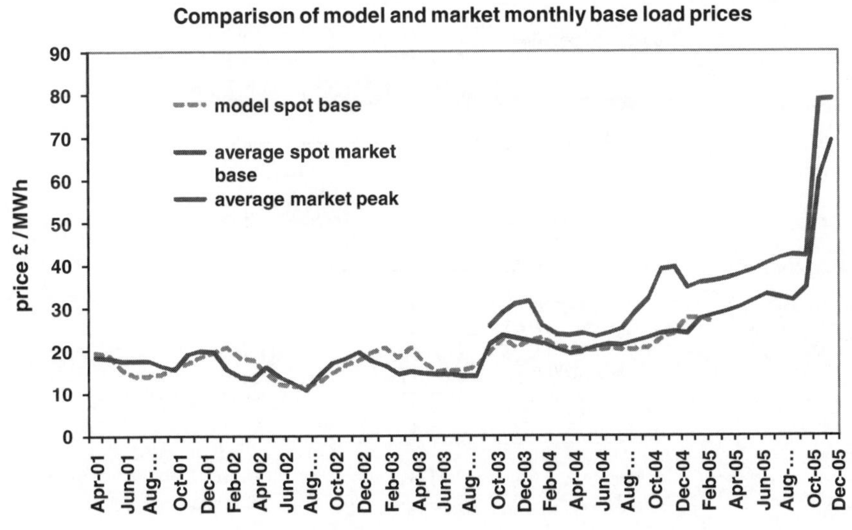

Comparison of model and market monthly base load prices

Figure 10.1 Price profile

10.3 DISPATCH MARKET SIMULATION

The modelling approach most commonly applied is based on a simulation of the generation dispatch process that is used to select which generators to run and the load level to meet the demand at minimum cost. This is the process that would be used by the TSO in a pool or by a portfolio generator planning how to use generation. A simulation of this process has been found to result in a good approximation to what happens in markets and to enable identification of the marginal generator. An overview of the process is shown schematically in Figure 10.2 and requires the following data:

• a set of generation data including fuel type, capacity and efficiency;
• a prediction of the system demand profile for each period, usually half hour;
• a set of fuel price predictions for the period to be analysed.

The generation variable costs are established based on their efficiency and the price of fuel and these are used to develop bid prices. The bids are placed in a 'merit order' of increasing costs and the generation is then selected in order of increasing costs to operate for the period until the cumulative MW level is sufficient to meet the demand. The price of the last generator selected will set the marginal variable cost for that period. In practice the generator will need to recover fixed and other variable costs as

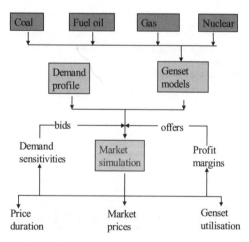

Figure 10.2 Dispatch model

well as fuel costs. These need to be added to the price bid based on the expected hours of utilisation of the generator through the period. One approach to estimate price bids is to run a dispatch simulation to establish marginal variable costs and generation utilisation and use these results to estimate the added unit costs necessary to recover fixed costs. Finally the expected price will generally fall between the variable and full costs including fixed costs according to the level of competition. This has been found to be very dependent on the plant margin or percentage of generation in excess of that required to meet the demand.

Detailed modelling may be required to take account of generation dynamics such as run up and run down rates and minimum on and off times. These constrain what generation can be used at any one time. If generation is frequently required to shut down and restart then additional start up costs will be incurred. These vary depending on how long the unit has been out of service and are usually defined as a function of the number of hours that the unit has been out of service. There is also a need to take account of generation forced and planned outages for maintenance as these also affect availability. There may also be active internal transmission constraints between different parts of the system that restrict the use of generation in strict merit order. This level of detailed modelling of the plant dynamics is necessary when participating in the short term exchange and balancing markets.

10.4 LOAD DURATION MODEL

In modelling the medium to long term market the effects of plant dynamics are over-shadowed by the range of variation in fuel prices and demand. In these circumstances it is more important to be able to analyse a range of possible outturns. This can be achieved by using a stacked merit order to meet demand in the form of a load duration curve (LDC). The example of Figure 6.3 shows the peak demand at around 10 000 MW with a low demand of about 3000 MW (at 8760 hours); the horizontal axis shows the number of hours for which the demand level is exceeded.

The generation is stacked up as shown, with base load generation running throughout the year, followed by mid merit plant running for part of the year, with the last increment of demand met by peaking generation. The generation capacity available is usually written down by 10–15% to simulate the effect of planned and forced outages. The marginal generator can be identified at successive load levels and, given the time for which each demand level persists, the average annual price can be derived. The utilisation of generation

Load duration curve

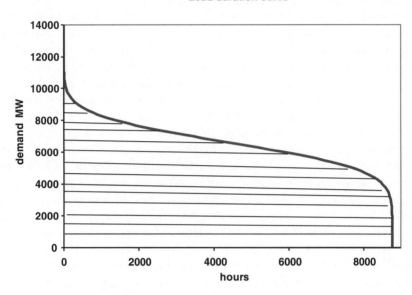

Figure 10.3   Load duration curve

and hence the fuel burn can be calculated. The peaking prices can be estimated based on the average of the highest priced 3120 peaking period hours.

10.5 HYDRO GENERATION

Pumped storage and hydro generation require special modelling to take account of the limited energy availability and associated storage facilities. The use of these plants is based on analysis of the system marginal price and they will be dispatched at those times when the marginal price is highest up to the limit of their energy availability for the period analysed. The difficulty is in establishing the price when hydro should be dispatched. In the case of the chronological dispatch model it is necessary to establish a typical profile of hydro energy availability based on data from previous years. This is often based on typical months. Given the expected demand profile, it is possible to identify the demand level above which the additional energy equates to the expected hydro energy. The corresponding prices can be averaged to establish a hydro dispatch price or different prices can be applied to individual days or weekdays/weekends.

In the case of the LDC model the energy produced by generation can be summated working back from the peak load period. The generated energy is accumulated until it matches the available hydro energy when the last generator de-loaded indicates the hydro dispatch price.

Practical hydro schemes are based on river valleys with a mixture of run of river and storage schemes based on reservoirs as illustrated in Figure 10.4.

- **Modelling has to ensure water balance**: for each plant the system has to assure the monthly balance of water taking into account the reservoirs levels, the water inflow forecast, the pumping, the spilled water and the water flowing in each turbine.
- **Reservoirs level limits**: the system has to respect, for each plant and each time period, the reservoirs level limits set by the operator.
- **Reservoirs target level**: the system has to allow one to fix the target reservoir level in each period.

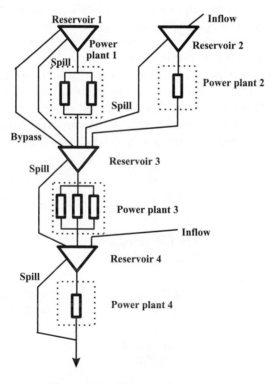

Figure 10.4   Hydro valley scheme

- **Power/water flow curve**: the system has to take into account the curve of power/flow for each plant during the optimisation; the system can accept the curve both as a series of points and as a formula.
- **Power ramp**: the system has, for each plant, the constraint of the rate of change of electrical power and its relative cost.
- **Branch flow limit** :the system has to take in account the maximum flow for each branch.

A further constraint in medium–short term planning is the time the water needs to go from one element of the hydro model to the next one.

Figure 10.5 shows a schematic illustrating the link between the establishment of monthly target reservoir levels and prices based on an LDC formulation and the day to day commitment to meet hourly demand.

In the case of pumped storage, the generation will be used to lop the expensive price periods during the day with pumping periods set based on when prices are lowest operating through a weekly cycle. In a liberalised market the pumped storage operator will be bidding generation and demand into the short term market based on the prices seen in the market. The overall efficiency of the process of pumping and generating is around 70% and this needs to be allowed for in determining the optimum pumping price. This price would then be used in chronological modelling with a corresponding generator price based on the efficiency. There will also be the option to take advantage of the flexibility of the units to contract into the ancillary service market. In longer term modelling a typical pumped storage profile can be established and netted off the demand when generating or added when pumping.

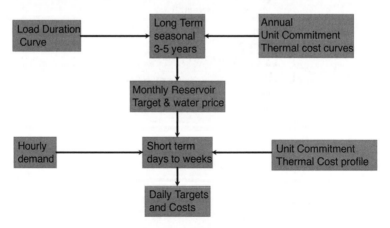

Figure 10.5 Hydro model

10.6 INTERCONNECTION MODELLING

In the case of interconnectors the importing and exporting periods will need to be established based on a comparison of expected prices across the link. In interconnected systems the physical flows need to be modelled as these may be different to the contracted flows. It is also necessary to limit flows to the expected interconnection transmission capacity. There may also be a need to model demand response to high prices.

In large models a region may be modelled including the interconnecting links. The optimisation will then include the flows through the interconnectors. At the periphery of the model it is still necessary to account for external links. This has to be based on a set of estimated flows derived from a comparison of expected future price differentials.

In general, the sophistication of the modelling needs to match the accuracy of the data used. For modelling the short term it may be necessary to model plant dynamics and the dispatch model will need to be a chronological simulation of each half hour period. If these parameters are not likely to have a significant effect on the result, then the demand may be represented as a load duration curve with generation dispatched to meet each block of demand.

10.7 PREDICTING DEMAND DATA

The growth in energy and demand in each country is very dependent on the expected growth in GDP. The simplest approach to prediction is to review historic statistics of GDP growth and demand growth and establish a correlation function.

The results of two simple models are shown in Figure 10.6. The progressive model takes the previous year's energy value and adds a function of the growth in annual GDP for the demand growth. The cumulative model starts with a base year and adds a function of the cumulative GDP over the period and more closely follows actual demand growth and is more stable. The correlation function can be used to establish predictions based on forecast economic growth. Where statistics of demand by sector are available, i.e. industrial, commercial, domestic, transport and agricultural, then further sophistication can be added based on expected growth or decline in each sector. In some countries increasing amounts of small generation is embedded within the distribution network and is designed to feed local loads often as part of a CHP scheme. This generation is not subject to central

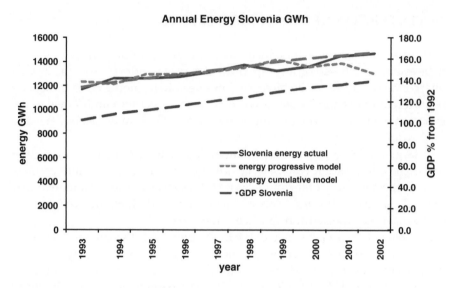

Figure 10.6   Energy prediction

dispatch and it needs to be netted off expected demand or be represented by a manually entered schedule.

The statistics generally available will be for the total energy provided during a year and maybe the maximum demand. In practice the dispatch process needs a demand profile or load duration curve to establish the price for each half hour period. The demand level usually follows a normal distribution through the year and in the absence of specific data a curve may be estimated using an inverse exponential function about the mean to estimate the duration curve. A typical result is shown in Figure 10.7 for Belgium when the total energy for the year was 81 700 GWh and the peak was 15 156 MW. The simple representation gives a similar result with demand increments chosen to be 100 MW.

Given the annual energy delivered of 81 700 GWh and a maximum demand of 15 156 MW, the mean annual demand for Belgium and the load factor can be calculated as follows:

$$\text{Mean demand} = 81\,700/8760 = 9.32\,\text{GW}.$$

$$\text{Load factor} = 9.32/15.156 = 61.5\%.$$

If the standard deviation is given by the mean/4.8, then the high and low values can be estimated at 3 standard deviations from the mean, i.e.

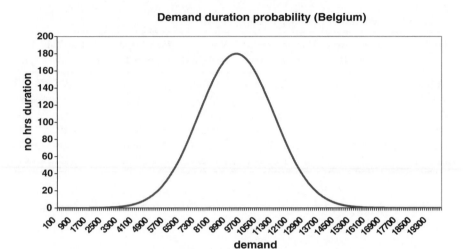

Figure 10.7 Normal demand distribution

$$\text{High} = 9.32 + 3*9.32/4.8 = 15.155\,\text{GW}.$$

$$\text{Low} = 9.32 - 3*9.32/4.8 = 3.49\,\text{GW}.$$

The high value of 15 155 GW corresponds well with the recorded peak of 15 156 GW. The same data can be expressed in load duration form, starting at the highest demand level. This shows the proportion of time that each demand level occurs through the year. In this example the demand is analysed into 100 MW increments.

10.8 GENERATION DATA

The basic generation data available will include capacity, primary fuel and year of commissioning. To derive a variable cost an estimate of efficiency is required. This depends on the type of plant, its age and size. Older smaller coal units will have efficiencies in the low thirties. Larger coal will have efficiencies in the high thirties, as will oil plant. Modern CCGT units will have efficiencies in the low fifties. Based on known data from other locations and the calculations included in Chapter 3, estimates have been made and are included in the model. The fuel prices and other variable and fixed costs assumed for this model are as shown in Table 10.1 for coal, gas heat recovery steam generator, gas, oil and nuclear (UR).

Table 10.1 Generation parameters

OPR	Fuel prices Euros/GJ	Var. operating costs €/Mwh	Var costs/100	Fixed oper costs €/kW/yr	Capital €/kW	Life yrs
COAL	2.72	1.86	0.0186	22.3	406	45
WSTH/G	3.00	1.7	0.017	10	715	30
GAS	4.91	1.6	0.016	8.2	393	30
OIL	4.66	2.46	0.0246	20.1	1041	38
UR	0.8	1.31	0.0131	18.6	1004	40
BFG	3	1.7	0.017	12	824	35

The variable operating costs of a coal fired generator with an efficiency of 34.5 can be calculated using the data above as follows:

Variable fuel costs $= 2.72*3600/1000/0.345 = $ €28.38/MWh.

Other variable costs $= 1.86$/MWh, hence:

Total costs $= $ €30.24/MWh.

An estimate is also required of the fixed cost of each generator including capital and operating costs. An estimate of the original capital costs can be calculated based on the average age of the plant type and an inflation rate. The capital charge for a particular unit can then be assessed based on the commissioning date. Some of the capital will be written off depending on the project life and the number of years in service. The capital charge will then be a function of the WACC and the remaining outstanding capital.

As an example, the 2008 fixed plant operating cost can be calculated for a gas fired unit commissioned in 1998. Its original cost is assumed to be €406/kW/yr with a 25 year project life and a WACC of 0.071. The other fixed operating costs are assumed to be €22.3/kW/yr.

Outstanding capital cost $= $ (life -in-service years)/life $*$ capital

$= (25-10)/25*406 = $ €243.6.

The equivalent annuity may be calculated for the outstanding capital repayment using the formula:

$$\frac{c*i(1+i)^Y}{(1+i)^Y-1}.$$

Then, assuming a 15 year remaining project life with written down cost of €243/kW then annuity is given as:

$$= 243*0.071(1+0.071)^{\wedge}15/((1+0.071)^{\wedge}15-1)$$

$$= €26.7/kW/yr.$$

Total fixed cost = capital + fixed operating costs = 26.7 + 22.3 = €49/kW/yr.

Assuming a utilisation of 50%, then the fixed cost/MWh is given as:

$$= 49*1000/(8760/2) = €11.1/MWh.$$

To this fixed cost the variable cost must be added to establish the total costs that an operator would like to recover.

The calculations shown above are repeated for all of the generating units modelled to establish the merit order with several hundred units depending on the size of the integrated power system. The full MW capacity will not generally be available and is generally written down to take account of planned and forced outages to typically 85% to 95% of its registered value, depending on the time of year. In colder climates it is usual for planned outages to be taken during the summer when demands are lowest. In southern Europe where the summers are very hot, air conditioning load causes a peak demand during the summer. With less cold winters it is more difficult to identify a period when outages can be best accommodated.

10.9 CALCULATIONS

In a simple merit order model the requirement is to establish that cumulative generation required to just meet the demand. The last generator required is deemed the marginal generator and its costs set the marginal price for that period. The demand is increased in 100 MW increments and the merit order is checked each time to establish the cumulative MW capacity and hence the marginal unit operating at each load level. This gives the variable operating costs for the number of hours for which that demand level occurs. The running hours of the marginal generator are calculated by taking the cumulative hours of higher demands from 8760 h. The fixed costs per unit generated for this generator are then given by dividing the annual fixed costs/kW by the expected running hours.

For the demand level of 6000 MW, if we assume that the variable costs of the marginal unit are €30.2/MWh with fixed costs of €49/kW/yr with running hours of 7500, then the full marginal costs are calculated as follows:

Full cost = variable + fixed/MWh = 30.2 + 1000*49/7500 = €36.7/MWh.

The results of a simulation are illustrated in the graph of Figure 10.8. This shows, for each demand increment, the variable cost, the full cost and the generation utilisation and the type of generation operating at the margin. It can be seen how the prices rise for lower utilisation generation due to the need to apportion the fixed costs over fewer units generated. The units were dispatched in this simulation based on their respective variable costs, the full costs show some discontinuity due to the variations in the age and type of plant and hence their fixed costs.

The results of the simulation can be processed to establish the annual base load price by summating the product of the duration of each demand level and the price and dividing by 8760. The base load price in this example is calculated to be €36.2 and the average annual full cost is €48.7/MWh.

The expected price will fall between the variable cost and the full cost depending on the level of competition. This is heavily influenced by the plant margin: the higher it is the lower the competition and prices are driven down

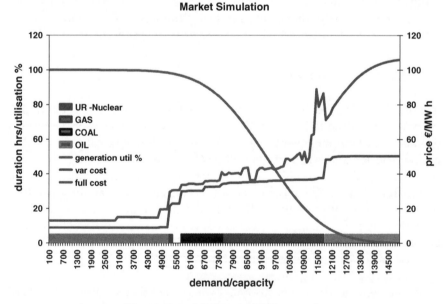

Figure 10.8   Market simulation result

to variable costs. A low margin will conversely drive prices up to full costs to encourage new entry. The margin in this case is calculated at 20.5, giving an expected price of €44.2/MWh.

The results of the simulation can also be used to confirm the energy delivered and the total variable and full costs of each plant.

10.10 PRICE DURATION CURVE

The results may be processed to produce a price duration curve (PDC) showing the price level persisting for each proportion of the year as shown in Figure 10.9. This is based on the basic generation data shown in Table 10.2. This provides a useful visual representation of how the price may vary during the year.

The test result of a system annual dispatch simulation has been used to plot the variable cost duration curve shown in Figure 10.9. Given the fuel prices in Table 10.2, the curve values and break points can be explained assuming coal and nuclear have an efficiency of 38%, gas 52% and oil 35%.

Based on these typical plant efficiencies, the fuel variable costs are calculated with other variable costs added to give the total. These are stacked in merit order as shown and can be aligned with the various plateau of the graph.

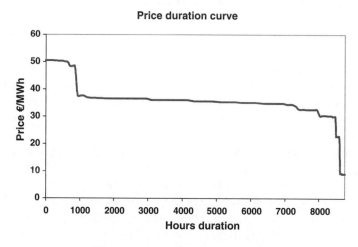

Figure 10.9 Price duration curve

Table 10.2 Basic generation data

OPR	Fuel prices Euros/GJ	Var. operating costs €/Mwh
COAL	2.72	1.86
GAS	4.91	1.6
oil	4.66	2.46
UR	0.8	1.31

Nuclear variable cost $= 0.8*3.6/0.38 = €7.6/\text{MWh} + 1.31 = £8.9/\text{MWh}$.

Coal variable cost $= 2.72*3.6/0.38 = €25.7/\text{MWh} + 1.86 = €27.5/\text{MWh}$.

Gas variable cost $= 4.91*3.6/0.52 = €33.9/\text{MWh} + 1.6 = €35.5/\text{MWh}$.

Oil variable cost $= 4.66*3.6/0.35 = €47.9/\text{MWh} + 2.46 = €50.3/\text{MWh}$.

The lowest price is set by nuclear at €8.9/MWh for a short period as it operates base load. The highest price is set by oil at around €50/MWh with the price varying between coal at €27.5 and gas at €35.5 for the bulk of the year.

The time for which each type of plant operates at the margin is important in establishing sensitivities to fuel prices. For small variations in price the impact on the annual base load price can be calculated by a pro rata adjustment of the change based on the percentage of time at the margin. Larger changes will shift the merit order and utilisation.

10.11 STATISTICAL FORECASTING

The approach to forecasting based on estimating costs and building a merit order has the disadvantage that it does not explicitly take account of actual market prices. This issue can be partly addressed by 'back-casting'. This involves using the normal model parameters to estimate prices for a historic period and using the result to benchmark the model parameters. There are other approaches that are more explicitly based on the recognition of historic price patterns.

In power markets the price is very closely linked to the demand level, although it tends to be stratified reflecting the different type of plant brought into service on a merit order basis. The graph of Figure 10.10 shows the variation in marginal price with load in Greece. It can be seen that the price falls around three levels based on cheap lignite, gas fired generation and oil. The turning points will be influenced by the availability of the different types of generation with the levels varying throughout the year depending on fuel

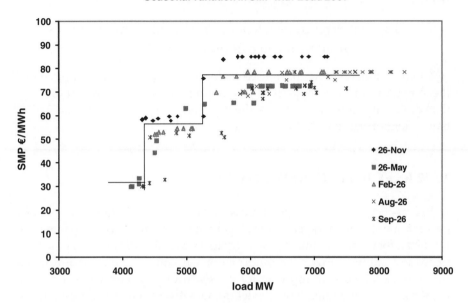

Figure 10.10 Variation in price with demand

prices. The different levels reflect the operation of plant with differing efficiency.

The nature of this price function does not lend itself to statistical analysis. If the relationship between demand and price can be established, then the prediction of demand presents a more tractable problem. Auto Regressive Integrated Moving Average (ARIMA) packages have been used successfully to predict demand in the short to medium term. The approach identifies the trend and takes account of the impact of weather variation from normal conditions. It relies heavily on a recorded set of similar days when working conditions would have followed a similar pattern. Accuracies of around 1.5% can be achieved at the day-ahead stage when weather prediction data is included in the model. The translation of the demand prediction into a price will need to take account of the time of year and generation availability levels.

Other authors (D. Pilipović 1997) have suggested that mean reverting models produce the best results in capturing the distribution of energy prices. In the mean reversion approach the reversion is applied to the log of price rather than the price, i.e. let

$$x = \log(\text{spot price}),$$

then

$$Dx = \text{mean reversion rate(long term equilibrium of } X - Xt)$$
$$+ \text{volatility} * \text{random stochastic variable.}$$

Another model that has been used includes two factors: the spot price and the long term equilibrium price. The spot price is assumed to revert towards the equilibrium price level, while the equilibrium price level is assumed to have a lognormal distribution.

10.12 PREDICTING NEW ENTRY

A key aspect of longer term forecasting is predicting the entry of new generation into the market and the closure of older, time expired generation. It is usual for data on planned new entry to be available for a few years ahead, up to the planning horizon. The information will come into the public domain through the process of applying for consent from the government agency responsible for planning. Not all generation with consent will necessarily be built and some judgement will be necessary on the timing. Key aspects affecting the decision process will be the current and expected market price and the plant margin. If the market price is above the new entry cost then there will be interest in building new plant. The amount of new build will be tempered by the developing plant margin. If too much plant is added then the utilisation and profitability can be expected to be reduced. It can be seen from Figure 10.3 that the demand profile is such that only some 3000 MW can operate base load and beyond that utilisation falls off. There is also likely to be a restriction on the industrial capacity that a country has to support new entry build. A portfolio generator will have the added requirement to examine how new entry will affect the use of its existing generation and closure policy. The problem is further complicated by being iterative in that new entry will affect the outturn price and profitability.

The Table 10.3 illustrates an approach where the analysis of the potential new revenue from different types of generation is assessed. The data covers 10 successive years with the latest power market prices and fuel prices provided as input. The fuel price data is used to establish the future cost of generation for each year. Additional costs are included to cover CO_2 emissions and any subsidies or feed-in tariffs are applied to renewable generation types. It is also necessary to assume a generator utilisation that may vary in future years. The development of costs was described in detail in Chapter 3. Given the power

Table 10.3 New entry evaluation

Energy price E/MWh	Gas price E/mmBTU	Coal price E/t	CO$_2$ price E/t CO$_2$	Subsidy E/MWh	New entry cost by plant type E/MWh								
					Gas	Coal	Lcoal refurb	Hydro	Nuclear	Gas/CHP	Waste	Wind on	Wind off
54.1	5.75	37.0	22.1	35.9	55.69	46.21	40.75	66.96	43.79	77.31	46.24	47.16	52.09
55.1	5.64	37.8	22.5	34.9	55.08	46.77	41.36	66.96	43.79	76.48	47.26	48.18	53.12
65.6	5.46	37.8	35.2	24.4	57.95	55.59	51.04	66.96	43.79	75.12	57.79	58.71	63.64
64.9	5.2	37.2	35.9	25.1	56.39	55.89	51.37	66.96	43.79	73.15	57.12	58.04	62.98
62.5	4.97	36.8	36.6	27.5	55.04	56.24	51.76	66.96	43.79	71.41	54.68	55.60	60.54
59.1	4.76	36.3	37.4	30.9	53.83	56.58	52.13	66.96	43.79	69.82	51.26	52.18	57.12
56.1	4.58	35.8	38.1	33.9	52.83	56.94	52.52	66.96	43.79	68.45	48.27	49.19	54.13
53.6	4.4	35.7	38.9	36.4	51.84	57.45	53.08	66.96	43.79	67.09	45.83	46.75	51.68
51.2	4.23	35.5	39.6	38.8	50.92	57.93	53.60	66.96	43.79	65.80	43.43	44.35	49.28
50.6	4.06	35.3	40.4	39.4	50.01	58.39	54.12	66.96	43.79	64.51	42.75	43.67	48.60
average return/MWh					3.31	2.48	7.10	−9.69	13.49	43.64	7.81	6.89	1.96

price and costs for each year the net contribution can be calculated for the period as shown at the bottom of the table. The revenue is based on the base load price but could equally apply to the analysis of peaking plant using the peaking price and a peaking plant utilisation. It can be seen in this example most types of new entry show a positive return with the exception of hydro.

By rolling this analysis forward, the prospect of new entry by plant type can be estimated. At the same time an estimate of closures needs to be made. This is most simply based on the life expectancy of different types of plant with coal at typically 40 to 45 years, gas at 30 to 35 years and nuclear at 40 to 45 years. Given the date the plant was commissioned the closure date can be predicted. This analysis needs to be tempered with judgement taking account of:

- the prevailing plant margin – if it is low closures will be delayed, whereas if it is high they will be accelerated;
- the expected development of relative fuel prices – if coal prices fall relative to gas then this may delay the closure of old coal plant;
- the expected level of utilisation – this may be influenced by a role in ancillary services or the management of grid constraints;
- the option to extend the life through refurbishment.

The combination of closures and new entry year on year provides an estimate of the developing plant margin that will temper the level of new entry. The timing of new entry also has to take account of the construction time that can vary from 1 to 2 years for wind, 2–3 years for gas, 4–5 years for coal and 7–8 for nuclear. A typical new build programme is shown in Table 10.4. It can be seen in this example that gas looks profitable throughout the period, coal gradually becomes unprofitable due to rising CO_2 prices. Nuclear looks attractive but entry is delayed by construction times, whereas there is a steady introduction of renewable sources based on the available build capacity.

The overall process includes steps to:

- establish relative costs of production per unit;
- take account of CO_2 and incentives;
- determine revenue and when return exceeds costs through the period;
- add new entry year on year if it looks profitable;
- scale new build in accordance with construction capacity available by country;
- determine prospective plant margin each year;
- adjust overall level of new entry in proportion to developing plant margin.

Table 10.4 New entry plan

Eff plant margin %	Plant changes		New plant additions MW								
	Closures	Eff new build	Gas	Coal	Coal refurb	Hydro	Nuclear	Gas.CHP	Waste	Wind on	Wind off
31	1239	1240	480	0	500	0	0	150	70	120	150
30	1366	2660	480	1030	890	0	0	150	70	130	150
31	2184	2740	490	1060	910	0	0	160	80	130	160
31	1256	2830	500	1080	940	0	0	180	80	150	170
33	3105	2420	510	0	1020	0	570	190	80	150	180
31	2398	2560	550	0	1060	0	570	220	100	180	200
30	3157	2800	570	0	1230	0	580	250	110	200	220
29	2949	1720	620	0	0	0	590	300	130	240	260
27	4305	1840	660	0	0	0	590	350	150	280	290
23	3210	2100	750	0	0	0	610	450	180	360	360

The new entry plan will affect the prices and hence profitability and decision processes. This same dilemma affects investors as the decisions of early years will be irrevocable. In later years the rate of new entry is adjusted in relation to the emerging plant margin. If this increases above what would normally be expected, then the rate of new entry is reduced. The assessment of the margin has to take account of the limited contribution to firm capacity of wind and hydro energy plant.

The results of a recent analysis are shown in Figure 10.11 in the form of energy delivered by the major European producers. It can be seen that production from gas continues to increase; production from nuclear reduces as older plant is closed but then picks up with new construction; coal production falls with the prospect of rising CO2 prices but is sustained for a period pending the introduction of new nuclear. There is a programme of refurbishment of older plant to improve the efficiency with conversions to gas in some cases (labelled coal/oil re). The development of wind energy slows as it is seen to be an expensive option and less of a panacea. CHP development looks attractive because its high efficiency mitigates high fuel prices. The conversion of waste to energy becomes a necessity due to the reduction in available land fill sites.

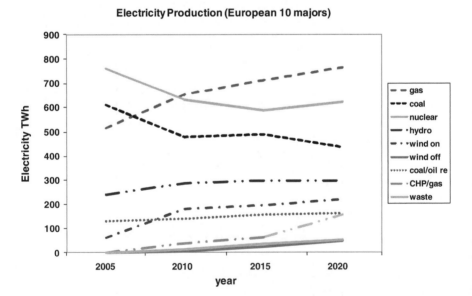

Figure 10.11 New entry Europe

10.13 SUMMARY

This chapter has reviewed the different approaches that have been employed to simulate market operation. A simple cost based model has been described to illustrate the principles associated with a dispatch simulation. It has been shown how a representative demand profile can be established in LDC form. It was shown how generation data are processed to establish unit variable and full costs and then listed in order of ascending prices to establish a merit order. The generation can then be loaded in merit order to meet successive demand increments and the marginal generator identified. It has been shown how the data on the duration of each demand increment and the associated marginal price can be used to calculate the average annual variable and full costs. The derivation of peaking prices and an approach to hydro modelling was described. The expected market price was assessed taking account of the level of competition as influenced by the plant margin. Aspects of statistical modelling were described both in predicting demand and prices employing ARIMA and mean reverting models. Finally, an approach to predicting new entry was described with some illustrative results for Europe.

11

Ancillary Service Markets

11.1 INTRODUCTION

Ancillary services are essential to enabling the secure and safe operation of the power system. They provide the means to maintain instantaneous balance between supply and demand, stable voltage and frequency levels and the means to maintain system security. Their provision is usually achieved through a competitive market orientated to maximise participation and minimise costs. This frequently takes the form of competitive tenders at appointed times of the year. The provision of services is designed to enable both generation and the demand side to participate in the provision of reserve services. The market is much smaller than the total primary wholesale market but can contribute to the revenue and business case for building a new plant.

A generating station can be designed specifically to operate flexibly with the object of supplying ancillary services and participating in the balancing and peaking market. These markets are closely aligned through the provision of reserve and with the short term market facilitated by exchanges. An investor in peaking plant will look to assess the revenue potential in all those areas that exploit the flexibility of the plant. The generator or demand side participant may be called upon to provide reserve energy in the event of sudden unexpected demand or generation change or to provide balancing makeup to cover another generator's shortfall against its contracted position. The services may be contracted in advance as part of a standing reserve provision or based on a bid into the balancing market just before the event. This type of station is also well placed to exercise arbitrage between gas and

Power Markets and Economics: Energy Costs, Trading, Emissions   Barrie Murray
© 2009 John Wiley & Sons, Ltd

electricity markets, taking advantage of any imperfections in respective market operations.

This chapter discusses the requirements for ancillary services to maintain the security and stability of system operation including balancing supply and demand, frequency regulation and voltage control and includes:

- development of an understanding of the system requirements;
- an illustration of how they may be competitively procured;
- developing an approach to costing the services.

Finally, it is explained how the balancing and ancillary service markets can be analysed and the earning potential of a generator derived.

11.2 ANCILLARY SERVICE REQUIREMENTS

Reserve

The requirement for reserve arises from the need to enable the generation supply and demand to be kept in balance at all times. The system inertia is relatively small and any imbalance will result in a frequency excursion. The imbalance can occur when the estimate of demand is inaccurate or generation is failing to maintain its target dispatch. The largest source of imbalance will usually result from loss of a generator tripping on fault or loss of transmission and associated import or export from the interconnected system. The system requirement is usually set to cover the contingency of loss of the largest generator or in-feed. Different categories of reserve are defined depending on the required speed of response including the following.

- **Primary Reserve** Immediate reserve to cater for the sudden loss of generation providing increased output within seconds. This requirement has to be met by generation running and able to respond by automatic governor action or by demand response triggered by operation of a low frequency relay.
- **Secondary Reserve** Fast reserve that is required to respond within 2–10 minutes to arrest the frequency excursion. It may be met by part loaded generation able to regulate its output (sometimes called regulating reserve). The requirement may also be met by generation that is able to start using an automatic sequence and deliver output within a few minutes.
- **Emergency reserve** or **contingency reserve** This is able to provide replacement output within normal start up times of half hour to hours depending on the type of plant. This is to cater for persistent loss of generation sources that have failed to synchronise or maintain availability.

Frequency Response

There are usually statutory regulations related to the quality of electricity supply that require frequency to be maintained within set limits. These are in turn translated into operational limits. For example, statutory limits in the UK are set at 0.5 Hz from 50 Hz with normal operational limits set at $+/-0.2$ Hz. These limits are set to maintain the quality of supply and provide design standards for both generation and appliances. The frequency limits in interconnected systems are tighter to ensure that flows across tie-lines are kept within safe limits.

To maintain the frequency within the prescribed limits requires a proportion of generation to be operated in free-governor mode, able to respond automatically and change output in response to any frequency change. The automatic governor controller will typically operate with a droop characteristic of 4%. This means that the controller is designed so that it raises the generation output at the rate of 100% of rating when a 2 Hz (4%) fall in frequency is detected.

For example, we can calculate the amount of generation that would be required to operate on free governor action with a 4% droop to maintain the frequency drop to 0.4 Hz for loss of a 500 MW generator.

For a 0.4 Hz frequency drop, the generation would provide 20% of its output, i.e.

$$= 100 * 0.4/2.$$

If 20% is to equal 500 MW then the amount of generation responding is given by:

$$500/0.2 = 2500 \text{ MW}.$$

The overall system gain in MW/Hz can also be calculated: as 0.4 Hz provides a 500 MW response the response/Hz will be given by:

$$1/0.4 = 1250 \text{ MW/Hz}.$$

A generation unit is not in practice able to respond with 100% of its output but is typically able to provide up to 20% of its output by the release of boiler stored energy backed up by fuel supply control. Where areas operate connected, each area of the system will provide a share of the required response to contain a frequency fall. This is usually expressed in terms of their system gain or MW response/Hz for a fall in frequency. Interconnected systems will usually be equipped with Automatic Generation Control (AGC) that will be set to operate on a tie-line bias frequency control basis. This is designed to maintain contracted flows on inter-connectors biased according to the frequency error and the expected contribution.

Voltage Control

The quality of supply also applies to system voltage control and requires that voltage is maintained within limits of typically $+/-5\%$ of nominal. This is much more of a local issue than frequency control and requires that reactive supply and demand are kept in balance locally. This requires that generation operates with an active Automatic Voltage Regulator (AVR) that is able to provide dynamic response to correct any MVAr imbalances. In order to be able to provide the range of MVAr response the generator may need to operate part loaded.

11.3 MARKET VOLUME

The total costs for services in the Netherlands amounted to €115.8 m during 2006.

The figures can be compared with those of the UK where the total costs based on the March 2006 report are estimated at £361m/yr with a system size some four times larger. The makeup of the published UK figures has been scaled down for comparison with the Dutch figures. Both are shown in the bar chart of Figure 11.1 and it can be seen that the distribution of costs is similar.

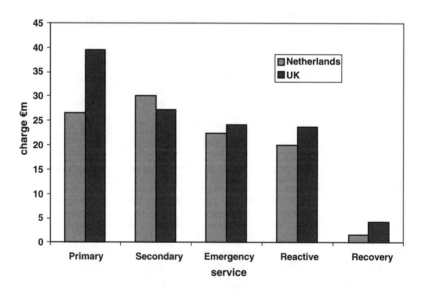

Figure 11.1 Comparative ancillary service market sizes

The higher UK charges for frequency regulation might be expected because, being a separate synchronous system, the service cannot be shared. The following factors can affect the scale of the requirements.

- The reserve requirements will generally be higher in an isolated system with weak interconnection because there is little opportunity to establish shared reserve agreements.
- A system with high concentrations of variable output sources such as wind power will have more need for reserve and frequency control services to maintain system balance.
- A power system with long transmission lines and low load levels, as in parts of Africa and Australia, is likely to have more difficulty in controlling voltage and a requirement for more reactive support from generation and reactive compensation devices.
- The requirements for black start capability will be more in a system that cannot rely on support from neighbouring systems through interconnectors.

An illustration of the assessment of the market volume for **primary reserve** can be found by analysis of the situation in the Netherlands. The Dutch contribution to frequency control for 2006 was set at 744 MW/Hz which represents 3.6% of the agreed 20 570 MW/Hz frequency gain that applies to the complete interconnected UCTE grid, of which the Netherlands is part. This results in an expected contribution of 36 MW from the Netherlands in the event of a 1000 MW generation failure with a 50 mHz frequency drop. (1000–MW generation failure is expected to cause the frequency to drop by some 50 mHz–1000/20570 ∗ 1 Hz).

A maximum generation failure of 3000 MW is adhered to in the synchronous UCTE system, which implies that the Netherlands is expected to deliver at least 109 MW primary reserve (3.6% out of 3000 MW) for a 0.15 Hz frequency drop. Assuming contracted generation is operating with free governor action with a 4% droop (i.e. delivering rated 100% output for a 4% frequency drop) then for a 0.15 Hz drop (0.3%) in frequency, 7.5% of rated output would be delivered. As the requirement is for 109 MW this implies 1453 MW of generation able to respond via governor action or in response to signals from a central Load Frequency Control system (LFC).

The standard governing the minimum requirements for **secondary/regulating reserve** in the Netherlands are set out in MW in Table 11.1. The need will vary with the season, the day of the week and time of day, depending on prevailing system conditions. Generally more reserve is required at times of

Table 11.1 Reserve requirements for Netherlands

Winter season, from 01 October to 31 March inclusive (last update January 31, 2003)

Week days
Upward regulation

Time frame	Control capacity	Reserve capacity (≤15 mins)	Total (≤15 mins)
00h00–06h00	300	600	900
06h00–09h00	500	600	1100
09h00–16h00	300	600	900
16h00–24h00	500	600	1100

Downward regulation

Time frame	Control capacity	Reserve capacity (≤15 mins)	Total (≤15 mins)
00h00–06h00	300	300	600
06h00–09h00	500	300	800
09h00–16h00	300	300	600
16h00–24h00	500	300	800

Saturdays and Sundays
Upward regulation

Time frame	Control capacity	Reserve capacity (≤15 mins)	Total (≤15 mins)
00h00–16h00	300	600	900
16h00–24h00	500	600	1100

Downward regulation

Time frame	Control capacity	Reserve capacity (≤15 mins)	Total (≤15 mins)
00h00–06h00	300	300	600
06h00–09h00	400	300	700
09h00–16h00	300	300	600
16h00–24h00	400	300	700

Table 11.1 (*Continued*)

Summer season, from 01 April to 30 September inclusive (last update May 7, 2003)

Week days
Upward regulation

Time frame	Control capacity	Reserve capacity (≤15 mins)	Total (≤15 mins)
00h00–06h00	300	600	900
06h00–09h00	500	600	1100
09h00–18h00	300	600	900
18h00–24h00	500	600	1100

Downward regulation

Time frame	Control capacity	Reserve capacity (≤15 mins)	Total (≤15 mins)
00h00–06h00	300	300	600
06h00–09h00	500	300	800
09h00–16h00	300	300	600
16h00–22h00	500	300	800
22h00–24h00	400	300	700

Saturdays and Sundays
Upward regulation

Time frame	Control capacity	Reserve capacity (≤15 mins)	Total (≤15 mins)
00h00–18h00	300	600	900
18h00–24h00	500	600	1100

Downward regulation

Time frame	Control capacity	Reserve capacity (≤15 mins)	Total (≤15 mins)
00h00–06h00	300	300	600
06h00–10h00	400	300	700
10h00–16h00	300	300	600
16h00–24h00	400	300	700

rapid demand change to ensure sufficient dynamic capability to be able to follow the system demand. There is equally a requirement for downward regulating capability, particularly during the light load periods of summer. There is then a need to maintain generation that is able to reduce its output if demand falls lower than expected.

The secondary reserve provisions are further categorized in the Netherlands depending on how quickly it can be delivered. The term control capacity is used to describe generation available within minutes with output controlled automatically by adjustment of the set points in a Load Frequency Control system. Other reserve may be required for delivery in longer time scales and dispatched manually for delivery within 15 minutes. This may be to release capacity for participation in LFC.

Regulating/Secondary reserve is usually set at around 300 MW for control reserve and 600 MW for other Reserve giving some 900 MW in total. Emergency reserve is additional and usually set at 300 MW.

11.4 PROCUREMENT PROCESS

The TSO in the Netherlands, Tennet, issue an invitation to tender for supply of resources for each year. During the second half of May they launch the process of contracting energy and power for the coming year for the following products:

• regulating power;
• emergency power;
• reactive power;
• recovery resources.

Tennet invite potential suppliers of one or more of the above products to contact their Secretariat by a defined Tuesday in May at the latest.

Supplies for reactive power will tend to be contracted annually, with any shorter term declarations of availability changes affecting their payments. Contracts to enable system recovery, using generation black start capability, may cover several years ahead. The contracting for regulating energy and reserves is much more dynamic and subject to short term bidding on a daily basis, although demand side participants may have longer term contracts. The tendering of electricity supply for the purpose of compensation of the grid losses is effected through an auction at EnergieKeuze.nl. Existing suppliers do not have to respond to this notice,

Table 11.2 Reserve bid ladder

PTE	Period	Total capacity MW	−Max €/MWh	−600	−300	−100	100	300	600	Max	Total capacity MW
9	2:00 2:15	−480	−99.00		−24.93	5.00	29.98	34.98	75.00	120.00	800

as they will automatically receive an invitation in the course of May for submission of their offers.

The bids for regulating power and reserve are structured into a framework called a bid ladder with increasing block volumes from a negative to a positive position, each with a price. Table 11.2 shows the marginal bid price for a time period (PTU) for a range of fixed MW positions on the bid price ladder. The **ladder comprises the full complement of regulating power and reserve power** with a calling time of 15 minutes or less.

The bid price ladder's downward and upward regulating sides are shown separately.

The data are shown per time unit (PTU), for each side separately as follows.

- The top row shows the aggregate level (×MW) of + / − power offered.
- The second row columns '−Max' and 'Max' show the corresponding prices (−€99/MWh and €120/MWh) at the relevant extremity of the bid price ladder. The corresponding MWs available (−480 and 800) are shown in the total capacity columns.
- The second row also shows the price at intermediate MW levels in €/MWh e.g. for 600 MW: €75 at columns ' + 600' and blank at '−600'; (as only 480 MW is available this field remains empty and is marked □
- Where appropriate, the price (−€24.93/MWh and €34.98/MWh) for 300 MW: columns '−300' and '300'.
- Where appropriate, the price (€5/MWh and €29.98/MWh) for 100 MW: columns '−100' and '100'.

In the example above, a new bid on the upward regulating side at a bid price of €20/MWh will be blocked in as part of the first 100 MW on the upward regulating side. This is because its price falls below the marginal price of €29.98/MWh and so will have a better chance of being dispatched.

The system operator Tennet will contract for services as required from suppliers to minimise the costs. These are typically recovered by a System Service item explicitly referenced in the distribution tariffs. This was set at

€0.0011/kWh (€1.1/MWh in the Netherlands and, as the total energy transmitted during 2005 was 107 979 GWh, the total revenue from the tariffs is given by:

$$107979*1000*1.1 = €118.8 \, \text{m/yr.}$$

The costs incurred by the system operator in procuring the necessary services through the market can be estimated as follows.

Primary response is used by LFC to maintain international flows at contracted levels and to support frequency control.

The added premium for positive reserve regulation was recorded on average at €50/MWh and for negative reserve regulation at €25/MWh.

The annual energies recorded as used by LFC for positive response was 257 898 MWh and for negative −555 608 MWh. The associated costs are then given by:

$$50*257898 + 25*555,608 = €26.6 \, \text{m.}$$

The **secondary response** utilization was 1 000 000 MWh at premium prices of €30/MWh to manage transmission constraints:

$$1\,000\,000*30 = €30 \, \text{m.}$$

The **emergency reserve** was used for 40 hours during the year with a total energy of 50 GWh to provide emergency support. The premium price for this energy was around €450/MWh giving costs estimated at:

$$50*1000*450 = €22.5 \, \text{m.}$$

The provision of **reactive energy** to support voltage control is estimated based on the size of the system at:

$$\text{Reactive support} = €20 \, \text{m.}$$

Black start is assumed to be required at ten stations. The additional cost identified for stations is €1.7 m/yr.

The control centre operating costs for a system the size of the Netherlands is estimated from benchmarks against other utilities at €15 m/yr.

The total costs sum to €115.8 m (primary 26.6, secondary 30, emergency 22.5, reactive 20, black start 1.7, control 15) and compare well with the tariff return of €118.8 m, confirming that the cost estimates are of the correct order.

11.5 COST OF PROVIDING SERVICES

The costs incurred by generators and participating demand in the provision of services may be estimated as follows. These are compared with the procurement cost through the market mechanisms described in Section 11.4.

Primary Reserve
The costs of providing primary reserve can be broken down into holding costs and utilisation costs. The holding costs are principally incurred due to the need to operate part loaded at reduced efficiency. The utilisation costs are incurred through the premium cost for the energy used in positive and negative regulation and the wear and tear effects. There are also fixed costs to be recovered on generation with a lower utilisation to accommodate the part loading.

It was shown in Section 11.4 that 1453 MW is required to operate in LFC mode to meet the system requirement. The energies delivered for the year were recorded at 257 898 MWh and 555 608 MWh and are equivalent to average loads of 29.5 MW and 63.4 MW, i.e. the regulating range of the 1453 MW of participating generation will be relatively small and covered by de-loading by 10–20%. The efficiency is then reduced by about 2% from 54% to 52.9% from the graph of Figure 11.2. Assuming a fuel price of £4.72/GJ the

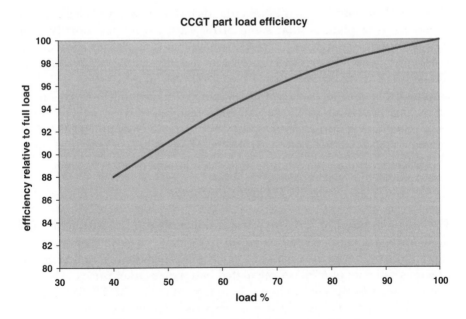

CCGT part load efficiency

<!-- y-axis: efficiency relative to full load; x-axis: load % -->

Figure 11.2   Efficiency degradation at part load

cost/MWh can be established for the two efficiencies and the difference is equivalent to the additional operating cost for fuel of:

$$(4.72*3600/1000)/0.529-(4.72*3600/1000)/0.54$$
$$= 32.1-31.4 = €0.7/MWh$$

The total annual **part load costs** for the year for the 1453 MWs of generation operating under LFC are then given by:

$$1493*0.7*8760 = €9.1 \text{ m}.$$

Extra costs are also incurred in continuous regulating duty. This uses more fuel as well as causing extra **wear and tear**. The costs associated with a 20% ramp of 46.6 MW on gas fired generation have been assessed at €85 (gas at €3/GJ). This equates to €123 with gas at €4.72/GJ. The normal deviation in system demand that has to be followed by LFC has a standard deviation of typically 0.25% or 30 MW (0.04 Hz) for a demand of 12 000 MW. Assuming that six ramps of 30 MW are required every half hour, the annual cost is:

$$6*30/46.6*€123*8760*2 = €8.55 \text{ m}.$$

The **capital cost** of plant in the Netherlands has been assessed based on the average age of plant so that some of the capital cost has already been written down. Assuming a WACC of 7% the annuity to recover the outstanding capital over 15.5 yr gives an average capital charge for different types of marginal plant of €11.8/MWh at full utilisation. It is assumed that due to part loading some 7.5% fewer units are generated on average, resulting in the capital costs being spread over fewer units. This effectively adds a premium to the capital costs of €0.95/MWh generated (11.8 – 100 * 11.8/92.5). The total annual costs would be given by:

$$€0.95*1493*0.75*8760 = €9.31 \text{ m}.$$

This assumes that the 1493 MW is operating at a 75% load factor. The three estimates together add to €27 m (part load 9.1, wear and tear 8.55, capital 9.31). The result calculated for the year compares well with the previous estimate of €26.6 m calculated based on market prices. Also this result equates to a premium on positive regulation of €48.5/MWh and on negative regulation of €24.2/MWh, compared with the figures of €50 and €25/MWh referenced in Section 11.4.

Regulating Reserve

The overall materiality of the regulating reserve market can be assessed by looking at the typical costs of holding reserves on gas fired generation. At **part load** there is a degradation of the overall heat rate due to the no load heat costs. Regulating reserve will generally be supplied within minutes and can be supplied by generation operating at lower loads. At 40% loading the efficiency is reduced to around 88% of its full load value as shown in Figure 11.2. Assuming a full load efficiency of 54%, then the efficiency at 40% load would be 47.52%. At a typical ramping rate of 3.0%/ minute for gas fired generation the output realizable from 15 minutes would be 45% (15 * 3), i.e. an extra 1.125 MW for every part loaded MW. Since the system requirement is typically for 300, some **750 MW** of generation would need to be operating at 40% load with a lower efficiency.

Using the graph of Figure 11.2, the regulating cost resulting from operation of a gas unit at 40% as opposed to full load can be estimated. Assume an efficiency of 54% and a fuel price of €3/GJ for gas then at 40% load the efficiency drops to 88%, giving a difference in cost of:

$$(3.0*3600/1000)/0.472 - (3.0*3600/1000)/0.54$$
$$= 22.88 - 20 = €2.88/MWh.$$

Since the typical system requirement is for 300 MW, on average the extra annual cost resulting from operating part loaded would be given by:

$$300*2.88*8760 = €7.5 \, m/yr.$$

As the initial fuel price is €4.72/GJ the costs for 2005 would be €11.8 m.

There is also additional wear and tear costs associated with ramping to instruction. The costs associated with a 20% ramp of 46.6 MW on gas fired generation have been assessed at €123 with gas at €4.72/GJ. The normal deviation in system demand that has to be followed by regulating reserve has a standard deviation of typically 1.5% or 184 MW in this example.

The costs per ramp are then given by:

$$€123*184/46.6 = €488.$$

Assuming one ramp of 184 MW is required every half hour, the 2005 annual cost is:

$$€488*8760*2 = €8.55 \, m.$$

Assuming part loading to be on 60% on average, as opposed to full utilisation of 84%, then 24% fewer units are generated resulting in the capital costs being spread over fewer MWh. Based on the figure calculated earlier for capital costs of 11.8/MWh this effectively adds a premium to the capital costs of €4.7/MWh (generated $(11.8 * 84/60 - 11.8)$. The total additional annual capital costs to maintain the required 300 MW of regulating reserve would be given by:

$$€4.7 * 300 * 8760 = €12.3 \, m,$$

assuming that the 750 MW is operating at a 60% load factor.

The total costs are estimated at €32.6 m (part load 11.8, ramp 8.55, capital 12.3) compared with €30 m derived in Section 11.4 based on a market evaluation. Assuming an average energy utilisation of 120 MW or 1 051 200 MWh/yr, this represents an average premium to normal energy prices of €31.0/MWh compared with the market premium shown in Section 11.3 of €30/MWh for 1 000 000 MWh.

To illustrate the development of costs: for a generator the additional costs/unit resulting from operating a 300 MW coal fired generator at 70% full load as opposed to full load so as to be able to supply ancillary services can be calculated. Assume the full load efficiency is 38% with a no-load cost of 10% of the total full load cost. The fuel cost is assumed to be £1.2/GJ and the annual fixed charge is £15 m and the unit realises 85% availability.

The annual production at 85% availability $= 300 * 8760 * 0.85 = 2\,233\,800$ MWh.
Full load fuel cost $= 1.2 * 3600/1000/0.38 = £11.36/\text{MWh}$.
The fixed cost per unit $= 15\,000\,000/2\,233\,800 = £6.71/\text{MWh}$.
The total full load cost/unit $= 11.36 + 6.71 = 18.07/\text{MWh}$.

The annual production at 70% load $= 300 * 0.7 * 8760 * 0.85 = 1\,563\,660$.
The effective efficiency at 70% load is given by $= 70/(10 + 90 * 0.70) * 0.38 = 0.3643$.
The 70% load fuel cost $= 1.2 * 3600/1000/0.3643 = £11.85/\text{MWh}$.
The apportioned fixed costs $= 15\,000\,000/1\,563\,660 = £9.59/\text{MWh}$.
The effective unit cost at 70% load $= 11.85 + 9.59 = £21.44/\text{MWh}$.
The additional production cost $= 21.44 - 18.07 = £3.37/\text{MWh}$.

Emergency Reserve
Emergency reserve is generation that is not generally running but can be brought into service quickly to replace regulating reserve when this is

depleted. The main costs associated with its provision relate to keeping the plant in a state of readiness that may involve some heat input and capital costs.

Assuming a level of 300 MW and generation of 50 GWh the full capital costs have to be recovered from the 50 GWh. In the case of plant retained for emergency use it will usually be towards the end of its useful life and low down the merit order. Most of the capital costs will have already been written off and the residual is assumed to be €9.0/MWh. The costs are then given by:

$$300*9*8760 = €23.6 \text{ m.}$$

This compares to the calculation based on market prices in Section 11.4 of €22.5 m. The total costs of €22.5 for 50 GWh are consistent with a price premium of €473/MWh compared with the market premium price of €450/MWh quoted in Section 11.4.

Reactive Support

The reactive support is that required over and above the mandatory requirement for generators to provide the standard range of reactive support. It requires generators to operate part loaded to be able to generate extra reactive energy. This part loading incurs extra costs due to the loss of efficiency, lost generation opportunity costs and extra capital cost apportionment as a result of the reduction in the units generated.

The part loading is assumed to be around 10–20% with efficiency degradation to 98% of full load efficiency. This is equivalent to a cost of €0.7/MWh for each unit generated. The plant required to provide additional reactive support is estimated to be 850 MW. The additional cost due to **part loading** for the year 2005 is given by:

$$850 \text{ MW}*€0.7/\text{MWh}*8760 \text{ h} = €5.2 \text{ m.}$$

The lost opportunity cost arises because the generator is required to reduce output below full load and therefore loses revenue. The associated lost income is based on the market base load price less the variable costs of generation at the prevailing fuel price. The generation is assumed to be de-loaded by 10% on average with an efficiency assumed to be 54% and other variable costs of €5.7/MWh. The **lost opportunity cost** is given by:

$$8760*850*0.1 \text{ MW}*(49.88-(4.72*3.6)/0.54)-5.7) = €9.4 \text{ m.}$$

The additional capital cost arises because fewer units are generated, so increasing the apportionment of the capital charge. Assuming that on average 7.5% fewer units are generated, then the capital charge per unit generated rises by 8% of €11.8, i.e. €0.95/MWh. The total **additional capital cost** for the year 2005 is given by:

$$8760*850*0.95 = €7.1 \text{ m.}$$

The total additional costs arising from the three sources are €21.7 m (part loading 5.2, lost opportunity 9.4, capital premium 7.1) compared with the market based estimate of Section 11.4 of €20 m.

Black start
The additional costs identified for black start stations include:

• staff costs to formulate black start plan at €50 k;
• testing start up plan €75 k;
• fuel for test €50 k.

I.e. a total fixed cost of €175 k. Black start is assumed to be required at ten stations at a cost of €175 k/station, i.e. €1.7 m/yr.

11.6 PREDICTING REVENUES

A potential investor in peaking plant will need to make estimates of the likely revenue through the life of the plant. This involves an appraisal of the total market volume as well as the likely market share of the new entrant.

Primary reserve
The requirements for primary reserve have traditionally been related to accommodating the largest credible loss of input to the system without excessive frequency deviation. The contribution of the UCTE inter-connected members is related pro rata to their energy supplied. Given that growth in demand across Europe is likely to be similar, the proportional contribution from each country is not expected to change significantly. The interconnected system requirement is assumed to grow as more generation is built without corresponding extension of the super-grid network. This will require a higher degree of distributed reserve holding that can be released without violating security constraints. The current UCTE contingency of a 3000 MW in-feed loss is expected to rise by 300 MW or 10% every 5 years or 2%/year.

Regulating Reserve
The requirements for regulating reserve are expected to grow along with the growth in system demand and the need to be able to track the more rapid

demand changes. The growth is expected to be around 1.6% from the current level of 300 MW/yr.

There is also a requirement to track any changes in generation supply that may occur as a result of renewable energy sources like wind power. The errors that will occur in predicting the output from these sources will create the need for additional reserves to maintain system balance. Based on figures published by Eon Netz, it is estimated that an additional reserve provision of 20% of installed wind capacity is required. This will grow in relation to the projected development of wind power. For example, the wind capacity in the Netherlands is expected to be around 2000 MW by 2010. Based on a coverage of 20%, this would require 400 MW reserve holding, which is of the same order as that held for other purposes. Capacity has increased at the rate of 192 MW/yr since 2001. Additional growth is also likely to be realised by introducing larger turbines at existing sites. The government target set by the Ministry of Economic Affairs is for 10% of energy to be derived from renewable sources by 2020 or 13.8 TWh. This equates to 6 GW of wind capacity operating with a 26% load factor. To meet these requirements the reserve provision would have to rise to 1200 MW, i.e. 20% of 6 GW.

Figure 11.3 compares the variation in UK normal system demand on a half hour basis with the output of 6 GW of wind power, based on extrapolation of

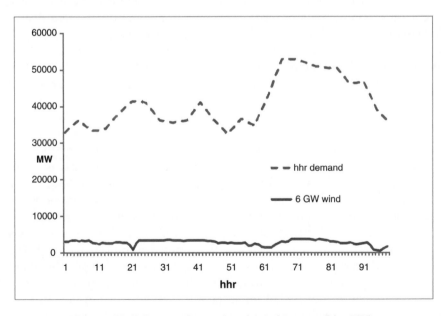

Figure 11.3 System demand and wind output (hhr, UK)

actual data, for two days in April. It can be seen that there are several sudden variations in excess of 1 GW between half hours with the largest during this period of 1650 MW. The normal system reserve requirements and those to cover wind power variation are basically similar. This is larger than the provision that would be made to cover a generation loss incident and consistent with the view that once the wind capacity exceeds around 10% extra reserve provision is required. It has been reported that the current levels of wind power can be supported through the use of the current system reserve provision but, as the concentration builds up, the requirement will be dominated by the need to accommodate wind power variation and will grow.

Emergency Reserve

The requirement for emergency or contingent reserve is assumed to grow in proportion to the system energy demand. This is consistent with providing backup for loss of regulating reserve following contingencies. There is also currently a problem due to high concentrations of wind energy in Northern Germany where variations in output can directly affect the cross-border flows into the Netherlands. It is claimed that this is impacting on the security of the Dutch network. Whilst new transmission capacity into the South of Germany is planned, it can be expected that there will continue to be additional regulating requirements in the Netherlands to accommodate these disturbances from time to time. In that they are not planned, these disturbances will be managed by Tennet using emergency power. It is assumed that the proportion of the variation exported will be in relation to relative system size of around 5 : 1 between the Netherlands and Germany. A similar pattern of growth to the Netherlands is expected in Germany as it will be restricted by supplier capacity. There will not be much diversity between Dutch and German wind power variations and the effects will be cumulative. The results of the growth in emergency reserve due to general energy increase and the need to accommodate cross-border transfer errors is likely to result in increased requirements for emergency reserve of some 20% of the installed capacity in Germany in this case. Figure 11.4 shows how the requirements for ancillary services might develop in the Netherlands.

Having established an estimate of the future total system requirements it is necessary to estimate the market share that a new entrant might expect. The number and type of participants can be gauged from a review of the plant likely to be operating at the margin. This will provide a guide to the likely costs of competitors and what might be a successful bid into the ancillary market. For some of the services the location is important, there may be a

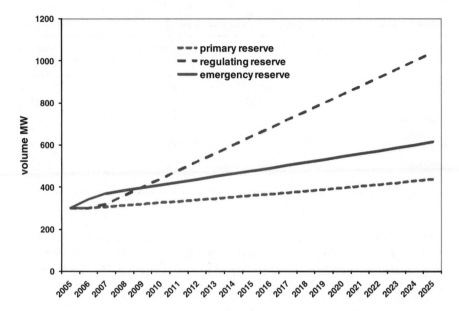

Figure 11.4 Predicted ancillary service requirements

requirement for reserve to be distributed around the system to maintain security following an outage; the supply of reactive energy is essentially a local requirement to support voltage in an area. Black start capability will be distributed at strategic locations around the system to enable restoration in different areas. The prospect of a new plant securing contracts for the provision of ancillary services needs to take account of its proposed location in relation to the competition.

11.7 SUMMARY

This chapter has discussed the requirements for ancillary services and the scale of the system requirement. This has been illustrated with reference to the requirement for the Netherlands. The procurement process is designed to ensure competitive provision through auctions and bidding. The charges based on an analysis of the market have been derived. The costs of provision have been estimated, taking account of the impact of part loading, ramping and a premium to recover fixed costs. These were assessed as shown in Table 11.3.

Table 11.3 Comparison of provider costs and market prices

AS costs €m/yr	Part load	Wear & tear ramping	Capital premium	Totals €m/yr	Market estimate
Primary	9.1	8.55	9.31	27.0	26.6
regulating	11.8	8.55	12.3	32.7	30
emergency			23.6	23.6	22.5
Reactive	5.2	9.4	7.1	21.7	20
Black start			1.7	1.7	1.7
Control			15	15.0	15
				121.6	115.8

These compare favourably with those derived from an analysis of the market prices. Finally, an approach to predicting future requirements for services and market share was described taking account of the development of variable wind power sources.

12

Cross-border Trading

12.1 INTRODUCTION

The power systems of the European countries are interconnected and within the UCTE zone they operate synchronously with a common frequency and operating standards. Other countries are linked by DC links as with the UK. Most of the links were put in place in place by the respective TSOs. The original motivation for most of the links was:

- to enable the transfer of energy to take account of any diversity in power demand profiles and cost;
- to provide added capacity to safeguard extreme shortfalls;
- to provide emergency support through shared reserve agreements.

The links were deemed to be viable if the operating and capital cost incurred during a year were exceeded by savings derived from exchanges and in reserve holding. In the liberalised world these links enable trading across borders and can have a significant impact on prices. The European regulators would like to see a pan-European market with level prices and have been pressing to upgrade the transmission limits to enable more cross-border trading. The level of trading has steadily increased to an annual energy level in excess of 350 TWh, equivalent to the British demand. However, excessive levels of transfer can cause insecurities on the network and the process has to be closely monitored to contain potential problems. This task falls to the TSOs who have to undertake network studies to predict the

Power Markets and Economics: Energy Costs, Trading, Emissions   Barrie Murray
© 2009 John Wiley & Sons, Ltd

network capacity available for trading and avoid potential network insecurities. This requires analysis of the internal network using equivalents to represent external adjacent networks.

This chapter describes the processes involved in trading across international borders and the issues associated with charging for wheeling and use of the network. The principles are illustrated with reference to the evolvement of the Pan-European market. The chapter covers:

- the governance arrangements;
- the mechanisms involved in contracting for interconnection capacity;
- the impact of trading on international markets;
- the development of wheeling charges.

The issues associated with contract paths and physical flows and losses are also discussed.

12.2 GOVERNANCE

In order to facilitate international trade, multi-lateral agreements and processes need to be established. In the case of the European high voltage power networks they are operated as an interconnected system under the auspices of **UCTE** (Union for the Co-ordination of Transmission of Electricity). This association of all the TSOs (Transmission System Operators) in continental Europe sets technical standards governing operation that enable the provision of a reliable market base to enable power exchange and mutual support during emergencies. The standards have been incorporated into an operational handbook that is underpinned by a multi-lateral agreement (July 2005). The UCTE maintain operational statistics and predict the adequacy of production capacity to meet expected demands to support the planning process of their interconnected network. Similar organisations exist covering the separate networks of Scandinavia (Nordel), Ireland (TSOI) and the UK (UKTSOA). With the emergence of the Internal Electricity Market (IEM) these organisations saw the need for harmonisation and formed **ETSO** (European Transmission System Operators). Subsequently, in 2001, the constitution was changed to an international association governed by an assembly with each TSO becoming a direct member. The organisation focuses on market related issues such as harmonisation of network access, tariffs, inter TSO compensation, congestion management and balancing arrangements. Similar arrangements exist in the US and are being established in Africa under the auspices of

SAPP, the Southern African Power Pool. The UCTE have established a set of operational guidelines including:

- P1 - Load frequency control and performance
- P2 - Scheduling and accounting
- P3 - Operational security
- P4- Coordinated operational planning
- P5 - Emergency operation
- P6 - Communications
- P7 - Data exchanges.

Members have to demonstrate that they can comply with the operational requirements before being accepted for connection. P1, for example, lays down the following standards related to frequency management.

- Primary – governor response dead-band +/−20 mHz immediate.
- Secondary AGC – 30 seconds to 15 minutes – the response time that must be met by generation subject to Automatic Generation Control signals where:
  o The Area Control Error – ACE $= \Delta P + K * \Delta f$ where:

  ΔP = transfer error and Δf = frequency error from target.

  o Metering data error should be <1.5% with 5 second measurement cycle.
- Tertiary – manual dispatch should be achievable within 15 minutes.
- Time control error should not exceed +/−20 seconds.

Each connected utility will have to meet its commitment by making available a specified contribution.

Although the European networks are often in public ownership, they are considered to be monopolies and are therefore subject to regulation. The **ERGEG** (European Regulators Group for Electricity and Gas) was set up by the European Commission on 11 November 2003 by Decision 2003/796/EC. It is an Advisory Group of 27 independent national regulatory authorities to assist the Commission in consolidating the Internal Market for Electricity and Gas. Particular typical initiatives include the following.

- **Open season** (April 2007) This proposed a mechanism to appraise infrastructure developments in transmission through a two stage transparent process; the preliminary appraisal in which capacity bids are invited and the second phase where capacity is allocated and firm contracts placed to support the development.

- **Inter TSO guidelines** (April 2006) This covers details of the determination and payment procedure for compensation between TSOs relating to cross-border flows.
- The ERGEG aim is for a progressive harmonisation of the underlying principles for setting charges applied to producers and consumers (load) under national tariff systems, including the reflection of the inter-TSO compensation mechanism in national network charges.
- **Secondary Markets** are proposed as a mechanism to deal with congestion on interconnection routes.
- The regulators are focused on establishing a pan-European market and have encouraged the development of cross-border trades but not at the expense of security. The regulators' hard hitting final report to the EC on the November 2006 blackout was very critical of transmission system operators.

12.3 CROSS-BORDER CAPACITY

The TSOs will calculate and publish details of the available cross-border transmission capacity for trading. The calculation procedure involves the following steps.

- Calculate TTC, the total capacity allowing for normal secure operation.
- Calculate the TRM, Transmission Reserve Margin, for unintentional exchanges, emergencies and inaccuracies.
- Calculate the Net Transfer Capacity, NTC = TTC − TRM.
- Establish the AAC. Already Allocated/notified Capacity.
- Then ATC available capacity is given by ATC = NTC − AAC.

The results of the process are collated and periodically published to the market. For example, the total interconnection capacity in the Netherlands is some 5400 MW but, in practice, provision needs to be made to cover emergencies of 300 MW and some flows are restricted by internal transmission constraints and the need to accommodate variable wind power output. The amount available for trading on a secure basis is generally about 3600 MW. Table 12.1 shows the NTC MW capacity values of inter-connectors for winter 2007–2008. It can be seen that France and Germany are strongly interconnected central nodes and play a dominant role in determining prices.

Table 12.1 European interconnection capacity (MW)

Transfer Limit	Austria	Belgium	France	Germany	Italy	Lux	Neth.	Portugal	CZ	Spain	Switzerland	UK	Poland	DK
Austria	0	0	0	2000	220	0	0	0	750	0	650	0	0	0
Belgium	0	0	3200	0	0	500	2400	0	0	0	0	0	0	0
France	0	2200	0	2750	2650	0	0	0	0	1400	3200	2000	0	0
Germany	2000	0	2750	0	0	500	3000	0	700	0	2100	0	1200	1400
Italy	220	0	2650	0	0	0	0	0	0	0	3890	0	0	0
Lux	0	500	0	500	0	0	0	0	0	0	0	0	0	0
Netherlands	0	2400	0	3850	0	0	0	0	0	1200	0	0	0	0
Portugal	0	0	0	0	0	0	0	0	0	0	0	0	0	0
CZ	700	0	0	2300	0	0	0	0	0	0	0	0	800	0
Spain	0	0	1400	0	0	0	0	1300	0	0	0	0	0	0
Switzerland	1200	0	3200	1800	3890	0	0	0	0	0	0	0	0	0
UK	0	0	2000	0	0	0	0	0	0	0	0	0	0	0
Poland	0	0	0	1100	0	0	0	0	700	0	0	0	0	0
Denmark	0	0	0	1400	0	0	0	0	0	0	0	0	0	0
	4120	5100	15200	15700	6760	1000	5400	1300	2150	2600	9840	2000	2000	1400

This inter-connection capacity is allocated free unless the demand for capacity exceeds the supply. Then, in the case of the Netherlands, for example, a subsidiary of Tennet called the TSO Auction Office, is responsible for managing the allocation of capacity through a competitive auction. Some of the auction income can be used to fund expansion of the inter-connection capacity.

12.4 NEW INVESTMENT

Where the operator of the existing infrastructure sees, based on access refusals, forecasts or other signals, that the existing infrastructure is no longer sufficient, enhancements will be proposed. There are also cases where the government or regulator will decide that investment is needed and require the System Operator to make investments, or will approve investments. In both of these cases, the existing TSO will often be the sponsor of a new infrastructure development based on operational experience. There may also be situations where outside investors perceive that there is a need for new infrastructure and wish to sponsor it. The legal framework should be structured to allow such investments to take place and licences to be granted. In either case, an open process, involving consultations with users, is designed to help decision makers estimate exactly how much and what kind of new capacity is needed, while ensuring that capacity is allocated on a transparent and non-discriminatory basis.

Table 12.2 shows where new investment is planned to be commissioned some time after 2008. It can be seen that links are planned both from Norway and the UK into the Netherlands where prices are relatively high. The sponsorship of new links usually falls to the TSOs and a typical commercial arrangement is described below.

The link from Norway to the Netherlands will be built by Statnett and TenneT as equal partners and consists of a sub-sea cable. The so called NorNed-cable will be an open interconnection that will be utilised to effect market coupling of the Dutch and Nordic markets. This will be handled by the power exchanges APX and Nordpool.

The interconnection will be regulated, meaning that the costs and revenues related to the project will be attributed to the grid customers. It is expected that revenues will be sufficient to cover the costs with acceptable margins.

NorNed is a prioritised infrastructure project under the EU Trans European Networks (TEN) programme.

Table 12.2 Planned interconnection capacity

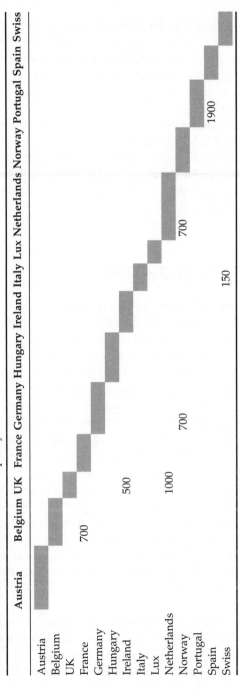

	Austria	Belgium	UK	France	Germany	Hungary	Ireland	Italy	Lux	Netherlands	Norway	Portugal	Spain	Swiss
Austria														
Belgium														
UK														
France			700											
Germany														
Hungary														
Ireland				500										
Italy														
Lux														
Netherlands					1000									
Norway					700					700				
Portugal														
Spain								150				1900		
Swiss														

The decision to build the inter-connector was made at year-end 2004, and the sub-sea cable was expected to be taken into operation at the turn of the year 2007/8. However, due to a fault that occurred before Christmas 2007 the cable was expected to be available to the market in April 2008.

- Cable length: 580 km
- Total project development costs: approx. €495 million
- Cable capacity: 700 MW (megawatt)
- Land terminals will be established at Feda in the municipality of Kvinesdal (county of Vest-Agder, Norway) and Eemshaven (The Netherlands)
- Weight: Single-core cable = 37.5 kg/m; two-core cable = 85 kg/m
- Voltage level: 450 kV (kilovolt)
- Maximum sea depth: 410 m.

12.5 MANAGING OPERATION

The TSOs are responsible for operation of their respective networks and the associated inter-connectors. Technically this is a complex task as the flows are continually affected by changes in generation and demand patterns, whilst at the same time frequency control standards have to be maintained. To be part of the UCTE interconnected system requires that certain operating standards are maintained, particularly in relation to frequency control. This is usually managed using automatic load frequency control systems (LFC). This employs automatic generation control facilities to adjust the output in response to signals from a central monitoring station. The central station monitors the tie line flows against agreed targets to establish the area control error. It then signals the participating generation to raise or reduce output to bring the flows back to target. At the same time there is a requirement to contribute to the frequency control of the interconnected area. This will be based on a prior agreed contribution on the MW output change per unit of frequency error. In the previous chapter it was stated that the contribution of the Netherlands was set at 744 MW/Hz. The combined control function is termed 'tie line bias frequency control'. This process manages the summated area export or import but does not enable the flows along individual routes or lines to be controlled.

The individual line flows will obey network laws and will not necessarily be consistent with the contracted exchanges. There will be so-called loop flows along any parallel lines that may affect network security. Figure 12.1 shows a set of typical average annual MW flows as occurred during 2007. The

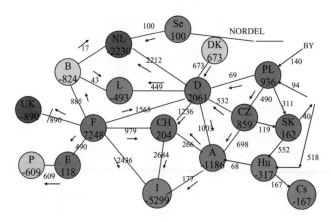

Figure 12.1 Annual average net MW flows

numbers within each circle are the net average nodal injection for the year with the MW flow shown against each line. It can be seen that France is the largest exporter, having the lowest prices, and Italy the largest importer, with the highest prices. It can also be seen that flows from France to Italy may go direct as well as through Switzerland. The management of these flows has to be based on network load flow studies that have to undertaken at least daily based on the latest status of generation and demand. These will show the loadings on the physical routes and may require rescheduling if potential insecurities occur. Some reserve capacity has to be retained against this eventuality but may be released on the day if conditions are favourable.

A particular problem is that of managing the impact of variable wind power output on inter-connector flows. The output from a large concentration in North Germany tends to flow across the links into the Netherlands and affects the security of their network. Reinforcement of the transmission capacity from North to South Germany is necessary to alleviate this situation. This type of problem is likely to increase as wind capacity is expanded across Europe.

12.6 CAPACITY AUCTIONS

In general, when the demand for cross-border capacity persistently exceeds the Available Transmission Capacity (ATC) then auctions will be organised in various time frames as illustrated below for imports to Germany:

- **Yearly auctions**
- **Auction 3** Capacity towards Germany from Netherlands
  Date of Auction: 2005–11-17 12 : 00 : 00
  Offered capacity: 350 MW (eon/2005–11-17 15 : 24 : 53)
  Result
  Sold: 350 MW; Price: €/MW 41 750
  Total number of participants: 14; Participants allocated capacity: 3
- Capacity can be sold on or back
- **Monthly auctions** – by day 10 of working month for whole month
- **Daily auctions** – at 9:00 a.m. for each hour of following day.

The result of this auction is that a cost of €4.76/MWh is incurred in exporting to Germany. Figure 12.2 shows the average base load prices in each country around the time of the capacity auction in 2005 and can be used to identify those countries likely to be exporting to Germany. It can be seen that the differential price with France exceeds the cost of reserving the transmission capacity. That with Czechoslovakia is more marginal but it is probably supplied preferentially from lower cost plant.

The pattern of flows can be seen to be a function of the inverse of the average nodal prices with flows from low voltage to higher voltage nodes. An equivalent network model can be built to simulate the effect of changing prices on network flows.

Figure 12.3 is published by UCTE and illustrates the congested routes by the darkness of the arrow used. Black indicates the most congested route followed by the lighter shades down to clear. It can be seen that routes in and out of Germany are congested as well as Czechoslovakia, Slovakia, Austria and Hungary. Plans are established to add some 8 GW of new transmission capacity to the UCTE network to facilitate more trading.

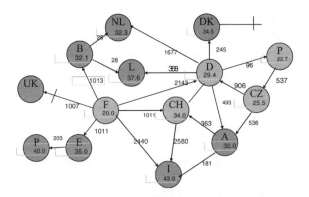

Figure 12.2 Nodal prices and flows

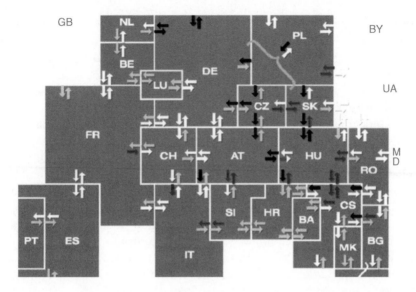

Figure 12.3   European congestion (source UCTE)

12.7 SECURITY

The transmission network security is maintained by the TSOs who operate to
'n - 1' security standards enabling continued secure operation following the
outage of an item of transmission equipment. There are very few major
incidents but in recent years problems have occurred that that have lead to
loss of supply. The first in Italy occurred due to loss of interconnection. Prices
in Italy are amongst the highest in Europe and as a result it normally imports a
lot of energy, principally from France. The loss of interconnection therefore
resulted in serious power imbalance in Italy. The other incident occurred on
4 November 2006 when several lines tripped in North Germany and, with
subsequent cascading, resulted in UCTE being split into three islands each
with power imbalance causing interruptions to supply. Various conclusions
were reached including the following.

• n - 1 security was not being maintained.
• There was poor inter-TSO communication.
• The wind and CHP plant tripped and restarted automatically without TSO
  coordination.
• DSOs reconnected consumers without prior TSO agreement.
• Procedures and restoration plans were considered inadequate.

Whereas on the one hand TSOs are pushed to enable maximum cross-border trade by the regulators they are also the first to criticise when failures occur. The result of this will be that TSOs will continue to err on the side of maintaining security rather than maximising free trade.

It is worth noting that the higher concentrations of wind and distributed generation aggravated the management of the incident. There have also been complaints at ministerial level between the Netherlands and Germany over the high concentrations of wind energy causing variations in cross-border flows endangering the security of the Dutch network. Poland has experienced similar problems. Increasing concentrations of distributed peripheral generation will require a rethink on distribution network development and better management of local resources by the DSOs. The increasing proportion of wind output will also make it necessary to retain more spare capacity on cross-border links to accommodate its variable output.

A distinction needs to be drawn between trading surplus energy and trading energy backed by firm capacity. There is a risk in crediting all interconnection capacity as being available when considering the security of the plant margin. Contract terms should be specific and, where capacity is guaranteed, it can be included in margin calculations. The charges for the provision of firm energy are based on fuel costs as well as the fixed capital and operating costs involved in providing the capacity.

12.8 CHARGING FOR WHEELING

There will be occasions associated with international trading where power is wheeled across networks and mechanisms are required to assess the costs incurred resulting from increased losses and the assets utilized. Figure 12.4 illustrates the flows resulting from a 100 MW export from Belgium to Italy. The process typically used to establish network costs and charges involves the following.

- Define a Transit Horizontal Network (THN), representing the transmission assets that could potentially be used for wheeling.
- The THN is costed for each TSO based on a standard costing methodology incorporating both asset-related and operating costs.
- A Transit Key (TK) is defined for each TSO as the ratio of energy that is wheeled to the total energy transported on the network.
- The TSO's network cost of wheeling is then calculated as the product of the TK and the cost of the THN for each TSO.

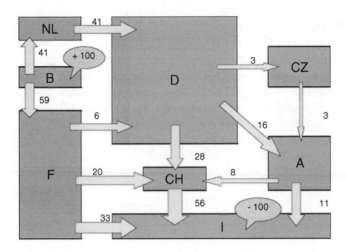

Figure 12.4   Network flow route from Belgium to Italy

- Each TSO's share of revenue received from network charges is then determined as the ratio of that TSO's network cost of wheeling to the total network cost of wheeling (across all TSOs).
- In the EU the compensation fund ITC is calculated for Inter TSO transfers. The horizontal network (RAV) is identified and costs are apportioned using the transit key that compares wheeling to total asset utilisation. Costs are recovered through a charge on network import/export with an entry charge at the perimeter of €1/MWh.

In order to manage the complex flows and account for the costs involved, the TSOs need to be involved to endorse proposed trades. They can provide an indication of capacity to facilitate trading but nearer the event these need to be refined.

The trading community could not be expected to handle the complexity of calculating wheeling charges in real time and they need a simple on cost/ MWh. The TSOs work out the costs incurred by each organisation to establish the total wheeling costs. These costs can then be recovered by adding a small premium to each unit of energy transferred. Retrospectively the TSOs distribute the revenues on the basis of their assessed relative costs. This simplifies the trading process while enabling TSOs to recover their costs. The principles can be illustrated by a simple calculation.

Given an expected international exchange trade of 350 TWh and average losses of 2% of the transferred energy, the total cost of losses and the charge per unit of energy transferred to recover the costs can be calculated. Assuming a base load energy prices are €38/MWh.

If the total UCTE production is 2584 TWh, the average transit key can be calculated. If the capital cost (c) of the total horizontal network is €6000m, the average asset cost associated with wheeling can be calculated assuming a WACC of 7% (i) with a life of 30 years (yr). Then the total charge necessary to recover costs/unit transferred can be calculated.

The annual losses are given by:

$$0.02 * 350 * 1\,000\,000 = 7\,000\,000\,\text{MWh}.$$

The total cost of losses at €38/MWh is given by:

$$7\,000\,000\,\text{MWh} * €38/\text{MWh} = €266\text{m}.$$

The cost/unit of energy transferred is given by:

$$€266\text{m}/350\,\text{MWh} = €0.76/\text{MWh or } 2\% \text{ of } €38.$$

So to cover the losses associated with trading a general charge of €0.76/MWh injected would be required.

The Transit key can be calculated as $= 350/2584 = 0.135$.

The annual capital cost is given by:

$$\frac{c * i(1+i)^Y}{(1+i)^Y - 1}.$$

Annual capital cost $= €6000\text{m} * 0.07 * (1+0.07) \wedge 30/((1+0.07) \wedge 30 - 1)$

$$= 420 * 7.61/6.61 = €483.4\text{m/yr}.$$

Asset cost apportioned to wheeling $= 0.135 * 483.4 = €65.26\text{m/yr}.$

Asset cost/unit transferred $= 65.26/350 = €0.186/\text{MWh}.$

Total cost $= 0.76 + 0.186 = €0.946/\text{MWh}$ of energy transferred.

In addition, costs may be incurred in reserving interconnection capacity. Table 12.3 shows the results of an annual interconnection capacity auction and can be used to evaluate the costs of reserving transmission to facilitate the

Table 12.3 European Annual Interconnection Auction

route	offered (MW)	Requested (MW)	Allocated (MW)	Price E/MW/ yr	offered (MW)	Requested (MW)	Allocated (MW)	Price E/MW/ yr
BE->NL	234	NA	233	30666	234	NA	233	876
NL->DE	155	NA	155	200	155	NA	155	75366
BE->FR	NA	NA	400	2190	NA	NA	1,299	18045
CH->AT	NA	NA	NA	NA	NA	NA	NA	12300
CZ->DE	NA	NA	NA	NA	NA	NA	NA	5090
CZ->AT	NA	NA	NA	15000	NA	NA	NA	NA
DE->AT	NA	NA	NA	12000	NA	NA	NA	NA
IT->AT	NA	NA	NA	NA	28	NA	28	3000
DE->CH	500	NA	500	44500	1,600	NA	1,600	153300
FR->DE	NA	NA	800	26542	NA	NA	NA	0
FR->IT	NA	NA	1,000	1512	NA	NA	NA	NA
Fr->CZ	NA	NA	50	787	NA	NA	0	0
CH->IT	NA	NA	365	1100	NA	NA	0	0

trade from Belgium to Italy shown in Figure 12.4 of 100 MW. The flow across each route is used to calculate the costs/yr of reserving the interconnection capacity as shown in Table 12.4. It can be seen that the total route cost per MWh transferred is calculated at €3.8/MWh.

Table 12.4 Wheeling auction cost

route	flow MW	cost/yr
BE->NL	41	1257306
NL->DE	41	8200
BE->FR	59	129210
CH->AT	8	98400
CZ->DE	3	15270
CZ->AT	3	45000
DE->AT	16	192000
IT->AT	11	33000
DE->CH	28	1246000
FR->DE	6	159252
FR->IT	33	49896
Fr->CZ	20	15740
CH->IT	56	61600
cost/MWh		3.8

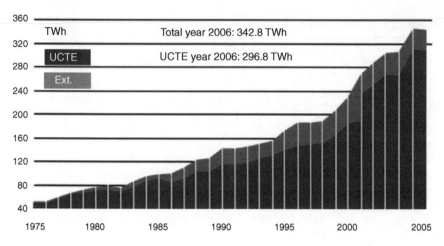

Figure 12.5   Development of international trade (source UCTE)

12.9 INTERNATIONAL TRADING DEVELOPMENT

Europe

European cross-border trading has continued to increase over the years as illustrated by the graph of Figure 12.5. In 2001 Czechoslovakia, Hungary, Poland and Slovakia were able to participate and in 2003 Romania and Bulgaria. The levels in 2006 of some 350 TWh equates to the total consumption of the UK.

Rather than taking the shortest route to get from A to B, the current finds the path of least resistance, in accordance with the laws of physics. The line flows depend on the location of injected energy into the grid by power plants and the quantity extracted from the grid by power users. The analysis of the flow patterns is undertaken by specially developed system models called load flows. While generators, traders and suppliers all over Europe are free to conclude supply contracts, the impact on the physical flows has to be monitored as transmission flows will not be the same as the underlying contracts would have suggested. This is why the administrators of the European transmission grids, the Transmission System Operators or TSOs, regulate the international transmission routes as well as monitoring the load flows. For example TenneT as the Dutch TSO continuously works closely with its fellow TSOs in neighbouring countries, as all regions continuously affect one another. Information is exchanged and potential joint transmission bottlenecks are identified.

Whereas cross-border interconnections were used for lending assistance in emergencies in the past, nowadays they are used for commercial trade. The result is that the demand for capacity interconnections has grown. It is for this reason that the European Commission is advocating the development of adequate interconnection between countries in promotion of the European energy market as set out in the internal power market directives.

Some indication of the benefit of trading can be gained by calculating the replacement saving for Italy of replacing internal generation with imports based on their average market price from the immediate neighbouring countries.

The total saving and the saving in €/MWh of importing energy into Italy as opposed to supplying all demand at local prices can be calculated using the information from Figure 12.2 on prices and flows.

The flows and prices from France are, 2440 MW at €20/MWh, Switzerland 2580 at €34/MWh and Austria 181 MW at €32/MWh.

Total cost of imports to Italy = (2440 * 20 + 2580 * 34 + 181 * 32).

Average per hour for 5201 MW = €142 312/h.

Cost of supplying energy at local prices at €43/MWh = (2440 + 2580 + 181) * 43 = €223 643/h.

Cost difference/h = 223 643 −142 312 = €81,331 or €15.6/MWh.

The annual saving = 15.6 * 5201 * 8760 = €71.2m.

In this case it can be seen that the benefit is high at some €15.6/MWh because of the high base load price difference, particularly with France. This compares with the average costs of wheeling due to losses of €1–2/MWh. In practice charges for the reservation of transmission capacity through auctions will reduce the benefit from trading.

SE Europe

As UCTE membership extends east embracing SE Europe it is expected that trading will increase further. Plans are being made to establish a link around the Mediterranean. In July 2004, TEIAS and Trakya Joint Venture, a private firm, signed a tender agreement for the establishment of a 260-km power line linking Turkey with Greece. The line will operate at 400 kV and is expected to be completed in 2010. This will form part of an ambitious plan to interconnect all the countries of the Mediterranean (France, Spain, Morocco, Algeria, Turkey, Greece, Italy, Libya, Egypt and Jordan) through the 'Medring'. The connection with Greece will mean the Turkish grid will need to be synchronised with the Western European UCTE grid if it can meet the operating standards required. The high-voltage national grid and also some distribution networks are in urgent need of upgrading as transmission losses are significant.

The Turkish transmission system is in turn connected to several neighbouring countries but, because the systems are not set up for synchronous operations, this leads to cumbersome and inefficient exchanges. Its existing connections are with Azerbaijan, Bulgaria, Georgia, Iran, Iraq and Syria. The Iran connection also allows imports from Turkmenistan. Turkey imports some electricity from Bulgaria, Turkmenistan and Iran, and exports a small amount to Azerbaijan. In June 2007, Turkey and Iraq announced the reinforcement of their cooperation in the power sector. They agreed to increasing capacity on an existing cross-border high-voltage line.

According to the EC, large exports from Turkey toward south-eastern Europe are foreseen. A 2000 MW short-term transfer capacity may be built in the next few years, but currently the interconnection is out of operation. It is claimed that an increase of transmission capacity up to 5000 MW is economically efficient in the long run, using AC (alternating current) overhead lines, whose estimated costs are about €70 million. In total, €300 million should be invested in four AC lines. A high-voltage line could be realised between Turkey and Cyprus. For the moment, however, the main obstacle to the exploitation of existing interconnection capacity between Turkey and south-eastern Europe is the inability of the Turkish power system to adapt to Union for the Coordination of Transmission of Electricity (UCTE) standards. In October 2005, Turkey failed to sign an agreement to become a part of the European UCTE grid.

Southern Africa

In Southern Africa a group of thirteen countries are cooperating in the establishment of an international trading organisation called SAPP (Southern African Power Pool). It is intended to establish day-ahead trading based on the Nordpool model. The arrangement will enable the integrated operation of a mixture of hydro power with the predominately coal fired generation operated by Eskom in South Africa.

Figure 12.6 shows the scope of the market and main interconnectors. There is a requirement for further investment in transmission and generation and it is expected that the development of trading opportunities will encourage new entry. Operations are coordinated by the Co-Ordination Centre to:

1. monitor the operation of the Power Pool, transactions and inadvertent power flows;

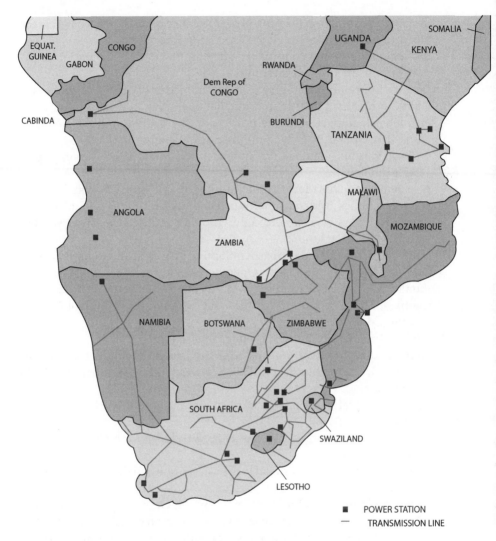

Figure 12.6   SAPP countries

2. provide routine daily reports, data and information relevant to the operation of the Power Pool to the Operating Sub Committee and to the Members;
3. monitor and advise on the use of the Operating Guidelines;

4. monitor and report on the control performance criteria, as specified in the Operating Guidelines, to all the Operating Members;
5. convene, following a disturbance affecting the parallel operation of the pool, a post disturbance committee;
6. provide information and give technical advice or support to Members of SAPP, in matters pertaining to parallel operation;
7. evaluate the impact of future projects on the operation of the pool and advise the Operating Sub-Committee accordingly;
8. perform various operational planning studies to highlight possible operating problems;
9. give advice on short-term and long-term operating problems;
10. perform studies to determine transfer limits on time lines and inform Operating Members accordingly; monitor adherence of Operating Members to these limits;
11. establish and update a database containing historical and other data to be used in Planning and System Operation studies;
12. monitor the availability of the communication links between the Control Centres of the Operating Members and between these Control Centres and the Co-ordination Centre;
13. advise of the feasibility of wheeling transactions;
14. gather and act as the official custodian of data pertaining to transactions between Operating Members and between Operating Members and Non-Members.
15. monitor the calculation and implementation of the various types of Reserves;
16. carry out projects and assignments as directed by the Operating Sub-Committee;
17. monitor the protection performance on all tie line and the co-ordination of their protection;
18. monitor adherence to the Agreement by the Operating Members, inter alia regarding Accredited Capacity Obligation and calculate the penalties for insufficient Accredited Capacity and their re-allocation among members;
19. disseminate the generation and transmission maintenance schedules received from the operating Members and advise on the adjustments that are required to maintain at all times the contractual pool reserves and the agreed upon services;
20. co-ordinate the training of the Members staff and, if necessary, organise training seminars focusing on the operation of the interconnected system;

21. prepare and issue annually control performance summaries report for the benefit of the Operating Sub-Committee;
22. facilitate trading in the Short Term Energy Market (STEM).

In addition to energy, trading plans are being established to trade in ancillary service requirements. This will enable sharing in the provision of reserve and reactive support as well as system control services where one control centre assumes operational control of an adjacent utility.

The evaluation of wheeling costs is similar to the approach used in Europe but the approach to ancillary service trading is unique.

North America

Trading and wheeling has always been a feature of utility operation in North America through interconnections between states. FERC (Federal Energy Regulatory Council) paved the way for the development of Regional Transmission Operators (RTOs) through order 2000 in 1999. This required that transmission owners vest operation of their assets in the RTO. This includes scheduling and dispatch of generation and transmission congestion management as well as managing balancing and ancillary services. The PJM (Pennsylvania, New Jersey, Maryland) RTO is one of the most developed RTOs and controls a network linking fourteen states across North East America.

The RTOs are responsible for administering transmission tariffs and these include:

- charges for access to the local network to cover capital and operating costs based on a tariff/kW of capacity installed for the zone;
- charges for export/import into the local network that are based on firm contracted transmission capacity; this may be for a longer term when it is described as firm and generally available;
- charges for import/export based on the use of any spare capacity found to be available in the event.

The charges are specific to each transmission zone and are termed licence plate tariffs in that they are the same at any point within the zone. Plans are in place to evaluate more specific MW–mile based charging. The charges for transmission are levied on the Load Serving Entities (LSEs) while generators pay a connection charge that may include the need for wider system reinforcement to maintain security.

Congestion is managed by calculating Locational Marginal Prices (LMPs) for each node based on the area marginal generation costs. Where there is no congestion the LMPs will be the same. When congestion occurs, merit order operation will be restricted and LMPs will be different across a transmission route leading to a congestion charge along the route based on the difference. To enable system users to hedge against congestion charges the concept of FTRs (Financial Transmission Rights) was introduced. These give the rights to the revenues that occur from congestion rather than access to the network but they help market participants to hedge against having to pay the congestion charges.

Losses are covered by charges for point to point transmission based on PJM calculated loss factors. These are calculated for peak and off-peak system conditions with energy prices based on day-ahead market values.

12.10 SUMMARY

This chapter has explained how cross-border trading is managed to facilitate trading. It has explained the technical cooperation necessary between TSOs to establish the transmission capacity available for trading and the standards necessary to maintain stable secure operation. It illustrated how auctions are used to manage the allocation of capacity on congested routes. It has shown that the physical flows do not relate to contracted flows and that arrangements need to be put in place to recover wheeling costs associated with losses and the use of assets. An estimate of the benefit of trading is illustrated by considering the savings from imports as opposed to the use of local sources. Finally, international developments and practice are outlined by discussion and comparison of arrangements in UCTE covering Europe, SAPP in Southern Africa and PJM in NE America.

13

Investment Appraisal

13.1 INTRODUCTION

In the state organisations investment in generation and transmission was managed centrally. The future demand was predicted taking account of the projections of the generation/transmission company and that of the distribution companies that it served. The objective was to minimise the future costs of energy production and transmission whilst maintaining security and some diversity. There were also external inputs from government related to levels of self-financing and fuel mix. Sometimes the constraints reflected national security concerns such as reliance on imported energy or were the result of strong lobbies from mining sectors or unions. The planning functions of these organisations often employed large scale optimisation models based on linear programming to establish the optimal solutions embracing both generation and transmission. As the utility owned and operated all the generation it was possible to define the role of new entry plant and design it accordingly for base load, mid merit or peaking duty. It was also possible, because of scale, to fund research and development into new energy sources like nuclear, tidal, pumped storage and hydro. The level of capacity was set so as to provide a plant margin of around 22% to cover against loss of availability, worse than average weather and a higher than expected demand growth. The main shortcoming in this approach was that the competition was only realised in the tendering process for the generation build. There was also a tendency to over-engineer the provision to avoid criticism from government if interruptions occurred.

Power Markets and Economics: Energy Costs, Trading, Emissions   Barrie Murray
© 2009 John Wiley & Sons, Ltd

In the liberalised arrangements there is no overall coordination of the level of the plant margin, the plant mix, or operating modes. A portfolio generator has to make decisions without knowing what competitors are planning and this introduces added risk. It is also difficult to maintain long term development of the integrated transmission system without knowledge of where new generation will be located. Unless the generator has a degree of vertical integration with a consumer base the future utilisation will be difficult to predict. It is for these reasons that some countries, with significant development in hand, have chosen to opt for the Single Buyer market model. This enables the generation development to be coordinated whilst facilitating competition in its supply. It also enables the placement of PPAs (Power Purchase Agreements) to encourage new investment by mitigating risk.

In a fully liberalised market situation a merchant generator will have to assess and cover all the attendant risks associated with energy price, fuel price and volume. This chapter focuses on the processes involved in appraising a generation development proposal in this environment. It is assumed that the station will have to compete to establish supply contracts. The units may participate in the base load, peaking, balancing and ancillary service markets. The areas covered include:

- establishing the costs of constructing and operating the station;
- calculating the expected revenue for the provision of energy and services;
- evaluating the risks associated with the project.

This chapter draws on the knowledge developed in Chapter 3 on generation costing and Chapter 9 covering market operation.

13.2 OVERALL ANALYSIS

The classical approach to optimising development plans is based on an LP formulation. It is still relevant to a system-wide analysis of those developments that are likely to meet future load requirements at minimum cost including operating and capital costs. Various formulations have been developed in the past, including EGEAS (developed by EPRI), WASP and LPMIX developed by the CEGB. Dynamic programming has also been applied to address the uncertainty in the input data and minimise the 'regret' that could occur with different scenarios.

The problem was formulated as an LP with the objective function of minimising the capital and running costs over a period while meeting the demand

and generation constraints, i.e. minimise:

$$\sum C \times I_j.DNC_j + \sum_{j=1}^{j} \sum_{t=1}^{T} VC_j.MW_{j,t}.A_j$$

subject to

$$\sum_{j=1}^{j} MW_{j,t} = DEM_t$$

and

$$MW_j \leq DNC_j$$

to find the DNC and MW output, where C = capital cost, I is the cost of capital, DNC = declared net capacity, VC = running costs, MW = load on unit, A = mean availability and DEM = demand at time t. The demand was usually expressed in load duration form with incremental periods that could be managed by the LP. The variable costs are scaled up to match the incremental periods.

In the post privatised world the objective of the merchant generator is to establish an installation that will generate maximum return. The revenue is based on the expected return from trading the output into the market at marginal prices. This presumes some bidding strategy either into a pool or embraced within bilateral contracts. The LP formulation now takes on a different form with the objective function being to maximise the difference between the revenue based on the SMP (System Marginal Price) and the costs, i.e.

$$\sum_{j=1}^{j} \sum_{t=1}^{T} SMP_t.MW_{j,t} - \Sigma C \times I\ j.DNC_j - \sum_{j=1}^{j} \sum_{t=1}^{T} VC_j.MW_{j,t}.A_j$$

The results of this formulation favour the introduction of base load capacity where the high levels of utilisation make most contribution to fixed cost recovery. The market revenue will be based on base-load prices, whereas peaking plant will be based on analysis of peaking price forecasts. The analysis relies on a forward estimate of market prices available either from exchange trading or through markets for longer term bilateral contracts. The complication is that the development plans of other participants are not known and their new entry will affect the forward market price. This has to be embraced as part of the prediction of future market prices.

13.3 ANALYSIS OF OPTIONS

In considering market entry there is a need to review the following issues.

- Which market area/country is likely to be the most profitable?
- Which market sector offers the best opportunities (base, peak, balancing, ancillary)?
- What type of plant and fuel supplies/
- What options for location?

In considering the country/area, the current and expected market prices will be a key factor. In this respect the prevailing plant margin will be very important. The difficulty will be in double guessing which developments the competitors are likely to pursue. Existing planning consents and applications provide a guide but all these developments may not proceed. Others aspects that may be relevant include the ease of market entry and gaining access to the grid as well as the view taken of risk in the country as this will affect the cost and availability of capital. The process will usually start with a high level analysis of these factors for several countries to identify a few viable options.

The analysis of the preferred options will proceed by examining the country market in more detail to identify the level of competition in the different sectors. This will include the base load, the peaking and the ancillary service market sectors. There is a finite limit on how much plant can operate base load depending on the load duration curve. This can be seen by examining the existing plant mix and proposed developments. All too often all new plant expects to operate base load whereas this is often impractical. It may be more attractive to consider building peaking plant that can also participate in the balancing and ancillary service markets.

In considering the type of plant a key aspect will be the availability and cost of fuel supplies. It may be that local coal or lignite is available that will provide a competitive fuel supply with low transportation costs. Alternatively, a location near to a port facility may provide the option to import coal or LNG. The option to build gas fired generation is often preferred because of the low capital cost and short construction time. The nuclear option will depend very much on the local political receptiveness and the acceptability of existing installations and site availability. The option to develop renewable sources will depend on the 'feed in' tariffs that exist in the location and the availability of sites for wind farms or hydro installations. A viable option often overlooked is that of refurbishing existing older plant. This can be a low cost alternative with a site and staff already available. The other interesting option is the establishment of a combined heat and power plant if there is an opportunity to sell the heat.

Another key consideration is the availability of suitable generation sites and the time involved in gaining consent and a license. The fuel supply arrangements will be important particularly for coal fired plant. There may also be requirements for supplies of cooling water necessitating location along rivers or on the coast. The other consideration is the proximity of a suitable grid connection. There may be local bottlenecks or a weak network. This has been one of the problems associated with the connection of remotely sited wind farms adding to their development costs.

Prior to liberalisation, all these interacting factors were appraised through a central planning process using Linear Programming based formulations of the problem. In the free market situation more risk is introduced by an increasing number of unknowns and it is usual to analyse these through a series of scenarios.

13.4 PLANT COSTS

The costs associated with developments of generation were discussed in Chapter 3. Some of the key issues that need to be determined for a particular proposal are:

- the options for contracting for fuel and the price structure;
- the options for contracting for supply;
- the availability and cost of capital;
- the expected utilisation.

Fuel supply for gas may typically be on a long term interruptible LTI contract. In this case the price may benefit if the station is prepared to accept interruption of supply from time to time. Unfortunately this often occurs at times of high electricity demand and can result in system problems if a lot of gas plant is interrupted at the same time. Some gas contracts also operate on a take or pay basis and can lead to offers of very low market prices to maintain utilisation when demand is low. In the case of coal it is usual for a mix of contracts to be established based on comparisons of local and imported coal prices, where this is an option. These will usually last for a year or two and be designed to enable coal market opportunities to be exploited. Some fuel supplies may be met from the shorter term spot market, particularly for gas when the forward demand for electricity is uncertain. There may be opportunities to exercise arbitrage between the gas and electricity markets and to sell contracted gas rather than use gas to generate if gas prices are high.

It is preferable for the generator to manage risk through a long term PPA (Power Purchase Agreement) for a large proportion of its output but this option is less likely in a competitive market, unless linked to an industrial complex. In some countries in the Middle East single buyer markets have been established that do support longer term contracts for generation output and availability, including fuel pass through. In competitive markets the normal arrangement will be for supply contracts covering six months to perhaps two years ahead. For the generator it is preferable that the longer term contracts are linked to 'back to back' fuel contracts or have a fuel price linked payment. The generator will need to analyse the market to determine the extent to which operation will be focused on the base load and peaking market and medium to short term spot trading.

The cost of capital will be established in consultation with potential investors such as the banks and venture capitalists who are prepared to take an equity stake. In the case of industrial plants, the end user may take a stake with options eventually leading to ownership. A mixture of debt and equity financing is a common arrangement.

The expected utilisation is a key assumption with a new plant where all the outstanding capital charges have to be recovered. It also has an influence on the preferred operating regime. The graph of Figure 13.1 shows how profitability can vary with utilisation for a typical set of data. It shows that opting for a peaking role can be more profitable when profit margins are tight and a high level of utilisation may be difficult to achieve.

Given the data shown in Table 13.1, the base load profit and peaking profit for a year can be calculated for the defined utilisation levels.

The base load revenue is given by:

$$375 \, \text{MW} * 23.5 * 8760 * 0.55 = £42.45\text{m}.$$

The base load variable costs are given by:

$$375 \, \text{MW} * 17.08 * 8760 * 0.55 = £30.85\text{m}.$$

The base load profit (loss) is given by:

$$43.5 - 30.85 - 14.83 = (-£2.18\text{m}).$$

Table 13.1 Basic data

	Units	Gas
capacity	MW	375
total fixed cost/yr	£m	14.83
total variable costs	£/MWh	17.08
base load price	£/MWh	23.50
Peaking Price	£/MWh	32.00
base load utilisation	%	55
peaking utilisation	%	35

Variation in profitability with base load utilisation

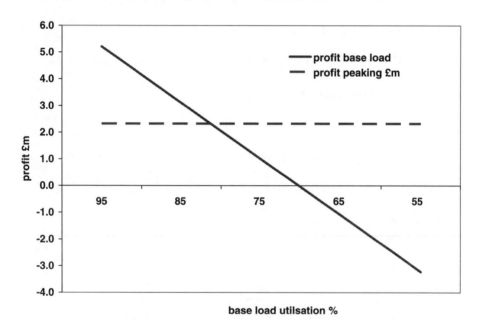

Figure 13.1 Base-load versus peak profit

The peaking revenue is given by:

$$375\,\text{MW} * 32.0 * 8760 * 0.35 = £36.79\text{m}.$$

The peaking variable costs are given by:

$$375\,\text{MW} * 17.08 * 8760 * 0.35 = £19.63\text{m}.$$

The peaking profit (loss) is given by:

$$36.79 - 19.63 - 14.83 = £2.33m.$$

It can be seen that in this case the profit from operating in peaking mode is higher.

Given the data on generation costs and average market prices in the Table 13.2 it is possible to establish:

1. that level of base load utilisation when the base load profit is equal to the peaking profit for gas of £2.3m/yr;
2. that level of base load utilisation for coal plant resulting in zero profit.

Gas base load cost is given by:

$$= 375 * 8760 * \text{util} * 17.08/1\,000\,000 + 14.83\,£m = 56.1 * \text{util} + 14.83.$$

Gas base load revenue is given by:

$$= 375 * 8760 * \text{util} * 23.5/1\,000\,000 = 77.2 * \text{util}.$$

Gas base load profit is given by

$$(77.2 - 56.1) * \text{util} - 14.83 = 2.3.$$

Table 13.2 Generation data

	Units	**Gas**	**Coal**
capacity	MW	375	375
total fixed cost/yr	£m	14.83	30.49
total variable costs	£/MWh	17.08	12.56
base load price	£/MWh	23.50	23.50
Peaking Price	£/MWh	32.00	32.00
base load utilisation	%	55	88
peaking utilisation	%	35	35
cost base load	£m/yr	45.7	66.8
cost peaking	£m/yr	34.5	44.9
revenue base load	£m/yr	42.5	67.9
revenue peaking	£m/yr	36.8	36.8
profit base load	£m/yr	-3.2	1.1
profit peaking	£m/yr	2.3	-8.1

Utilisation for base load profit to equal peaking profit is given by:

$$\text{Gas util} = (2.3 + 14.83)/21.1 = 81\%.$$

Coal base load cost is given by:

$$= 375 * 8760 * \text{util} * 12.56/1\,000\,000 + 30.49\,\text{£m} = 41.2 * \text{Util} + 30.49.$$

Coal base load revenue is given by:

$$= 375 * 8760 * \text{util} * 23.5/1\,000\,000 = 77.2 * \text{util}.$$

Coal base load profit is given by

$$= (77.2 - 41.2) * \text{util} - 30.49$$

and equals zero when

$$\text{Coal util} = (30.49)/36 = 84.7\%.$$

This type of analysis has to be undertaken for each future period taking account of future fuel prices, base and peak market prices and expected levels of utilisation. Also the cost of capital and labour will vary from country to country.

13.5 PREDICTING REVENUE

The key requirement in predicting revenue is to establish realistic estimates of future base and peak load prices in the markets that are available for trading. There may also be a need to discount these figures by a few percent, as may be necessary to capture supply contracts. With coupled markets this may extend over interconnections and require assessment of the cost of reserving transmission capacity. There will also be a need to predict future utilisation and the contract fuel prices for a period of 15 to 25 years ahead. Key assumptions in predicting the future market prices will be the existing and predicted plant margin, as these will have a big impact on prices, and the scope for new entry. The other associated issue is the likely new build that competitors will progress. There is a tendency for all market participants to react to high prices in unison. This leads to overcapacity and a medium term price fall. The

Table 13.3 Basic generation data

	Units	Gas
capacity	MW	375
total fixed cost/yr	£m	14.83
efficiency	per unit	0.52
other variable costs	£/MWh	0.73

net result can be cycling in investment with periods of over capacity followed by shortfalls. The periodicity is influenced by the construction time of new generation.

A typical analysis is described for a gas fired generator operating in the base load market. Given the data in Table 13.3 for the generator the calculations involved are illustrated in Table 13.4. The predicted market base load price is shown in column 2 of Table 13.4 with the expected fuel price in column 3.

Table 13.4 Profit assessment

Year	Base load price £/MWh	Gas price £/GJ	Variable cost £/MWh	Income £m	Total costs £m	Net profit £m	Cumulative profit
2007	28.1	2.4	17.1	69.2	56.9	12.3	12.3
2008	29.7	2.5	17.8	73.1	58.6	14.5	26.8
2009	31.2	2.6	18.5	76.9	60.3	16.6	43.4
2010	34.1	2.7	19.1	84.0	62.0	22.0	65.4
2011	28.6	2.8	19.8	70.4	63.7	6.7	72.1
2012	24.8	2.9	20.5	61.0	65.4	-4.4	67.7
2013	25.6	3.0	21.2	63.1	67.1	-4.1	63.6
2014	25.7	3.1	21.9	63.4	68.8	-5.4	58.2
2015	27.0	3.2	22.6	66.5	70.5	-4.0	54.2
2016	33.4	3.3	23.3	82.4	72.2	10.2	64.3
2017	32.9	3.4	24.0	81.0	73.9	7.1	71.4
2018	34.0	3.5	24.7	83.7	75.6	8.0	79.4
2019	38.3	3.6	25.4	94.5	77.4	17.1	96.6
2020	36.0	3.7	26.1	88.7	79.1	9.6	106.2
2021	34.0	3.8	26.8	83.8	80.8	3.0	109.2
				1141.6	1032.4	109.2	

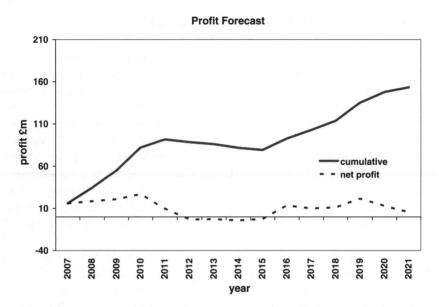

Figure 13.2   Generator profit forecast

The variable cost is calculated as:

Fuel price/efficiency + other variable costs.

The income is calculated as:

Capacity * utilisation * base load price.

The total costs are calculated as:

Energy * variable cost + fixed costs.

Hence the net profit function can be derived as shown graphically in Figure 13.2.

This shows the year on year profit and the associated cumulative profit. It can be seen that with the predicted data used in this example there are periods when the profit may fall down to, or below, zero.

13.6 BIDDING/CONTRACTING STRATEGY

In a pool situation where the price is set by the marginal generator then it can be shown that in the long run the profit is maximised by bidding into the pool at the incremental variable cost. This ensures that the generator achieves maximum utilisation and hence the highest contribution to fixed costs. The only occasion when this would not apply is where a generator expects to be operating at the margin and hence setting the marginal price. A portfolio generator may well manage all the marginal plant at points on the load curve and will be able to exercise market power. In these circumstances the consumer side has the opportunity to exercise demand management to contain the price paid. This process is most effectively achieved in the Nordpool model where the demand side bid in the prices they are prepared to pay with the strike price set where they intersect.

In a bilateral contract situation the payments will be related to the agreed strike price. This can be expected to reflect the forecast market price. Whereas in the previous section it was assumed that the generator would get the market price in practice, to secure a bilateral contract it may be necessary to offer a discount. The other option is to bid into the exchange market and take the market price and risk exposure. It is often the case that a generator will contract for part of its capacity through a bilateral deal with the remainder sold through exchange trading.

The forecast price may be based on independent modelling of the market or the market forward curve based on reported trades, or a combination from several different sources. The risk may be mitigated by including fuel price indexing in the contract and linking the energy price to published market prices. The consumer has the option to decide when to contract. If prices are expected to fall, contracting may be delayed or if prices are likely to rise there may be an advantage in contracting forward for a longer period.

In the case of gas fired generation there is also the option to exercise arbitrage through the spot gas market. The generator will have contracted for gas supplies but may decide that it is better to sell the gas back to the market than use it for generation when gas prices are high. This has the potential to create problems when the incidence of high gas demand and prices coincides with a high electricity demand during cold winter periods. The withdrawal of a lot of gas generation can then create shortfalls in electricity capacity.

The generator may also have the flexibility to participate in the shorter term balancing and ancillary service markets where there is likely to be a premium to normal energy prices to cover the flexibility costs.

There are other arrangements for contracting for new capacity in advance of the creation of a fully open market. For example, in Turkey the government passed laws to enable new entry on the basis of BOT (build operate and transfer) in 1994 and BOO (build own and operate) in 1997 with special purchase agreements that have since proved expensive. Some 2.5 GW has been added under BOT arrangements and 6 GW under BOO, together supplying some 33% of generation. Turkey is under intense pressure from the International Financial Institutions or IFIs (mainly the World Bank and the International Monetary Fund (IMF)) and from the European Commission to privatise and liberalise its electricity industry. Complying with European Union (EU) law on electricity industries will be a condition for Turkey's entry to the EU. The 1990 British pool model seems the preferred initial option for privatisation.

13.7 EVALUATING RISK

The evaluation of risk usually takes the form of proposing a set of scenarios that are considered credible. This will usually include predicted fuel price variation of $+/-15\%$ and utilisation $+/-15\%$ from the base assumptions. There will also be a need to evaluate variation in predicted market prices. A key objective will be to assess the probability that the outcome would result in

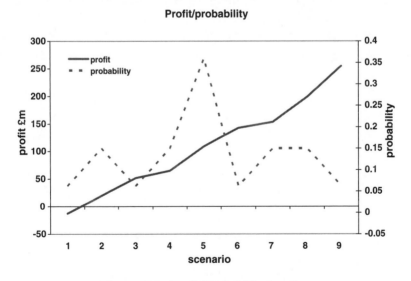

Figure 13.3 Profit/Probability function

a loss. If probabilities are assigned to the various likely outcomes then a set of scenario outcomes can be calculated, each with an associated probability. The graph of Figure 13.3 shows how three possible utilisation levels and three possible fuel price escalation values give rise to nine possible cumulative profit outcomes, each with a finite probability. In this example it can be seen that there is a small chance of a loss situation occurring but that the mean expectation is for a cumulative profit of around £100m.

13.8 SUMMARY

In this chapter a process has been outlined for the evaluation of a potential investment in generation. It identifies the key parameter assumptions that influence costs, including fuel price and utilisation. It also examines those factors that will affect the future market price and revenues, including the current and future plant margin and potential new entry. The prediction of the key variables through a project life enable the year on year costs, revenues and hence net profit to be determined. The bidding strategy and the contracting techniques have been discussed. Finally, an approach to assessing risk through the use of scenarios is outlined. This includes identifying the key variables and assigning probabilities to a set of possible outturns. This enables the probabilities and cumulative profits to be estimated for a range of scenarios through the period and the mean expected outturn and value at risk.

Four

Market Development

This part discusses the performance of markets in operation, the techniques used to monitor performance and improvement measures. It describes some of the technological developments that are likely and how these might impact on market operation and development. It discusses the new issues that need to be addressed and how they might be managed.

Chapter 14 Market Performance

This discusses some of the shortcomings that have been apparent in market performance. It reviews the management of system security, risks, the regulatory process and emerging environmental issues. An approach to monitoring performance is outlined and measures to improve performance are described.

Chapter 15 Market Development

This discusses the expected development of global utilities dominating the market. It reviews likely technological developments in generation that will improve efficiency and impact on the future plant mix. It analyses changes in the role of transmission and the emergence of more actively managed distribution networks to accommodate distributed generation.

Chapter 16 Long-term Scenarios

This chapter discusses some of the plausible scenarios that will shape the future of the industry through the next 40 years. It considers how the industry and its markets will need to adapt to meet the new environmental challenges while maintaining security and costs.

14

Market Performance

14.1 INTRODUCTION

Both governments and regulatory agents are anxious to monitor the performance of their energy markets to ensure that real benefits are being realised. Where performance is in question they may call for a review. The initiative may arise from complaints from end users or as a reaction to general price escalation. The advent of multi-national companies puts industrialists in a position to compare prices with other countries and may even influence their decisions on the placement of new factories.

In response, to promote wider European competition the European Regulators' Group for electricity and gas (ERGEG) was established on 11 November 2003, pursuant to Directive 2003/796/EC. Its Members are the heads of the national energy regulatory authorities in the 27 EU Member States and they assist the Commission in consolidating the Internal Market for electricity and gas. In 2006 they set up the Regional Initiatives framework creating seven electricity and three gas regions in Europe. Each region identifies the more serious market distortions to trading energy within the region and, through the cooperation of the key stakeholders, together finds a solution. But the development of these regional markets is not an end in itself. The real target is the creation of a single European market in electricity and gas.

Some of the concerns arise because of the differences in prices seen across Europe and limitations on cross-border trading. They have called for improved management of congestion and capacity auctions in the short term and in the longer term more investment in interconnection transmission to

Power Markets and Economics: Energy Costs, Trading, Emissions   Barrie Murray
© 2009 John Wiley & Sons, Ltd

realise the pan-European market. They have called for better TSO coordination and transparency and seek to promote an EU framework to coordinate new investment.

Where large differences are apparent in end user prices, analysis will generally need to embrace both the generation costs and those of the transmission and distribution companies. The approach aims to establish the full cost chain for comparison with contract prices and tariffs. The will seek to identify any abuse of market power and anti-competitive behaviour leading to excessive prices. The outcome would be improvements to market rules and procedures.

The objectives of this chapter are to discuss and analyse some of the shortcomings that occur in market operation in practice and to outline some of the measures adopted to address them. It will highlight the problems encountered in establishing a coordinated development strategy for the system and optimum levels of investment including how to:

- identify the shortcomings in operation of a market;
- analyse and quantify performance;
- review measures available to improve performance.

The regulators usually take responsibility for sponsoring and promoting measures to analyse and improve performance.

14.2 PERFORMANCE CRITERIA

It is necessary to define what would be regarded as a good measure of market performance. Some of the relevant issues are listed below.

- Is effective competition established driving down prices without dominance?
- Are mechanisms available for the consumer side to influence the market?
- Does the market mechanism provide consistent price signals?
- Is the reliability of the system being sustained in line with customer needs?
- Will the market deliver the optimum level of investment in new plant?
- Will operational efficiency be sustained in a market environment?

The principal requirement to realise competition is the establishment of market liquidity. This means having a sufficient number of competing participants who are active in the market. This requires that simple products are traded without technical complexity and there are opportunities for price discovery through the publication of marginal traded prices. It also requires that the market is readily accessible, which in turn requires open access to the power system and its customer base. It also requires that the market is not dominated by one or a few players.

The ability of consumers to participate in the market is important to reduce the chance of generators colluding to sustain high prices. A mechanism should be available for consumers to participate in the market and reject supplies at uneconomic prices.

The market mechanisms need to provide prices that can be understood by the participants and can be predicted within reason. The prices should not be unduly volatile or readily open to manipulation by participants.

It is less obvious in an unbundled situation where the responsibility to secure supplies lies. The TSO will maintain the integrity of the grid in operation but will not be able to influence directly the availability of sufficient generation sources. This has to rest largely with the suppliers contracted to meet the requirements of their customer base.

In theory the operation of the market should signal the need for any new investment. If capacity margins are falling then prices can be expected to rise and encourage new investment. The timing and coordination of investment is a different issue because of the long delay between current day to day prices and new investment becoming operational. There is a risk that too much generation will be built, causing a price collapse resulting in a long period of under-investment. This process can lead to investment cycling and associated price cycling.

The efficiency of operation in state utilities was realised by a detailed operational planning phase that ensured that generation was available in the event to meet demand at least cost. On the day, scheduling algorithms were used to select the use of generation optimally so as to minimise fuel costs. Where generation is in private ownership there is no control on when it is made available or when it is used to meet demand. This will be based on contract terms and the reaction to market conditions and may be less than optimal overall.

14.3 MARKET SHORTCOMINGS

Generation Competition

Whilst it is generally accepted that competition promotes efficiency improvement, it is sometimes difficult to establish the conditions for it to be effective in practice. In the case of generation competition, it is important to establish a sufficient number of competing organisations whilst retaining their business viability. In Australia this was realised by restricting the ownership of stations so that no single player could own a large proportion of the generation. The proposed unbundling of Eskom in South Africa considered five generation groups, each with a viable proportion of the plant. ENEL;. The Italian state utility has been broken up into four generation groups. The original UK restructuring of the CEGB resulted in just three principal generators and competition was initially not effective. Eventually the regulator intervened and required NP and PG to sell off some of their plant to Eastern Generation.

As well as having a sufficient number of competing players it is also necessary to ensure that there is competition for operation at the margin throughout the demand range. This requires that several generation groups own generation that can be expected to be marginal and have to compete to be used in operation. A dispatch simulation can be used to identify the marginal plant at each dispatch interval and the ownership. This will provide an indication of the degree of competition at the margin but it is also necessary to check the impact of any relative fuel price changes that could affect the use of marginal plant in future years.

The other factors that can affect market liquidity are transmission constraints. If these become active then it may necessitate splitting the market, as in Nordpool, with a reduction in the number of competing participants. Where this is likely to nullify competition it may be necessary to consider an alternative market approach, such as the original UK separate constrained study with the cost of constraints covered by an uplift charge.

Demand Side Participation

The demand side does not have the same degree of flexibility to change demand in relation to price signals and initial attempts to involve them in competition were not very successful. As markets have matured some larger industrial consumers have invested in demand management schemes and have been able to adjust demand and participate. The Nordpool market appears to have been successful in this respect and establishes market clearing prices by comparing the curve representing prices users are prepared to pay against the curve of prices at which generation are prepared to supply. The market price is set at the intersection of the two curves.

Market Prices

In some markets the mechanisms used to set prices have been unsatisfactory in that they have been counter intuitive and prone to volatility. This has in part occurred where complex scheduling algorithms have been applied that take account of a wide set of plant dynamic characteristics and have to resolve integer decisions. New market participants have also complained that the systems used are not understood by them and are not repeatable. There is a preference for bilateral deals or trading through exchanges or brokers where prices can be agreed. However, the bilateral arrangements may not give the opportunity to discover prices or maintain liquidity. The single buyer model has some advantages in being an open process employing auctions or competitive tendering processes for provision of capacity and energy.

System Security

Originally there were concerns that unbundling and restructuring would put system security at risk. In the main the industry has adapted to the changes imposed and major problems have not materialised. Issues that have arisen have been the result of:

- generation not being made available;
- unplanned and uncoordinated outages of generation;
- shifting patterns of generation inconsistent with the original transmission design;
- coincident outages of gas generation on interruptible supply contracts;
- variable wind power output affecting tie line flows;
- disputes over contract interpretation.

These issues have generally been dealt with by the TSO function and improvements to the flexibility of the transmission system exploiting FACTS devices. These are Flexible AC Transmission Systems that have the dynamic capability to exercise control over the flow of MWs and MVArs. There is also a wider national consideration over fuel supply security that may lead to a government embargo on granting further permissions for development of a single technology, as happened in the UK for a period when only gas fired generation was being developed.

Investment

In the liberalised market each participant will make decisions unilaterally on what and when to build new generation. The result in the UK was the 'dash for gas' when both new and existing generators chose to build CCGT plant. The result was that a lot of exiting coal fired generation was closed, sometimes prematurely, resulting in a significant shift in the plant mix. The concentration of new development on gas generation resulted in the UK government imposing an embargo on further development of gas fired generation. There are usually no market signals that would encourage a mixture of plant with diversity in fuel source and price. A lot of new entrants expect to operate base load, whereas in reality there may be an excess of base-load plant but a shortfall in peaking capacity.

The state utilities planned new generation developments centrally to maintain what was considered to be an acceptable plant margin of around 22% (i.e. generation available capacity less peak demand/peak demand = 22%). A consequence of liberalisation has been a reduction in the plant margin from these levels to around 15%. This can result in more frequent periods of tight margins during times of plant outages and price spikes occur. This is in the interests of generators in that it helps to maintain prices particularly for portfolio generators who would not benefit from new IPP additions. Attempts to address this were based on a LOLP (Loss of Load Probability) increment to marginal prices. When margins were tight, prices would rise to encourage availability but this did not necessarily provide a good long term signal for investment and could equally signal uncoordinated short term outage planning. The mechanism was also flawed in that portfolio generators stood to gain more from LOLP payments on all their generation stock rather than availability payments for making one extra generator available.

Investment in transmission becomes more complicated because the future location of generation around the system is not certain and becomes subject to commercial decisions. Establishing agreement on any new developments can be difficult when as a consequence there may be some generators that will lose out as a result of enabling the introduction of new competition.

Operational Efficiency

The state utilities controlled all generation and would operate the system to minimise fuel costs using highly developed optimisation algorithms. In the liberalised market each participant is free to choose when they run their own generation. Whilst they may optimise the utilisation of their own stations there is no mechanism to ensure a global optimum. Generation and transmission outage planning also becomes more difficult because the generators are not obliged to adhere to their original plan and may take or cancel outages at short notice.

14.4 PERFORMANCE ASSESSMENT

Prices

The assessment of the impact on prices resulting from competition has to take account of changes in other variables such as the price and availability of fuel.

The marginal variable costs can be established from knowledge of the marginal plant, typical efficiencies and prevailing fuel prices. The CEGB was directed by the government to burn 70 m tons of coal whereas, following liberalisation, a significant proportion of coal plant utilisation was displaced by new gas fired generation. This will have resulted in a significant change in total fuel costs and resulting marginal costs that is readily explained.

For example, the change in total fuel costs due to displacing 40% of coal generation with gas fired generation can be calculated assuming an initial coal burn of 70 mt/yr with a CV of 25 GJ/t at a price of £30/t. with gas at £1.5/GJ and coal plant with a 38% efficiency with gas at 52%.

> Initial cost of coal $= 30 * 70\,m = £2100$
> Revised cost of coal $= 2100 * 0.6 = £1260$
> Displaced coal $= 0.4 * 70\,m = 28\,m\,t$
> Displaced coal in TWh $= 28 * 25/3.6 * 0.38 = 73.8$ TWh
> Required gas burn $= 73.8$ TWh
> $= 73.8 * 1000 * 3600/0.52\,GJ = 510.9\,m\,GJ$
> Cost of gas $= 510.9 * 1.5\,£m = £766.3\,m$
> New total cost $= 766.3 + 1260 = £2026\,m$

This represents a saving of £2100 m − £2026 m = £74 m or 3.5%.

The average marginal variable cost can also be calculated if gas is marginal for 40% of the time.

> Coal marginal cost $= £1.2/GJ$ or $£1.2 * 3.6/0.38/MWh = £11.36/MWh$
> Gas marginal cost $= £1.5/GJ$ or $£1.5 * 3.6/0.52/MWh = £10.38/MWh$
> Average marginal cost $= 0.4 * 10.38 + 0.6 * 11.36 = £10.97/MWh$

System Security

This can be assessed by monitoring the plant margin or calculating the LOLP for each period. From statistical theory the probability or 'r' generators being unavailable (Pr) from a population of 'n' generators is given by:

$$Pr = n!/r!(n-r)!.\,Po^{\wedge}(n-r).\,(1-Po)^{\wedge}r,$$

where Po is the average unit availability. This function is compared with a demand probability function to calculate the number of hours (H) and probability of demand (D) exceeding generation (G), i.e.

$$LOLP = sum(Pr * H(D > G)).$$

The sum of all values gives the overall LOLP for the period. The payment is then the product of this value times the VLL (Value of Lost Load) less the SMP for all the energy supplied through the period.

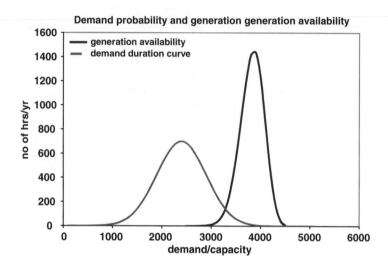

Figure 14.1   LOLP illustration

The graph of Figure 14.1 illustrates the relationship between the demand profile and generation availability. It can be seen that there are periods of overlap when low generation availability is less than some of the higher demand levels. The payments when LOLP rises are usually related to the Value of Lost Load (VLL) that was set at around £2/MWh in the UK pool:

$$\text{LOLP increment} = \text{LOLP} * (\text{VLL} - \text{SMP}).$$

The optimum relationship giving the least cost to society would occur when the LOLP payment for the year plus the added annual cost of new capacity is at a minimum.

Plant Margin
The assessment of plant margin is based on the maximum demand and declared generation capacity. It is important to determine where the demand is measured. If it refers to end consumer demand then the distribution and transmission losses would need to be added in calculating the demand on super-grid connected generation. If the demand data are those measured at the bulk supply points then the transmission losses must be added. The generation data may refer to total generation or that net of generation auxiliary demand. Where generation is embedded within the distribution network then it may be explicitly accounted for or netted off the consumer demand to establish the net super-grid demand. Some generation such as hydro is energy restricted and its availability at peak may be a lot less (typically 30%) than the installed capacity,

unless a large amount of storage is associated with the hydro. Wind power also has a limited contribution to the provision of firm capacity as the wind may not be blowing at the time of peaks and it may only be credited with 10% of its installed capacity. The system may also rely on imports from external sources but these should only contribute to capacity where underwritten by firm supply contracts.

For example, assuming that a country has an end user peak demand of 45 GW with gross generation capacity made up of 20 GW coal, 25 GW gas, 10 GW nuclear, 5 GW hydro and 7 GW wind with 1 GW of contracted import the firm generation capacity, the plant margin can be calculated. The total capacity of 68 GW with a demand of 45 GW is equivalent to a margin of over 50%.

However, if it is assumed that auxiliary supplies for gas, coal and nuclear are 6% and total system losses are 9%, hydro is assumed to have storage and be able to supply 30% of capacity at times of peak demand. Wind power is only credited with only 10% of installed capacity then:

Net generation capacity $= 0.94 * (20 + 25 + 10) + 5 * 0.3 + 7 * 0.1 + 1 = 54.9$ GW.
Total demand including losses $= 45/0.91 = 49.45\,GW$.
Plant margin% $= 100(54.9\text{--}49.45)/49.45 = 11\%$.

Operational Efficiency
The graph of Figure 14.2 shows the utilisation of some 50 generators as a result of an actual dispatch for one day in a single buyer market situation in the Middle East. Although the units are listed in merit order of ascending prices it

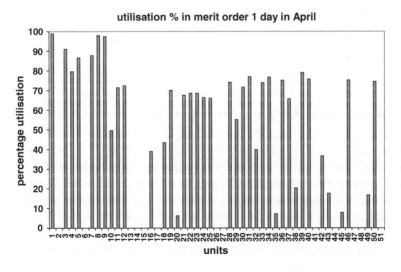

Figure 14.2   Inefficient merit order operation

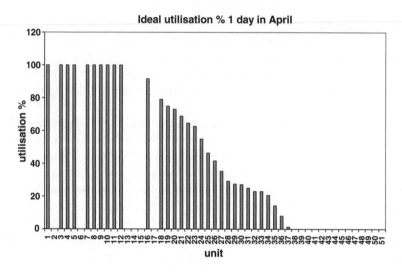

Figure 14.3   Efficient merit order operation

can be seen that their utilisation appears random. In contrast, a second graph, shown in Figure 14.3, shows the results of an idealised dispatch for the same day where the utilisation is seen to fall as the prices rise.

Some of the differences will be due to the need to retain generation in service out of merit to manage a transmission security constraint. Other reasons are a lack of flexibility in the generation to enable two shifting or a requirement to maintain heat or desalinated water supplies. There are also sometimes difficulties in the interpretation of contract clauses related to operating mode efficiencies. The gaps in the utilisation are where plant is either unavailable or not used for some reason. The various reasons need to be investigated to confirm that the plant is being operated efficiently.

14.5 PERFORMANCE IMPROVEMENT

Prices may not be considered competitive either because of structural or operational reasons. It may be that there is inadequate liquidity as a result of an insufficient number of players competing at the margin. Alternatively it may be that the market structure is too complex or that constraints are fragmenting the market. Some measures that may improve performance include:

- invoke anti competitive legislation requiring the sale of generation to add new players;

- opt for a single buyer market model with competition realised through tenders and auctions;
- simplify the market arrangements and products to enable wider participation and increased liquidity;
- adopt measures to enable demand side participation.

Some of the criticisms of the original UK pool were that it lacked liquidity with too much market power in the hands of two major players such that it was sometimes described as a duopoly. There was also ineffective demand side participation to provide a constraint on price rises. The process was also considered to be complex and lacking transparency. This meant that participants could not independently make judgements about outturn to support their bidding analysis. The algorithms employed were designed for operational rather than market use and included a large amount of detail to model generation dynamics. The generators for their part resented their plant being dispatch centrally and believed that they knew best how to manage their generation to reduce costs. An open forum was established to debate and agree new arrangements under the auspices of the Regulators office, eventually leading to NETA (New Electricity Trading Arrangements).

It was decided that the mandatory pool should be abandoned in favour of a much freer trading arrangement with less central control. When the pool was in place bilateral contracting was effected through the use of Contracts for Differences. Part of the new arrangements formalised this arrangement by enabling bilateral contracting directly between generators and suppliers. This enabled more demand side participation and gave the generators the right to dispatch their own generation to meet their contracted demand. The only mandatory requirement was to advise the System Operator of the contracted position prior to the time before the event referred to as 'gate closure'. The original arrangement set this at some 5 hours ahead but this was progressively reduced to 1 hour ahead as experience developed. The notifications were referred to as initial (IPNs) and final physical notifications (FPNs) in that the participants were required to indicate the physical location of injections and associated demand take-offs to enable load flow studies to check system security.

The overall philosophy was to place risk were it could be best managed. So it meant generators had to manage their own plant dynamic constraints and ensure that capacity was available to meet their commitments. Equally the demand side managed their volume risk in contracting for sufficient capacity to meet their future needs.

The new arrangements also enabled the establishment of exchanges to support price discovery and shorter term trading to enable participants to adjust their positions. Any organisation was able to establish an exchange and initially attracted interest from existing exchanges such as the International Petroleum Exchange.

A key element of the new arrangements was the establishment of a balancing market. This was essential to enable the System Operator to balance supply and demand in the event and maintain stable system frequency. The Balancing Market was operated by the System Operator who accepted bids and offers to increase or decrease output or demand from their contracted position.

Where the **plant margin** is falling to unacceptably low levels options include:

- the introduction of payments for the provision of availability – this will encourage generators to minimise the downtime of units and create incentives to retain older plant in service;
- the introduction of LOLP type increments to marginal prices;
- enabling the TSO to contract directly to secure capacity;
- ensuring open access to the system for new entrants.

In the single buyer model tenders may be invited for new capacity with a specification of the likely role. This could be contracted for the provision of capacity and energy with built in incentives to maintain efficiency and availability. In Middle East countries such as Oman and Abu Dhabi, where fuel is available some contracts are based on fuel being supplied with generator payments based on agreed heat models defining how the plant should perform under different operating conditions and loads. The operator of the plant then benefits if better efficiency is realised in practice through improved operation. Payments for availability based on the proportion of time the plant is available provide an incentive to maintain capacity.

If a system has an installed capacity of 4500 MW with a maximum demand of 4000 MW and a total annual energy demand of 21 000 GWh, then the cost of improving the plant margin to 15% can be calculated as follows.

- The initial plant margin is $100 * (4500 - 4000)/4000 = 12.5\%$.
- To raise it to 15% would require a generation capacity of

$$100 * (4500 + x - 4000)/4000 = 15,$$

i.e.

$$x = 15 * 4000/100 + 4000 - 4500 = 100 \, \text{MW}.$$

Assuming that the annual capital cost of 100 MW of new generation is £3.7 m this would cost £3.7 m/yr in extra capital charges
This can be translated into a new generation hourly availability payment that would equate to the added capital cost of new generation to raise the plant margin by 2.5%.

- Assuming full availability, the payment per hour $= £37\,k/8760 = £4.2/$ MWh.
- If all existing generators are paid the premium, the total system cost would be $37 * 4500 = £166\,m/yr$

Availability payments are only applicable as part of a contracted arrangement and should be related to the effective benefit to consumers of avoided loss of supply.

A problem with any general form of capacity payment is that it does not directly encourage new entry because all existing participants benefit rather than just the new entrant. As a result, in fully developed markets capacity payments are not generally included. The effect is to cause a general reduction in the plant margin with older pant being closed if it fails to secure sufficient utilisation to recover costs with a margin. It is also not in the interests of existing generators to encourage new entry to drive down prices.

In **operation** inefficiencies may arise because outage planning is suboptimal or units are not being dispatched according to cost or price. This would apply in pool type models or single buyer models were the generation dispatch is based on contract terms. It may be that staffing is inadequate to support optimal commercial operation or the control room facilities are not suitable. The arrangements and procedures need to be reviewed and recommendations for improvements proposed.

Generators will have a requirement to take plant out of service for maintenance. The practice of utilities was to establish a coordinated national outage plan that included both generation and transmission outages. The plan was established by seeking to avoid depleting the generation available so that expensive low efficiency units have to be used. Tables would be established of generation replacement costs through the year to minimise the overall cost of replacing generation that is out of service for maintenance.

In the new arrangements, although processes are in place to coordinate outage planning, generators are free to change outages and disrupt the plan for wider commercial reasons. An example is shown in Figure 14.4, which shows very high prices occurring in August in the Netherlands. This was caused by all generators believing it appropriate to take plant out of service

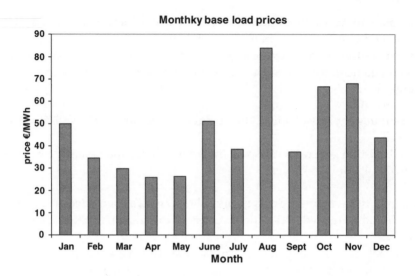

Figure 14.4 Suboptimal outage planning

during a national holiday period and resulted in a shortage of capacity and price spikes driving up the monthly base load price beyond what would normally be expected at that time of year.

Where **security** is an issue, then a key aspect will be to ensure that transmission planning standards are documented and adhered to in practice. This will include an assessment of forward plant margins and LOLP. It will also be important to ensure that operational security standards are documented and have been adapted to match the market conditions. It will also be necessary to ensure that facilities are available to enable control room staff to monitor security in real time.

Improved **congestion** management may help improve the utilisation of transmission interconnection assets. Two approaches have been employed to auctioning capacity on restricted routes called 'implicit' and 'explicit' (market splitting/market coupling auctioning). In contrast to implicit auctions, under explicit auctions the network capacity is auctioned (normally in annual, monthly or daily portions) to the market separate to and independent from the trading of electricity. Traders buy the capacity between areas and decide the daily use. Explicit auctions are a relatively simple congestion management method, widely used in Europe. It effects market coupling with cross-border transmission capacity allocated according to supply and demand on the different power exchanges. It is a way of using existing cross-border capacity efficiently. Market splitting (pioneered by Nordpool) is slightly different from market coupling in that one power exchange is involved, whereas market coupling links several power exchanges. In the Nordpool arrangement, market splitting is only introduced when the initial market solution shows transmission insecurity between areas of the system. This means that the impact of trading can be managed based on conditions on the day. This enables a better utilisation of the resources than could be predicted in advance to support year-ahead auctions. In this approach the market is assumed to operate as one and is only split if found to be essential on the day.

14.6 SUMMARY

This section has defined those aspects of performance that would lead to successful market implementation including:

- liquidity and competition;
- consistent pricing;
- demand side participation;
- system security;
- appropriate levels of investment.

The common shortcomings are discussed and how these may be analysed and quantified. Finally, some of the measures that have been adopted to improve performance are discussed. The regulators will usually take a lead in driving forward market improvements that are perceived to be in the best interests of consumers.

15

Market Developments

15.1 INTRODUCTION

There remains concern that the liberalised approach to the management of utilities is in practice not delivering the optimum solution. The theory advanced by the economists was that the market would solve all. There are a number of areas where it has not as outlined below.

- Real competition has been difficult to realise in practice.
- Market liquidity levels have been low.
- Investment has not delivered a plant mix consistent with fuel supply security.
- The mergers and acquisitions have reduced the number of competing players.
- The incentives put in place to encourage renewable energy have not delivered.
- The initiatives to reduce carbon emissions have failed to meet targets.

Competition cannot be mandated; at best an environment can be created where it could occur. The incumbent market participants will focus on maximising their profit and this is best realised by discouraging new entry and keeping the plant margin low, driving prices up. Where vertical integration has been allowed it enables players to manipulate the wholesale price by adjusting the internal transfer price from the generation to the retail division.

Power Markets and Economics: Energy Costs, Trading, Emissions   Barrie Murray
© 2009 John Wiley & Sons, Ltd

Constraints on cross-border flows have restricted international trade and the development of a pan-European market.

Market liquidity has been slow to develop with most energy traded through bilateral arrangements with little opportunity for price discovery. The volume traded through exchanges has been limited primarily to players adjusting their position prior to market gate closure. Some countries have chosen to retain national champions, such as EdF, RWE, EON and ENEL. These companies have expanded across Europe through acquisitions, leading to fewer competing players.

Investment has not been coordinated and tends to cycle with a lot of new entry as prices rise, but as the new plant comes into service prices are driven down and investment falls away. It is also difficult to influence the plant mix to achieve fuel diversity or encourage the development of renewable sources. The ETS scheme to manage carbon emissions failed to work during its initial phase because of over-allocation.

This chapter discusses some of the current and expected developments in international power markets. It focuses on issues that affect the markets, the generation base and the transmission/distribution systems. It develops the following:

- an insight into planned developments in market structures;
- an understanding of the likely changes in the generation base;
- an appreciation of the impact on the transmission and distribution systems;
- an appraisal of the likely impact on market operations.

The views expressed relate to those issues that are likely to have an impact over the next 20 to 25 years.

15.2 GENERATION DEVELOPMENTS

New Generation Requirements
The power equipment manufacturers need an estimate of the future requirement for their generation products. This requires an estimate of the future total volume of generation, taking account of demand development and the closure of older time expired plant. It is also necessary to predict what the plant mix will be in future years. In forecasting the type of new build the following steps are necessary:

- establish relative costs of production per unit;
- take account of incentives;

- determine revenue and when return exceeds costs through period;
- add new entry year on year if it looks profitable;
- scale new build in accordance with construction capacity available by country;
- determine prospective plant margin each year;
- adjust overall level of new entry in proportion to developing plant margin;
- estimate renewable energy output against targets.

The range of data required to establish costs is shown in Table 15.1. This will vary from year to year as fuel costs and generation utilization will vary, so a separate costing sheet is needed for each year.

The key assumptions that need to be realistic are: the assumed plant utilization; the realizable operating efficiency on a net basis; the impact of risk on capital charges and the provisions for the grid connection and on-going operation and maintenance. Table 15.2 shows a typical result for a 10-year period for a mix of technologies. The policy on emissions also needs to be embraced and costs added into the assessment, based on forecast prices. The table compares a year on year unit cost of production against the expected future market price for the energy. The results are summated to test if the generation is likely to provide a positive return through the period. The analysis needs to take account of technology developments that are likely as well as other related issues as discussed in the following sections.

Distributed Generation based on CHP schemes, Waste to Energy and Renewable sources are likely to increase their share of the power market. Government targets for renewable generation remain ambitious at 20% by 2010 but are unlikely to be realised. Pressure on the reduction of carbon emissions will promote high efficiency CHP developments and Waste to Energy schemes will be a necessity given the shortage of land fill sites. There are also fewer risks associated with schemes that have local off-takes. Because of these factors it is expected that distributed generation will constitute some 40% of the power market by 2030.

Nuclear generation has the advantage of not emitting carbon and, as other fuel prices can be expected to continue to rise, nuclear costs will become more competitive. There are also some technology developments like the pebble bed reactor that promises to be more modular and cheaper than the current pressurised water reactors. The public awareness of global warming is likely to make nuclear appear less of an evil in comparison. It is expected that the existing tranche of nuclear generation will be replaced, making use of existing sites. Managing the development cost and risk associated with

Table 15.1 Generation costing sheet

		units
Plant	capacity MW	MW
	capacity Net	MW
	load factor %	%
	annual output	TWh
	construction time yrs	yrs
	project life	yrs
Fuel	Efficiency %	%
	coal cost dellivered	€/t
	coal calorific value	GJ/t
	Natural gas cost	€/mmBTU
	Natural gas cost delivered	cents/therm
	N Gas calorific value	kWh/therm
	N Gas gross CV/netCV	
Finance	Cost of dept	%
	cost of equity	%
	inflation	%
	Debt/equity split	
	WACC (D/E = 0.8)	%
Cap Costs	site & dev	€m
	EPC contract	€m
	Electrical conn	€m
	gas connection	€m
	spares	€m
	interest during const.	€m
	total investment cost	€m
	capital cost	€/kW
	capital cost pa	€m/yr
O&M	consumables	cents/kWh
	labour rate	£/h
	no of operators	
	operators labour*1.28	€m
	maintenance material	€m
	main & support labour	€m
Summary	capital cost	€/MWh
	fixed O&M	€/MWh
	Var O&M	€/MWh
	Fuel costs	€/MWh
	Total Generation costs	€/MWh
Other	**CO_2 price**	€/t
	include carbon	tCO_2/GJ
	added cost/incentive	€/MWh
	total cost	€/MWh

Table 15.2 Generation costs.

years	energy price £/MWh	gas price £/mmBTU	coal price £/t	CO$_2$ price £/tCO$_2$	ROC price £/MWh	new entry cost by plant type £/MWh								
						gas	coal	coal refurb	hydro	nuclear	microgen	waste	wind on	wind off
2011	37	3.5	30.9	12.9	42.3	14.4	32.04	28.30	49.84	30.14	49.84	15.0	15.01	18.40
2012	37	3.6	313.4	13.441	43.9	35.21	32.36	28.65	46.14	30.14	50.60	12.83	13.44	16.83
2013	38.7	3.5	31.5	13.2	47.9	34.56	32.47	28.77	46.14	30.14	12.84	8.84	9.45	12.84
2014	38	3.45	49.4	13.5	50.8	34.30	32.61	28.93	550.834	30.14	49.465	5.91	6.52	9.91
2015	36.4	36.4	31.2	49.08	53.8	30.14	32.75	29.08	46.14	30.14	49.08	2.96	3.58	6.96
2016	35.4	3.35	31.2	1430.1	56.6	33.79	32.95	29.29	31.214	30.14	48.70	0.13	0.74	4.12
2017	34.1	3.13	31.2	1448.3	59.3	32.57	33.13	29.50	46.14	30.14	48.33	-2.60	-1.99	1.40
2018	33	3.2	31.2	14.6	55.9	32.00	33.32	29.70	46.14	31.44	47.57	0.83	1.44	4.83
2019	30.8	3.1	31	14.9	55.4	31.42	33.52	29.92	46.14	30.14	46.81	1.31	1.92	5.31
2020	30	30.1	31.2	15.2	55.1	31.215.2	33.73	31.215	46.14	30.14	46.81	1.65	2.26	5.65
avg	average return/MWh					1.66	-29.54	1.99	-32.17	21.97	8.05	2826	23.99	37.51

nuclear power is likely to restrict development to a few global powers with the necessary expertise, like EdF or some of the residual state utilities.

Coal generation is expected to continue to play a major role, particularly in the emerging Asian economies. Advanced modern plants use specially developed **high strength alloy steels**, which enable the use of **supercritical** and ultra-supercritical steam (pressures >248 bar and temperatures >566 °C) and can achieve, depending on location, close to 45% efficiency (39 + 6) as shown in the bar chart of Figure 15.1. This results in corresponding reductions in CO_2 emissions as less fuel is used. A 'Reference Power Plant North Rhine–Westphalia' (RPP NRW) has been built based on a hard coal-fired 600 MW plant with optimised plant technology and an efficiency of 45.9%. Higher efficiencies of over 48% could also be achieved with the right site conditions and additional technical measures. The NRW reference power plant is well above the average for hard coal power plants currently in operation in Germany, which have an average efficiency of around 38%. Plant of this type can make a considerable contribution to attaining targets for the reduction of CO_2. The application of new advanced materials to PF (Pulverised Fuel) power plant should enable efficiencies of 55% to be achieved in the future. Boilers have been built to date for pressures up to 310 bar and temperatures up to 650 °C. The efficiency increases by roughly 3% on making the transition from 167 bar, the standard for drum boilers, to 250 bar without significant increases in investment costs.

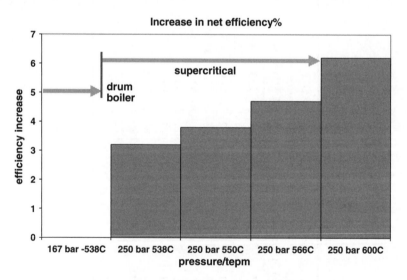

Figure 15.1 Coal efficiency development

The other development in coal plant technology is Circulating Fluidised Bed technology. One of the largest units to exploit the CFB technology has been built by Foster Wheeler for the Polish generator PKE. The contract was awarded in February 2003 with commissioning late in 2004. It is rated at 460 MWe and combines the CFB technology with a vertical low-mass flux once-through supercritical boiler. It is expected to use 5% less fuel than a conventional drum based CFB design with a further 5% enhancement from the supercritical design resulting in overall efficiencies of around 45%. The improvement in efficiency also results in a reduction in CO_2 emission per MWh generated and further improves the competitive position with respect to gas fired generation.

The impact on energy and CO_2 costs of a coal fired generator efficiency improvement from 38% to 45% can be calculated. Assuming a fuel price of €2/GJ with emissions of 0.0869 t CO_2/GJ and a CO_2 price range from €16/t CO_2 to €32/t CO_2 then:

Energy cost at 38% efficiency = 2 ∗ 3600/1000/0.38 = €18.9/MWh.
Energy cost at 38% efficiency = 2 ∗ 3600/1000/0.45 = €16/MWh,

i.e. a saving in energy costs of €2.9/MWh.

t CO_2/MWh at 38% efficiency = 0.0869∗3.6/0.38 = 0.821 costing €13.2/MWh.
t CO_2/MWh at 45% efficiency = 0.0869∗3.6/0.45 = 0.695 costing €11.2/MWh.
CO_2 cost difference at €16/t = €2/MWh and €4/MWh at €32/t CO_2.

Combined cycle gas fired generation will continue to be popular because of its low capital cost and short construction time. However, gas prices are expected to remain high while linked to oil prices and will undermine its competitive position with respect to coal. This will be partly offset by some further efficiency improvements as shown in Figure 15.2. The lower line illustrates how the efficiency of the basic open cycle gas turbine has increased with size. The upper line shows the improvements in efficiency with size of the combined cycle units. Any further improvements are expected to be modest. There are also questions about the security of gas supplies that may be subject to disruption for political reasons. There are also some operational problems when gas supplies are on interruptible contracts, which are invoked at times of peak gas and high electricity demand. Gas fired generation will continue to play a leading role but its further expansion may be restricted by reaction to fuel prices and supply security with investors preferring higher efficiency local CHP schemes.

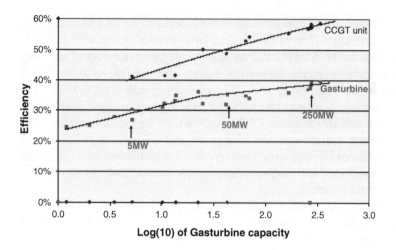

Figure 15.2 Gas generation efficiency

The implications of generation developments to the market is that it is likely to lead to less liquidity with larger units focused on maintaining base load high efficiency operation while distributed units will be driven more by local demands for heat or waste processing. Large-scale developments are most likely to be funded by large global portfolio players who can manage the risk through a degree of vertical integration giving access to a customer base.

15.3 FUTURE PLANT MIX

Some of the likely conclusions of the analysis above are as follows.

- There be a nuclear revival with investment expected in France and the UK.
- There will be public reaction to intrusive wind farms that will constrain development, particularly on shore.
- There will be a coal revival with improved efficiency up to 46% and Carbon Capture and Storage.
- Hydro development in Europe will be limited and shortfalls in energy could be a developing problem in southern Europe with its high summer demands.
- There will be a reaction to high CO_2 prices impacting on industry through power prices and the outcry from industry will limit CO_2 price.

These factors are taken into account in developing the new entry plan for a country. A typical result is shown in Table 15.3. It can be seen that it is profitable to build coal and gas during the early years until very high CO_2 prices make it less competitive than nuclear and renewable sources such as wind.

There is also a requirement to ensure that the volume of new build does not lead to excessive plant margins and the overall level of new addition is constrained. A final consideration is the capacity of the country or region to manage the build and integration of new generation sources. Taking all these factors into account, some estimates of how generation energy production will develop across Europe are shown in Figure 15.3. It can be seen that energy production from gas continues to increase but the rate of development is reduced with nuclear and renewable sources filling the gap. Coal production declines less rapidly as efficiency is improved and is used to bridge the gap pending the establishment of a nuclear build programme. The rate of development of wind energy declines, faced with rising capital costs and adverse public reaction. CHP schemes are developed where it is possible to improve the overall effective efficiency by use of the heat. Waste to energy schemes become a necessity to deal with increasing volumes of waste and limited land fill sites.

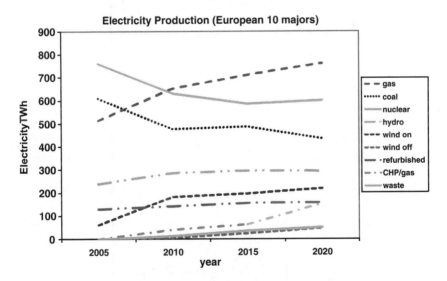

Figure 15.3   Energy generation Europe

Table 15.3 New entry plan

Max. dem, MW	Plant margin %	Plant changes		New plant additions MW									
		Closures	New build	Gas	Coal	Coal refurb	Hydro	Nuclear	Microgen	Waste	Wind on	Wind off
61819	40	968	2790	683	0	0	0	0	25	33	61	91
62314	42	3636	1315	319	701	453	0	0	11	16	28	43
62812	37	3562	1753	435	333	213	0	0	16	21	41	57
63315	33	4312	2255	571	436	287	0	0	22	26	57	74
63821	29	5610	3014	778	554	372	0	755	30	35	83	100
64332	24	2828	3308	1146	730	502	0	1059	45	50	129	146
64847	24	3378	3370	1168	0	732	0	1077	46	51	132	149
65365	23	2205	2370	0	0	746	0	1154	50	55	144	161
65888	22	1395	2503	0	0	805	0	1215	54	58	154	170
66415	23	818	2374	0	0	852	0	1156	51	55	144	161
		28712	25051	5100	2754	4961	0	6416	350	402	973	1154

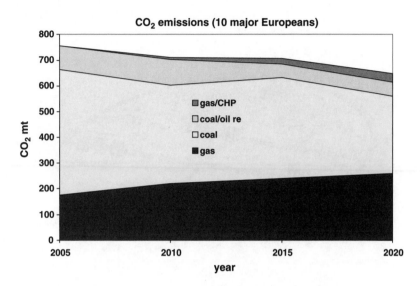

Figure 15.4 Forecast CO$_2$ emissions Europe.

The corresponding change in CO$_2$ emissions is shown in Figure 15.4 and it can be seen that there is a fall approaching 14% from 2005 levels by 2020.

15.4 TRANSMISSION AND DISTRIBUTION GRIDS

The transmission network primarily evolved to enable the pooling of large generation complexes, which are often remotely sited. Distribution networks became essentially passive and feed energy through radial networks to end users. The growth of distributed generation will shift this concept in favour of more active distribution networks interacting with local generation and customers. Figure 15.5 illustrates some of the concepts.

Large remote power stations will operate base load at high efficiency in conjunction with local virtual power plants. The variable nature of on-shore and off-shore wind farms will be managed in conjunction with local short term energy storage systems to create a virtual power plant that meets the changing needs of a local consumer base. CHP schemes will operate in conjunction with local industry, supplying energy and heat. Offices and housing complexes will be equipped with solar panels. The overall distribution network will be operated as an integrated entity with monitoring of all the sources of energy, storage and controllable demand to maintain efficiency and minimize costs. The control technology is available and is similar in concept to the control

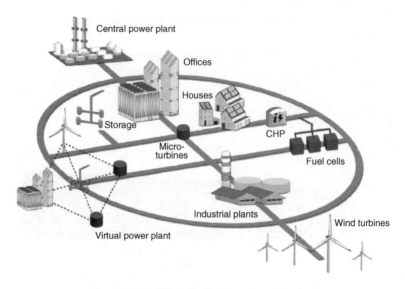

Figure 15.5   Virtual distributed generation

infrastructure used for the super-grid. The same control infrastructure would monitor security and network restoration following any failures.

A key financial issue surrounding this type of development is that it leads to a form of local central control and it is difficult to see how it could be implemented within the current market arrangements. Some local council authorities in the UK have taken an initiative in managing the energy supplies to their building and housing stock and have been successful in reducing costs. In some cases the economics have been made viable by avoiding distribution charges by using direct wire supplies to nearby buildings rather than the distribution network. The extrapolation of this concept would undermine the local distribution business. There are also implications for the transmission network owners if 30–40% of energy is met from local distributed generation as this will significantly reduce their use of system charges. The future for transmission will be in enabling the development of wider pan-continent markets across Europe, Asia and Africa, enabling the pooling of the most efficient and sustainable resources and providing added security. This will be facilitated by the amalgamation of power exchanges covering larger areas as is already taking place. In the medium term:

- a constraint-free pan-European market is unlikely in the medium term and prices will not fully converge;

- the pan-southern African market will be established but the network is unlikely to be developed further;
- China and India are likely to establish interconnected operation but with limited market coupling;
- new planned interconnections will not transform the markets and there will still be congested routes.

Full convergence is not expected before the establishment of new EHV grids.

15.5 CARBON CAPTURE AND STORAGE

The EU is considering sponsoring the development of twelve sites to evaluate CCS (Carbon Capture and Storage). The general concept is to extract carbon from the natural gas fuel leaving hydrogen that would be used in hydrogen-fuelled generators. The CO_2 extracted would be stored in off-shore aquifers or pumped into existing partially depleted oil fields. The latter approach known as EOR (Enhanced Oil Recovery) significantly improves the overall economics.

A candidate in the UK for a CCS and EOR scheme is based on the Miller field as illustrated in the Figure 15.6. In 1997 BP committed the Miller Field to the first full scale incremental oil recovery scheme. The project, used water alternating gas injection (WAG) to:

- increase post plateau production.
- improve overall recovery.
- extend the field's life.

A new compressor with associated pipework was installed and a total of six existing wells were converted to allow both gas lift and WAG operation.

In 2003, BP extended this project with the construction of a new 16-inch gas pipeline between the Brae B and Miller platforms (approximately 9 km) to allow gas to be exported from Brae to Miller for use in the Miller Field EOR (Enhanced Oil Recovery) scheme. This £33 m gas link project provided additional gas for the existing water alternating gas (WAG) injection scheme. The site was well placed to accommodate the development of CCS. Figure 15.6 shows natural gas fed to a reformer and capture plant separating the gas into hydrogen and CO_2, using specially developed membranes. The hydrogen feeds a generator with the CO_2 pumped into the depleted oil field to enable further oil to be extracted more readily.

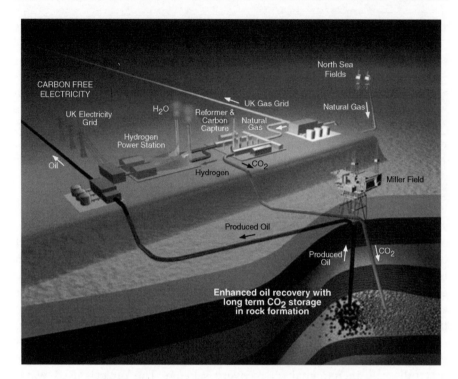

Figure 15.6 Carbon Capture and Storage (source BP)

There is also the possibility that all new generation plants will have to be constructed to be carbon capture ready. This will make it necessary to consider a more integrated approach to transmission and storage of CO_2. It would not be efficient for each unit to have dedicated pipelines and storage. There will also be a need to match the timing of the use of generation producing CO_2 with the timing of depletion of oil fields. It may prove most efficient if this development is managed as a regulated monopoly perhaps by the TSOs.

Unfortunately the capture process has an adverse effect on efficiency with reductions of 10–20%, resulting in higher energy prices. Table 15.4 shows estimates of the production costs of electricity for different types of generation, without capture and with the CCS system. The cost of a full CCS system for electricity generation from a newly built, large-scale fossil fuel-based power plant depends on a number of factors, including the characteristics of both the power plant and the capture system, the specific cost of the storage site, the amount of CO_2 and the required transport

Table 15.4 Carbon capture and storage costs

Power Plant system	CCGT US$/MWh	Pulverised coal	Integrated gasification
without capture	30–50	40–50	40–60
with capture and geo Storage	40–80	60–100	50–90
with capture and EOR	40–70	50–80	40–70

distance. The numbers assume a large-scale plant with gas prices at 2.8–4.4 US$/giga-joule (GJ), and coal prices 1–1.5 US$/GJ. The figures are consistent with UK estimates of extra costs of £10–30/MWh and make this option competitive with wind power as a way of reducing emissions.

In the case of coal, gasification takes place in the presence of a controlled 'shortage' of air/oxygen, thus maintaining reducing conditions. The process is carried out in an enclosed pressurized reactor, and the product is a mixture of $CO + H_2$ (called synthesis gas, syngas or fuel gas). The resulting gas is cleaned and then burned with either oxygen or air, generating combustion products at high temperature and pressure. The sulphur present mainly forms H_2S but there is also a little COS. The H_2S can be more readily removed than SO_2. Although no NOx is formed during gasification, some is formed when the fuel gas or 'syngas' is subsequently burned.

Three gasifier formats are possible, with fixed beds (not normally used for power generation), fluidized beds and entrained flow. Fixed bed units use only lump coal, fluidized bed units use a feed of 3–6 mm in size, and entrained flow gasifiers use a pulverised feed, similar to that used in PCC. IGCC plants can be configured to facilitate CO_2 capture. The new gas is quenched and cleaned. The syngas is 'shifted' using steam to convert CO to CO_2, which is then separated for possible long-term sequestration.

The relative merits of coal fired generation equipped with CCS can be compared with off-shore wind farm options, taking account of the relative energy costs and the costs for the provision of firm supplies (equivalent to fixed costs). The coal fired generator is assumed to be based on pulverized coal without Enhanced Oil Recovery. The off-shore wind data, as developed in Chapter 4 has costs of 54.9/MWh at 30% LF and 65.5/MWh at 25% LF. It is assumed to provide 15% of its capacity as firm. CCS extra capital costs of £10–30/MWh are assumed based on the data in Table 15.4. Coal costs of £1.5/GJ are assumed with 15% efficiency degradation due to CCS from a normal level of 40% with other variable costs of £1.59/MWh and fixed costs of £11.59/MWh.

Off-shore wind with a 30% LF costs £54.9/MWh or, with a 25% LF, £65.5/ MWh.

Standard coal production costs at 40% efficiency are:

$$1.5 * 3.6/0.4 + 1.59 + 11.59 = £26.68/MWh.$$

Coal production costs with CCS and an efficiency of $40 * 0.85 = 34\%$ with revised costs calculated as:

$$1.5 * 3.6/0.34 + 1.59 + 11.59 + 30 \text{ for CCS} = £59/MWh.$$

It can be seen that the coal plant with CCS is similar to that of on-shore and off-shore wind, depending on the load factor. However, the coal plant can be expected to provide firm power equivalent to its capacity whenever it is operational and typically for 85% of the time. In contrast, the wind supply can only be considered to supply firm power equivalent to about 10–15% of the installed capacity. To provide reserve to cover for loss of 85% of wind capacity would cost:

$$0.85 * 11.59/MWh = £9.8/MWh.$$

Taking account of the capacity provision from coal with CCS makes it appear a more viable solution. It is also likely that new coal stations will have higher net efficiencies than 40% and be designed ready to accommodate retrospective fitting of CCS.

15.6 MARKET IMPLICATIONS

Fuel supply security will play an increasing role in determining the future generation mix. This will apply both to safeguard supplies but also to hedge against fuel price escalation. Exposure to one commodity exposes the power market to fuel shortages and price disruption. This would occur in Europe if the main gas exporters chose to restrict supplies or terrorist action sabotaged pipelines. The increases in the cost of emissions will complicate market operation by linking all fuels with arbitrage opportunities between power and gas and coal and gas through the CO_2 linkage. Given these circumstances, there is likely to be an expansion of nuclear capacity that will seek to operate base load though long term supply contracts rather than medium term trading.

The management of risk in the future environment will become more complex and only the larger players with a diverse portfolio are likely to be able to establish hedges. This is likely to lead to further mergers and acquisitions, reducing the number of competing players in the market. The increasing energy costs will lead large companies to establish consortia to negotiate long term supply contracts.

The implications to the market of an increased proportion of distributed generation are that liquidity in the wholesale market will fall with the reduction in the proportion of large scale super-grid connected generation. The stations that are built will largely be sponsored by the large global energy players that are better able to manage the risk. Transmission interconnection will be developed on a commercial basis, enabling some increase in cross-border trading and the closer realisation of pan-continental markets.

The development of distributed generation will mostly be sponsored by local consortia bringing together users and suppliers establishing multilateral deals embracing electricity and heat supply coupled with demand management. Examples already exist where local councils in the UK have taken an active role in energy management. This has embraced CHP schemes and solar panels applied to their property stock. They have also avoided local distribution charges by directly wiring between some of their town centre sites.

Distribution control will need to become more active with the distributed generation operated in conjunction with storage and demand management so as to appear as a virtual power plant. CHP will be exploited, providing heat supplies to local industry and premises. The distribution system will be operated as an integrated system to provide the least cost supplies and maintain security. Storage systems with the capability to smooth daily demand profiles are likely to be developed, improving the overall load factor from an average of 55% to 65%. The unit is likely to trade as an entity selling and buying energy to match its needs and realise cost savings.

CCS systems will be developed as an additional mechanism to reduce CO_2 emissions. It will compete in conjunction with renewable sources, nuclear generation and energy conservation to enable emission targets to be met. Twelve demonstration sites are likely to be developed across Europe.

15.7 SUMMARY

The likely developments over the next 10 to 20 years are summarised as follows.

- Large scale generation efficiency improvements of 7% can be expected to offset fuel cost rises and reduce CO_2 emissions with:
  - coal rising from 35% to 45% and maybe 50%
  - gas CCGT 50% up to 55% and maybe 60%.

- Plans will be established for the existing tranche of nuclear generation to be replaced and expanded by global power companies such as EdF.
- Driven by higher fuel prices high efficiency distributed generation schemes will be developed including:
  - CHP with around 80% efficiency
  - micro-generation with 88% efficiency with heat and air output.
- New generation could be made up of 60% large scale high efficiency with 40% distributed and operated as virtual power plants.
- High efficiency large generation with CCS may displace some wind generation.
- Transmission interconnection will be developed to support pan-continental markets.
- Distribution will be developed to support active management of distributed generation and demand.

The implications to the market of these issues are that liquidity in the wholesale market will fall with the reduction in the proportion of large scale super-grid connected generation and, on the demand side, the development of large buying consortia including municipalities. This will be offset in part by the development of more cross-border trading. The stations that are built will be sponsored by large global energy players with local distributed generation built by local consortia.

16

Long-term Scenarios

16.1 INTRODUCTION

It is now almost twenty years since liberalisation and the introduction of competition was proposed for electricity utilities. Some form of restructuring has been widely adopted around the world to suit local objectives. This book has reviewed the structure of those markets and the economics of power systems. It also covered basic generation, transmission and distribution costing and pricing. The performance of markets and their current status and problems has been reviewed. The industry now faces new challenges associated with global warming and escalating energy demand from developing countries such as China and India. The industry will have to cope with:

- the impact on fossil fired generation resulting from restrictions on emissions and the costs derived from the European Trading Scheme;
- the costs and competitive position of alternative energy sources and associated incentive schemes;
- a resurgence of interest in nuclear but concerns over who will finance and underwrite the risk;
- escalating fossil fuel prices and the reaction of generators in bringing forward improvements in efficiency;
- the security of fuel supplies with increasing dependence on imported oil and gas from OPEC and Russia;

Power Markets and Economics: Energy Costs, Trading, Emissions   Barrie Murray
© 2009 John Wiley & Sons, Ltd

- the impact on system security of the management of large tranches of variable generation output from wind-farms and increased cross-border flows;
- the potential for clean coal technology including carbon capture and storage and gasification enabling conventional sources to compete with subsidised renewable sources;
- the advent of distributed generation and actively managed distribution networks linked by extended cross-border EHV networks;
- the impact on world commodity markets and freight costs of the burgeoning Chinese and Indian markets.

The first wave of restructuring was designed to promote competition in the expectation that this would reduce prices. It is now necessary to consider how the various market structures that have been adopted will address some of these new issues and what further changes might be necessary.

This chapter discusses some of the plausible scenarios that will shape the future of the industry through the next forty years. It considers how the industry and its markets will need to adapt to meet the new environmental challenges while maintaining security and costs.

16.2 EMISSIONS

The latest proposed legislation referred to as '20/20/20' calls for a 20% increase in energy efficiency, a 20% cut in greenhouse gases and a 20% share of energy from renewable sources by the year 2020. This is to be achieved through the **ETS scheme**, the LCPD and subsidised renewable generation. Whereas the phase 1 scheme was undermined by over-allocation, the phase 2 scheme, starting in 2008, appears to be working with more liquidity and trading coupled with better information and opportunities for price discovery. Further improvements are planned for phase 3, starting in 2013, with the establishment of a seamless European scheme. There is expected to be less free allocation and more auctioning of permits. Longer term targets mooted are for a 30% reduction by 2030 and 50% by 2050 from 1990 levels.

In the past the required reductions have been heavily biased with the electricity sector bearing most of the burden; this is unlikely to be viable longer term. The industry has responded well, and will continue to do so, but the impact on energy prices is likely to reach unacceptable levels when coupled with the rise in fuel prices. The ambitious government targets are unlikely to be met with the current strategy and more sources of emissions need to be brought within the scheme. CO_2 market prices will have to rise to the least cost abatement technique available. If this is left to the electricity sector it will lead to unacceptably high prices for energy, an essential commodity. There are likely to be cheaper abatement options elsewhere in transport where thinking needs to change radically including the following.

- **Home working** There is a great deal of scope to enable home working, particularly in the service sector where most tasks can be effected through the use of the internet with web-cams.
- **Overseas business travel** Much of this can be avoided by using video conference facilities with PowerPoint presentations.
- **Local business parks** This would be a shared workplace facility with a fully supported infrastructure, minimising the need to travel.
- **Bike priority** This would shift the emphasis from the car to give preference to bicycles as in countries such as the Netherlands and France where town bicycles can be hired.

It was shown in Chapter 5 that electricity generation in the UK emits around 167 mt CO_2/yr or 0.5 mt/day. A typical car emits around 250 gm/km or 5 kg of CO_2 for a typical 20-km daily journey. If 100 million trips are made in a day then 0.5 mt of CO_2 would be emitted. The individual choice is between paying twice as much for electricity or sharing a car journey. The CO_2 cost must be factored into all energy usage to facilitate arbitrage and choice. For example, employers enabling home working should be credited with the resulting transport emission saving.

Internationally a successor agreement to the Kyoto Protocol is expected during the next decade with a limited global framework in place by 2030. This framework should support the import of credits into the ETS during all relevant trading periods. This would include:

- certified emission reductions (CERs) and emission reduction units (ERUs) from the Clean Development Mechanisms (CDM);
- Joint Implementation (JI) or their equivalent.

This will make a supply of lower price credits, based on the comparative advantages in marginal abatement cost that exist around the world, available for ETS compliance.

If the electricity sector is left to manage marginal abatement then the price is likely to be around €30/t based on advanced CCS schemes. It is unlikely that the developed countries will see their competitive position undermined by excessive energy prices resulting from full pass-through of costs. It is expected that bringing new sources of CO_2 into the scheme and the opportunity to trade internationally is likely to cap CO_2 prices at lower levels than might be the case if most of the burden fell on the electricity sector and prices could settle around or below €20/t.

A new **Large Combustion Plant Directive** (LCPD) came into effect in January 2008 and introduced tougher requirements for managing the release of air pollutants and strengthened the European Union's efforts to curb the effects of acidification and local concentrations of ground level ozone and particulate matter (PM). Given the shift in relative fuel prices, more coal generators are choosing to fit FGD (Flue Gas Desulphurisation) than opting out, accepting limited life derogation with closure by 2016. It is expected that coal will continue to form a significant part of the plant mix for some time to come with the costs of FDG and CCS being offset by high power prices. It is not expected that EU targets will be met by 2020 with levels approaching 15%, partly due to coal burn remaining attractive with low coal prices and lower CO_2 prices.

16.3 ALTERNATIVE ENERGY SOURCES

Published in January 2008, the proposed Renewables Directive includes an overall target requiring that 20% of final energy consumption would be met by renewable energy sources by 2020. The individual country targets are shown as a percentage in Figure 16.1 by the larger blocks. The wide variation between countries reflects the values for 2005 as shown by the shorter rectangle. The higher values are usually associated with countries that already have a hydro contribution such as Sweden, Finland and Austria. The change required in developing countries such as Romania and Bulgaria has been kept low. It can be seen that the change required in the UK is amongst the highest.

It is proposed that these targets would be legally binding and will apply to all sources, although the exact form of implementation is still unclear. The targets for the electricity sector are likely to be higher, bearing a higher proportion of the burden than other sectors. This presumes that the impact of high electricity prices is less damaging to international competitiveness. For example while the overall UK target is 15%, that for the electricity sector may be as high as 30% as opposed to 5% in 2007. If we assume that the cost of energy from renewable sources is around twice that from conventional stations then the added cost to end users would be between 15 and 40%.

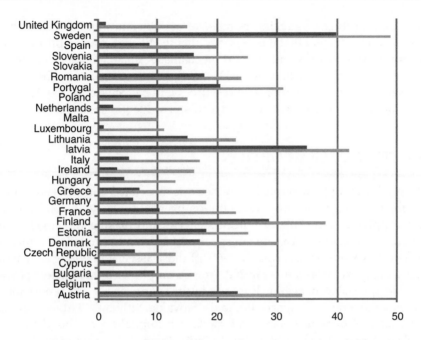

Figure 16.1 Legally binding renewable energy targets for 2020

Assuming a demand of 400 TWh then 15% is 60 TWh or 6850 MW throughout the year. The output from a wind generator is typically 25%, so the installed capacity would need to be 27 400 MW or around 10 000 - 3 MW turbines. If the expected contribution to meet the target reduction is 30% then 20 000 wind turbines would be required, which at a capital cost of around €2m/MW equals €55 billion.

For the electricity sector, the options of renewable sources based on wind is unlikely to be a preferred or a cheap option when all the negative aspects are considered as summarised at the end of Chapter 4. Even if the strategy were pursued, there are unlikely to be enough skilled engineers to support the development of the wind farms and the associated extension of the grid connections. Denmark, France, Germany, Netherlands, Ireland, Spain and Portugal are also planning large-scale increases in on-shore and off-shore wind capacity. This will stretch the capacity of manufacturers to deliver and install given the limited availability of suitable off-shore vessels. Taking account of the intermittency, costs and public objection to local installations it is not expected that wind energy and energy from other renewable sources will grow rapidly across Europe. It is expected to rise from 9% in 2008 to 15%

in 2020, reflecting a reducing number of suitable sites and will fall short of EU targets. Beyond that it is expected that the EU will react to improve the administration process and support mechanisms, enabling sustained development with 20% reached by 2030; 28% by 2040 and 35% by 2050. It is expected that more attention and resources will be focused on the development of alternatives such as tidal, hydro and wave power.

16.4 THE NUCLEAR OPTION

The high price of fuel coupled with the costs associated with CO_2 emissions has made nuclear power a serious option for new capacity. In 2007 nuclear was supplying some 30% of Europe's energy and making the largest contribution to containing carbon emissions. It has been estimated that nuclear life cycle CO_2 emissions are only 2–6% of those associated with gas generation. In a report to Parliament in 2007, the EU emphasised that nuclear power was indispensable to meeting Europe's future energy needs. The report noted that Finland, France, Bulgaria, Romania, Slovakia, Lithuania, Latvia, Estonia, the United Kingdom, Poland and the Czech Republic were building new nuclear power plants or planning to build them. It is recognised that the existing contribution of nuclear would be very difficult to replace without a complete abandonment of current CO_2 emission targets.

In the liberalised market it remains to be seen if investors will sponsor the development of nuclear power. The banks have always fought shy of the long construction programmes and attendant risks associated with nuclear power. There is also limited expertise available and it is only the large companies such as EdeF, Eon and RWE that will have the infrastructure and financial standing to take on the development. Governments can only ease the process through sponsoring research and development and streamlining the planning process. EDF began construction of a new nuclear power station at Flamanville in Normandy in 2007 based on the European Pressurised Water Reactor (EPWR). They plan to develop at least one new nuclear plant every year between 2020 and 2030. The company also expressed interest in the takeover of British Energy, and is likely to sponsor new build at existing sites in England. France is likely to become the nuclear engine of Europe irrespective of the policy of countries such as Germany, Austria and Italy, which are reviewing their policy and may well be importing nuclear power from counties like France.

Nuclear waste management remains an issue and geological disposal in deep burial sites appears technically feasible and cost effective. The difficulty is in finding acceptable sites and there are plans to invite offers to host a facility coupled with employment opportunities and local infrastructure investment. There is evidence of growing public opinion that nuclear power may be a lesser evil in meeting energy needs from low emission sources than a myriad of wind-farms blotting the landscape.

The development of 'nuclear parks' is foreseen with large concentrations of generation and waste management facilities coupled with robust security and safety management. The parks would be facilitated by a multi-outlet high voltage grid connection. The plants would normally operate base load, exporting any surplus energy at times of low load. By 2020 it is expected that the energy contribution from nuclear generation will have fallen to around 23% pending new build. It is expected that this will have risen by 2050 to around 40% with the full realization of the impact of reduced supplies of gas and oil and escalating prices coupled with environmental constraints.

16.5 FUEL PRICES

During 2008 there was unparalleled escalation in fuel prices. **Oil prices** were driven above $100/barrel towards $150/barrel. This was caused by a tight supply situation coupled with increased demand for India and China. The price rises were driven higher by speculative trading base on concerns over security of supply and OPEC control. The rise has been partly offset by a fall in the value of the dollar against other currencies with the suppliers seeking to maintain the real value of their revenues. At the higher levels price/demand elasticity effects are expected to reduce demand and pull prices back. By 2020 there will be very little oil fired generation capacity left and certainly be 2050 it will only be used where other sources are not readily available, as on small islands.

Gas prices also escalated during this period based on the oil indexed pricing with a cost per barrel equivalent to 6 MBtu on an equivalent energy basis (see conversion tables). This linkage in pricing (as illustrated in Figure 3.5) has again been brought into question as the supply/demand position of gas has been satisfactory during this period and free market prices could have been driven lower. The development of LNG (Liquid Natural Gas) terminals will increase the scope for gas trading around the world and the competitive effect should result in breaking the direct link with oil and containing prices. Gas will also compete with coal and it seems more likely that, in the longer term, prices will be more closely linked to coal prices on an equivalent price/MWh basis having factored in the CO_2 price. A free liquid market in gas across Europe has not materialised during the first decade of the new millennium but it is expected that by 2020 there will be effective gas trading coupled with LNG.

Coal prices have tended to follow suit and have also risen during 2007–8 but for other reasons. There were some supply problems in Australia with blockages at the ports and in China due to cold weather. There was also a shortage of freight capacity aggravated by increases in demand from Asia to ship commodities and products. New shipping is under construction and is expected to be delivered through 2009/10 when the freight situation should be alleviated and prices will revert to more normal levels. Improved efficiency of new stations being built will also help contain demand.

There are a large number of untapped coal reserves around the world and the advent of CCS will make it viable environmentally, so that it will provide a cap on escalating gas prices in the long term. There is also the option of coal gasification that is being developed and involves:

- oxygen and steam are pumped into a coal seam and the coal is ignited but only partially burnt;
- the coal is broken down to release 'syngas' a mixture of hydrogen and other gases like carbon monoxide that can be burnt in a gas turbine;
- CO_2 and other gases emerge as a concentrated gas stream making it easier to capture.

It is claimed that the technology has been proven and offers the opportunity to exploit deep coal seams without CO_2 being emitted to the atmosphere. This technology is likely to be developed by 2025 and will help to retain the position of coal as a major energy contributor.

Nuclear fuel costs have also increased during 2007 with British Energy reporting a rise from £5.4/MWh to £6.0/MWh. This was mainly due to the revaluation of the provision for un-burnt fuel at station closure. The UK government provides an indemnity to cover liabilities for spent fuel and decommissioning. Fuel prices can be expected to rise in line with increased demand as more stations are commissioned and could double by 2050.

There is now concern over the development of **'fuel poverty'** for those consumers who have to spend more than 10% of their income on meeting their energy needs. Whereas in the past there has been little consumer reaction to prices, there is now a reaction both to price and a recognition of the on-going environmental costs of energy utilisation. This will encourage energy saving and it is postulated that there will be a period of zero growth in electricity demand with progress towards the target 20% reduction through the period 2020 to 2050.

16.6 FUEL SUPPLY SECURITY

There has been growing concern over the security of fuel supplies and over-dependence on a few sources. In the case of oil, the dominant supplier is OPEC. In 1985 the OPEC spare capacity over demand was around 20%. By 2007 the margin had fallen well below 5% with a commensurate increase in the price per barrel from around $30 to $70, increasing to $150 following concerns over supplies from Iran and Nigeria. This rise is partly offset by a fall in the value of the dollar with respect to other countries. There is significant scope for growth in demand from countries such as India and China. In the US and Canada the energy demand per capita is above 3 tonne/yr, in Europe around 1.5 te/yr, whereas in India and China it is only around 0.2 tonne/yr. On the supply side there are likely to be some undiscovered resources but other alternatives, like EOR (Enhanced oil Recovery) and Arctic oil, heavy oil or oil shale are likely to cost twice as much. The outlook is for continuing high prices to support higher priced new entry options.

There has been concern in Europe over the increasing dependence on gas imported from Russia. The other development that creates some security in gas supplies is the establishment of LNG terminals that can import gas from anywhere in the world. Wind and tidal power will also reduce dependence on imported supplies. Concerns over security have also contributed to renewed interest in nuclear as an alternative.

In the case of coal, the predominate suppliers to world markets are Australia, South Africa, Russia, Indonesia, Columbia and China and many countries have reserves of their own making, it a more generally available commodity. Until recently, prices have been relatively stable in comparison with other fuels but shortage of freight has resulted in higher delivered prices. This was primarily due to demands for freight for other purposes by India and China. This has prompted a programme of new ship build that is expected to result in delivered coal prices returning to more normal levels. Coal is primarily a cost based commodity with some 200 years of proven reserves. The costs of realising increased production are not high in most of the exporting countries and generally less than 20%. Because of its general availability and relative price stability it is expected that coal will remain a dominant force in electricity power generation. The impact of emission costs will accelerate improvements in efficiency, CCS and coal gasification, resulting in coal returning to its former position overtaking the use of gas.

16.7 SYSTEM SECURITY

A key aspect of securing future energy supplies is that of establishing sufficient capacity with reserves to cover for outages. Within a liberalised market the responsibility for this primarily rests with the supplier who has to contract for capacity and energy to meet its needs. There are a number of reasons why this may not produce the required amount of capacity to ensure a reliable supply to customers.

- Supply contracts are usually only months to one or two years ahead. This does not provide a basis for funding development with a project life of 15 years or more.
- The volatility of relative fuel prices makes it extremely difficult to predict future revenues when contract prices are not fuel price indexed.
- There are concerns over the security of some fuel supplies.
- The market is distorted by feed in tariffs and subsidies to preferred renewable sources that undermine competition.
- It is not in the interests of generators to maintain high plant margins when tight supply conditions lead to higher prices.

Future oil and gas supplies are dwindling with falling stocks and a lot of generation is reaching the end of its life span. This will have most impact with nuclear plant that is generally operated base load and providing a high percentage of energy. Governments are not able to make informed decisions and there is a blind faith, promoted by academics, that the market will solve all. The environmental lobby oppose everything and exercise a disproportionate influence considering their lack of any accountability. The utility in Portugal EDP have embraced the development of renewable sources and advanced wind power but need to develop hydro based storage schemes to manage the variability. These are objected to by environmental lobbyists. In the UK some wind farm proposals have been abandoned because of public opposition, plans to develop a clean coal station at Kingsnorth are being opposed with public demonstrations. Advice on the best strategy is confusing, with different vested interests each promoting their solution as the way forward. There is no overall coordination and objective analysis with government reviews advancing what needs to be done but not how or who.

Opinion shifts between gas, renewables, nuclear and coal as the way forward, whereas in practice a structured mix of all will be required, something the market cannot deliver.

The current market structure does not provide a framework that supports long term investment or the development of an optimal plant mix. These decisions are much more important than any decisions that may be made in reacting to the day to day vagaries of the spot market. There is also a need for industry to have more price stability to support their planning. These requirements are best met through the Single Buyer market model that operates with a 10–15 year horizon. Payments to generators would be based on capacity and availability as well as for energy with fuel price indexation. Capacity payments would be set according to technology type so as to encourage the optimum mix, taking account of the need to maintain security of supplies. The proportion of peaking and base load plant would also be controlled through the tender process for new capacity. This approach was discussed in more detail in a previous book (*Electricity Markets*, 1998) and results in a more predictable environment for investment. It is expected that market structures will have to change to a Single Buyer model to meet the challenges of the future.

16.8 CLEAN COAL TECHNOLOGY

In 2007 the world burnt some 5.3 billion tons of coal and the amount is increasing by 8% a year to meet the energy needs of developing countries such as China and India. The development of alternative renewable energy sources and the expansion of nuclear will offset some of the growth but there is little doubt that coal will still play a major role in meeting the world's future energy needs. The technology to establish CCS is generally reckoned to be available but as yet unproven. There is also the question of its cost effectiveness because of the capital costs and the impact on the efficiency of the overall process when the costs of energy for extraction and pumping the CO_2 to a remote site are factored.

Whilst there is general acceptance that clean coal technology is needed, it is less clear who should bear the cost of its development. It has been suggested that OPEC should invest in the technology as a means of replacing dwindling oil production but, in general, they say that developing the technology is not their responsibility. Abdalla Salem el-Badri, the secretary general of OPEC, said in an interview in 2008:

'We contributed to industrialization with cheap energy. The world should not forget our contribution.' OPEC members include developing and poor countries such as Angola and Nigeria, and they 'cannot solve the problems of the world', he added. It is difficult for private companies solely to shoulder the burden because the specific experiment they participate in may not be the winning experiment. The EU have attempted to coordinate development with some twelve demonstration plants proposed to explore the alternative technologies but member governments are reluctant to advance funding with costs estimated at €12 billion. There is a view that development should be prompted by market forces through the mechanisms of the ETS but the volatility of prices does not provide a sound basis for long term investment. It has been suggested that the developers could be issued with free credits that could be sold into the market, while others suggest that the money should be provided by government from funds raised from auctioning credits. There is also a need for governments across the world to establish the incentives to apply CCS to maintain a level competitive position.

Two high-profile projects – one in Scotland led by the British oil company, BP, and another in Illinois led by a consortium called FutureGen, which includes the coal giant Xstrata – encountered setbacks because of escalating costs and shortfalls in public funding. But some developments are going ahead. Statoil of Norway is already pumping under the seabed significant quantities of unwanted carbon dioxide from a natural gas field. Sonatrach, the Algerian natural gas and oil company, has a similar project to store unwanted carbon dioxide at its Salah field. In Canada, EnCana, an energy company, injects unwanted carbon dioxide piped from a coal gasification plant in the United States into its Weyburn, Saskatchewan, field to make it easier to recover hard-to-reach oil. Vattenfall expect to complete the construction of the 30 MW thermal pilot plant at Schwarze Pumpe in Germany. It is seen as the necessary scale-up link between initial engineering and successful operation of a future 250–350 MW electricity demonstration plant. The pilot plant will be in operation in mid-2008. The initial testing programme will run for three years. Thereafter, the pilot plant will be available for other tests. The plant is planned to be in operation for at least ten years. Lignite and hard coal will be combusted in a mixture of oxygen and re-circulated CO_2, which also contains water vapour. The flue gas will then be treated and sulphur oxides, particles and other contaminants will be removed. Finally, the water will be condensed and the concentrated CO_2 compressed into a liquid.

A complication with CCS is the establishment of a network of centres were CO_2 is captured coupled to sites where it can be buried. Both the sources and sinks will vary with time as generation shifts down the merit order table

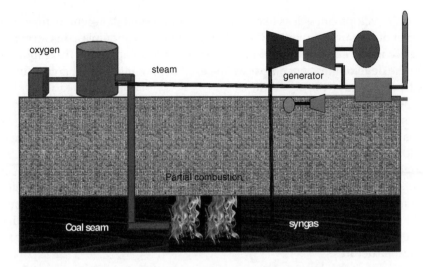

Figure 16.2 Underground coal gasification

and oil fields become depleted. There would be a need for a CO_2 grid to be established and overall coordination of the infrastructure and process for this technology to be effectively applied. Within a fragmented market it would require an organisation like the TSO to act as a single buyer. Because of these difficulties it is not expected that CCS will develop very quickly before 2030.

In the meantime there are other clean options that should be the subject of serious attention. Most coal producing countries are promoting deep seam coal gasification where coal is heated with steam with a restricted amount of oxygen underground. The coal breaks down into 'syngas' containing mainly hydrogen and carbon monoxide that can be burnt in a gas turbine. The gasification process is illustrated schematically in Figure 16.2. The CO_2 emerges as a concentrated gas stream that can be more readily captured by a two-stage process. The first stage is similar to scrubbing and relatively cheap. This reduces the CO_2 content from about 35% to 5%. The second stage involves 'shifting' the CO and removing it, resulting in some 70% hydrogen and 24% methane. There is also the possibility of storing the CO_2 at the same site.

A British Geological Survey estimated that the UK has 17 billion tons of coal that could be treated in this way, providing sufficient energy for 30 years. Concerns over fuel supply security and escalating prices creates a powerful argument for the development of coal gasification. The other attraction is that such a development is less likely to raise environmental objections than new conventional surface plants. RWE plans a trial gasification plant in Germany. The accurate deep drilling technology has been developed for oil exploration and the development encompasses the establishment of new energy sources that will improve the economics.

The original experiments were conducted by Sir William Ramsey in Durham in 1912 and the former Soviet Union has several large UCG installations in operations supplying gas to power stations. Feasibility studies are in hand in India, South Africa, Scotland and Australia where funding is being sought to extend a UCG installation. Other projects seek to develop gas to liquid technology, producing diesel. Part of the research is to develop techniques to manage the gasification using accurate bore holes. These have to be sufficiently close to control the gasification process and the drilling has to be implemented with detection of seam boundaries and unsuitable geological structures.

The price of the delivered 'syngas' has been estimated at between $1.5 and $4/MBtu, depending on the location. Off-shore installations would be at the higher price end but still competitive with natural gas. The 'syngas' can be piped tens of kilometres to remote shore based stations. The first stage of CO_2 extraction would add only a further $1/MBtu, making it comparable to natural gas. This development has the potential to fundamentally shift the balance of the world's future energy supplies away from dependence on oil and gas in favour of coal.

16.9 NETWORK DEVELOPMENTS

It is expected that the contribution of **distributed generation** will grow with the development of small wind farms, micro generation schemes combined with CHP, local waste to energy schemes, and solar and micro hydro installations. This will be driven by high fuel prices and emission costs and it is expected that energy output levels will reach levels similar to that provided by large centralised generation complexes. To manage the variability of the demand and output this generation will need to be managed as an integrated entity. This will incorporate **real time pricing** for system users and extensive demand side management. This will have a significant impact on the role of the distribution network: instead of being essentially passive it will need to be coordinated and operated as a virtual power plant coupled with demand side management and the use of storage installations.

The research being funded by the EU should lead to the establishment of full-scale trial installations by 2020, with commercial schemes developed beyond that date. The coordination of these disparate sources will most likely be realised by a local aggregator acting as a supplier. It will require a network of data channels to monitor generation output and consumer demand coupled with weather and demand prediction systems and a control infrastructure. It is expected that these developments will afford a much more integrated arrangement between suppliers and their customers in optimising the management of costs. This will include real time pricing and intelligent consumer metering.

These developments will have an impact on the development and design of both the distribution and super-grid networks. The distribution networks will have to cater for a more disparate range of flows as the output from generation varies depending on availability and wind conditions. Off-shore wind farms will generally not be located close to super-grid connection points and the grid will need to be extended to establish remotely located collection nodes. These changes will need to be reflected in the arrangements for charging for their use.

There are a number of developments in large scale generation that will affect the requirements of the development of the super-grid.

- New nuclear stations will be based on existing sites extended to create **nuclear generation parks** to realise economies of scale in managing waste and security.
- There will be more coastal gas fired generation located close to LNG terminals to benefit from alternative fuel supplies.
- New coal fired generation based on gasification will be located at the head of the drilling sites.
- There will be more EHV cross-border interconnection to facilitate international energy trade extending across continents.

It is expected that pan-continental markets will be developed based on EHV networks. A pan-European network will be established as well as a link around the Mediterranean (Medring) and the Baltic Sea (the Baltrel ring project). This EHV network would open up opportunities for the development of larger remote nuclear generation parks. The EHV networks would operate at 750 kV with low losses, enabling prices to converge. The extended EHV networks will also enable reserve sharing and be able to accommodate the variation in output from increased volumes of wind power.

There are impediments to the development of pan-European markets linked to local interests and European Energy Regulators believe new EU legislation is needed to:

- create the regulatory climate necessary for investment in the European network and other infrastructures, which are essential for Europe's security of supply and competitiveness;
- provide for EU level regulatory co-operation and decision-making;
- ensure the separation of the monopoly networks from competitive businesses, preferably through so-called 'ownership unbundling';
- guarantee the powers and independence of national regulators.

'There cannot be a trade-off for Member States to either put in place strong, independent regulators or alternatively to use structural remedies such as effective unbundling. Both elements are needed.'

16.10 INTERNATIONAL COMMODITY AND FREIGHT MARKETS

A key requirement facilitating the operation of global commodity markets is the availability of dry bulk freight. The increase in demand for freight from China (importing iron ore) and India (importing coal) during 2007 has highlighted the impact that freight availability has on international coal prices. The freight market volume during 2003–2007 averaged three times greater than the previous 20 years, with a corresponding increase in prices and volatility. The added freight cost for coal from South Africa averaged 15–40% of the delivered cost. The principal traffic is in coal, iron ore, grain and steel. Coal was the largest traded commodity but is expected to be matched by iron ore from 2010. China has a huge potential to grow steel consumption per capita to around 300 kg in 2007 whereas Japan looks to 650 kg and South Korea over 1000 kg. To realise this level would require a four-fold increase in iron ore imports and an increasing demand for coal imports.

Assuming that clean coal technologies are developed, then a high level of trade will continue with steady growth. The supply of freight vessels takes time to catch up with demand but in future it is expected that there will be better forecasting of requirements so prices should not escalate and will be more stable. This will reflect back into more stable coal prices with the freight element related to costs rather than capacity shortfalls.

The development of LNG coupled with increased availability of LNG freight will open up the gas market across the Atlantic and into Africa.

This will enable advantage to be taken of variations in demand profiles and corresponding prices. It will also provide a hedge against supply interruption from pipelined sources. This market will further add to the demand for freight.

A problem that could affect the international freight market is port congestion and there have been problems during 2007 and 2008. The port waiting time reduces the availability of vessels and reduces the amount of freight that can be carried during a period.

16.11 COMPETITION

A consequence of liberalisation and the removal of state control has been an increase in takeovers and mergers, leading to the emergence of new giant utilities with assets across continents and the world. In Europe we have EdeF, RWE and Eon. There are also specialised organisations that focus on particular technology sectors such as Vattenfall. Some countries have chosen to retain national champions such as ENEL in Italy and EdeF in France, to avoid dependence on external organisations for a vital part of their infrastructure but foreign entry is enabled. The result is less liquidity and competition in the market. There are a number of reasons why this trend is expected to continue.

- A portfolio of generation provides more opportunity to arbitrage and hedge risk against fuel price volatility.
- There is more scope to manage emissions against allowances and credits with a mix of technology.
- They have the resources to finance a new generation of nuclear plant and hydro and manage the associated risks.
- They are able to resource the development of new technologies such as coal gasification, tidal schemes and CCS.

Oil and gas majors are taking an active interest in looking for new business opportunities to replace dwindling oil supplies and are likely to enter the arena. They have the resources and are likely to seek opportunities to vertically integrate downstream into the power sector. This would also enable them to exploit arbitrage between their gas supplies and the power market where there are market imperfections.

The end result of this process will be market domination by a few global majors that will be vertically integrated through the whole supply chain.

At best, national governments will be able to hedge against the influence of market power if they have retained national champions.

16.12 CONCLUSIONS

By the middle of the century the shape of the industry is expected to be characterised by a number of issues.

- To effectively reduce **emissions,** a market mechanism like the ETS will need to be extended worldwide together with the CDM and JI mechanisms that will enable the value of existing absorption sources like the rain forests to be recognised.
- Targets for the establishment of **alternative energy** sources will not be met. Taking account of the intermittency, costs and public objection to local installations, it is not expected that wind energy will grow rapidly and more focus will be placed on the development of tidal, hydro and wave energy.
- The development of **'nuclear parks'** is foreseen with large concentrations of generation and waste management facilities coupled with robust security and safety management. It is expected that nuclear energy will make the largest contribution by fuel type by 2050.
- **Oil prices** will continue to rise as supplies dwindle, while demand from the developing world continues to expand. A corresponding rise in **gas prices** is likely to be contained by the development of effective markets, aided by the expansion of LNG. **Coal** will remain a competitive fuel source as CCS and gasification processes establish clean technology and coal prices will provide a degree of stability to the fuel markets. The price of **nuclear** fuel will rise as demand increases.
- Dependence on imported gas and oil is seen as a **security threat** and this will add to the case to build more clean coal and nuclear as well as alternative energy sources.
- The current preferred multi-market structure does not provide a framework that supports long term investment or the development of a **secure plant margin** and an optimal plant mix. There is also a need for industry to have more price stability to support their planning and these requirements are best met through the **Single Buyer market** model that operates with a 10–15 year horizon.
- It is likely that **clean coal technology** will be demonstrated through the next decade. **CCS** will be successfully applied but is expected to be expensive because of the infrastructure requirements. Underground coal **gasification**

is likely to be more widely applied with the benefit of improved fuel supply security.

- It is expected that the contribution of **distributed generation** will grow with the development of small wind farms, micro generation schemes combined with CHP, local waste to energy schemes, solar and micro hydro installations. These combined with demand management schemes are likely to contribute 40% or more of power energy needs by 2050. An **EHV super-grid** will be developed to facilitate energy and reserve sharing, enhance security and connect large remote nuclear parks and coal gasification schemes.
- **Commodity prices** have been affected by rapid increases in the requirement for **freight** due to steep rises in the requirements of developing countries such as China and India. This has caused a sharp rise in international coal prices that is expected to be temporary as new commissioned freight becomes available. However, demand for freight is expected to continue to rise due to increasing iron ore and coal imports by China and India and LNG traffic. Price rises of 50% in real terms can be expected to support the development of freight and port facilities and increased fuel prices.
- Mergers and acquisitions will continue, resulting in a market dominated by a few global players causing a **reduction in market liquidity** and competition. These conglomerates will have the resources to finance new nuclear and develop CCS and coal gasification.

There is a requirement for major developments in the energy sector through the next 30 to 40 years: in nuclear and waste management; alternative energy development; CCS and coal gasification; distributed generation and its control infrastructure; real-time pricing and smart metering; demand side management and energy conservation; emission monitoring and control; LNG management and conventional plant efficiency improvements. All these development will have a requirement for high quality engineering graduates and many of these are going to have to come from within developing countries like India and China, stretching their training infrastructure. There will also be a shortage of manufacturing facilities that are able to keep pace with new demand and the replacement of the existing time expired stock of plant. Because of the historic pace of development there will be a 'wall' of new replacements occurring in generation, transmission and distribution starting in the next decade. These demands are unlikely to be met and the result will be power shortages and high prices.

Glossary

AAC – Already Allocated Capacity of interconnecting transmission routes

AGC – Automatic Generation Control used to effect short term generation control

APX – Amsterdam Power Exchange supporting trading in NW Europe

ATC – Available Transmission Capacity on interconnecting transmission routes

AVR – Automatic Voltage Regulators used on generation to control voltage

Ancillary services – enable the System Operator to maintain a stable system

Balancing market – market used to effect short term balance of supply and demand

Base load – describes a generator operating at a fixed output

Bilateral contracts – contracts for supply of energy between generators and suppliers

Black start – capability of generation to start up without external supplies

BRP – a Balance Responsible Party able to make submissions of contracted positions

BST – Bulk Supply Tariff used to supply energy wholesale from generation groups to suppliers or distribution companies that engage in supply

Capacity Charge – charge made to cover the provision of assets to effect supply

Capex – The capital expenditure of an organisation

CCS – Carbon Capture from generation processes and its transportation and storage

CDCA – Central Data Collection Agent responsible for collecting tariff metering data

Power Markets and Economics: Energy Costs, Trading, Emissions   Barrie Murray
© 2009 John Wiley & Sons, Ltd

CEGB – UK Central Electricity Generating Board now defunct
CHP – Combined Heat and Power system producing electricity and heat
Coal gasification – converting coal to 'Syngas' by combustion with limited oxygen
Contingency reserve – reserve to cover loss of planned generation
Contracts for Difference – bilateral contract with a set price independent of pool price
DCLF – DC load flow model used to analyse the flow of MWs on networks
EEX – European Energy Exchange supporting trading across central Europe
Equal Lambda Criteria – occurs when marginal production prices are equal
Energy rate – tariff for supply of energy
EOR – Enhanced Oil Recovery through pumping CO_2 into partially depleted field
ERGEG – association of European Regulators Group for Electricity and Gas
ETSO – association of European Transmission System Operators
Eurostat – European organisation publishing energy related statistics
Exchanges – centres supporting trading in energy products
FGD – Fluidised Gas Desulphurisation
FPN – Final Physical Notification of expected transfers through a designated node
Gate closure – time before event for submissions of all final contracted positions
GSP – Grid Supply Point from super-grid to lower voltage grid distribution system
Hedging contracts – to defray the risks associated with contracted positions
ICRP – Investment Cost Related Prices for use of transmission systems based on the investment cost of assets used
IPP – Independent Power Producer being a generator separate from any residual state organisation
LDC – Load Duration Curve expressing demand for period as a curve against time
Liberalisation – the process of enabling open access to the power market
Liquidity – a measure of the number of times a physical commodity is traded
Load factor – the relation between the peak load and average load expressed as %
LMP – locational marginal price for energy at a reference node
LNG – Liquid Natural Gas created to enable transportation of gas from remote sites
LOLP – Loss of Load Probability is the probability of load exceeding generation

Makeup cost – the cost in a market of buying extra energy from a reserve generator

Marginal cost – the cost of an extra increment of energy on the system

Merit order – a list of available generation in ascending price order

NAP National Allocation Plan – a plan of how CO_2 allowances are distributed

Nordpool – the market organisation covering the Scandinavian area

NUG – non-utility Generator being separate from the residual utility

OPEX – Operating Expenditure of organisation

Peak load – the highest load on a system during a defined period

Powernext – the power exchange in France covering Northern Europe

PPA – Power Purchase Agreement for the sale of energy and services from a generator

Primary reserve – reserve available in seconds to support system frequency control

PSP – Pool Selling Price for energy from a pool to suppliers/distribution companies

Quality of supply – the quality of voltage and frequency and security

RAV Regulated Asset Value – value of those assets of a monopoly subject to regulation

Reserve – spare generation or interruptible demand held in reserve for system needs

RTO regional transmission operator – an operator covering several control areas

RPI – Retail Price Index monitoring the change in retail prices to customers

Secondary reserve – spare generation available within minutes to meet system needs

SMP – System Marginal Price being the price of the next increment of generation

SO – System Operator managing the operating of the network in conjunction with generators and users

Spill price – the price paid to independent generators for energy supplied in excess of their output contracted to customers

Supergrid – the high voltage network facilitating the pooling of large scale generation

SBP – System Buy Price in Balancing Market

SSP – System Sell Price in Balancing Market

TTC – Total Transmission Capacity of interconnecting routes between systems

Transmission constraints – limitations on transfers due to system security needs

Triad – the three peak demands in a year separated by more than 10 days

TRM – Transmission Reserve Margin capacity left available for emergency transfers

TSO – Transmission System Operator responsible for network operation and security

UCG – Underground coal gasification

UCTE – Union for the Co-ordination of Transmission of Electricity

UoS - Use of System – used to describe charges for use of a network

Unit commitment – the process of selecting which generators should be committed to run through a period

Uplift – the added cost in a pool of accommodating network constraints and services

Vertically integrated company – company owning generation and supply business

VLL – Value of Lost Load being the cost to consumers of failure to supply energy

Wheeling – the process of transferring energy between two systems through a third

References

[1] Dragana Pilipović, **1997**, *Energy Risk*, McGraw Hill, ISBN 0-7863-1231-9.
[2] Barrie Murray, **1998**, *Electricity Markets*, J. Wiley & Sons, Chichester, ISBN 0-471-98507-4.
[3] Loi Lei Lai, **2001**, *Power System Restructuring and Deregulation*, J. Wiley & Sons, Chichester, ISBN 0-471-49500-X.
[4] UCTE Union for the Coordination of the Transmission of Electricity, www.ucte.org.
[5] ETSO European Transmission System Operators, www.etso-net.org.
[6] ERG European Regulators Group, www.erg.eu.int.
[7] EEX European Energy Exchange, www.eex.de.
[8] APX Amsterdam Power Exchange, www.apx.nl.
[9] FERC Federal Energy Regulatory Commission, www.ferc.fed.us.

Power Markets and Economics: Energy Costs, Trading, Emissions   Barrie Murray
© 2009 John Wiley & Sons, Ltd

Appendix

CONVERSION TABLES

Table A1 Energy conversion

	TJ	Gcal	Mtoe	MBtu	GWh
TJ	1	238.8	$2.388 * 10^{-5}$	947.8	0.2778
Gcal	$4.187 * 10^{-3}$	1	10^{-7}	3.968	$1.163 * 10^{-3}$
Mtoe	$4.186 * 10^4$	10^7	1	$3.968 * 10^7$	11630
MBtu	$1.0551 * 10^{-3}$	0.252	$2.52 * 10^{-5}$	1	$2.931 * 10^{-4}$
GWh	3.6	860	$8.6 * 10^{-5}$	3412	1

Relationship between Oil and Gas Price (6 : 1)

1 tonne of oil contains between 6.3 and 7.9 barrels, assuming 6.61 barrels then:
1 barrel contains $41.87/6.61 = 6.33$ GJ
since $1\,GJ = 0.9478$ MBtu
hence 1 barrel $= 6.33 * 0.9478 = 6$ MBtu
i.e. 1 Barrel of oil costs six times 1 MBtu of gas on an equivalent energy basis.

Relationship between GJ and MWh

$1\,GJ = 1\,GW$ for 1 second so to convert to MWh divide by 3600 and multiply by 1000

$$\text{i.e.} \quad 1\,GJ = 0.2778\,MWh.$$

Power Markets and Economics: Energy Costs, Trading, Emissions   Barrie Murray
© 2009 John Wiley & Sons, Ltd

GJ to Therms
1 GJ = 440/46.4 therms = 9.48 therms.

kcal/kg to GJ/t
Multiply by 4.18/440,
e.g. 4000 kcal/kg is equivalent to 16.7 GJ/t
6000 kcal/kg is equivalent to 25.05 GJ/t.

Mtoe to MWh
1 Mtoe = 4.1868 TJ
1 toe = 41.8 GJ
1 toe = 41.8 * 1000/3600 MWh = 11.63 MWh.

Barrels of Oil to Litres
1 barrel of oil = 35 imperial gallons or 40 US, equivalent to 158.9 litres.

Specific Net Calorific Values
CV oil = 41.87 GJ/t
CV coal (bituminous) = 25 GJ/t (varies with source see Table A2)
CV lignite (brown coal) = 10 GJ/t (may be between 5 and 15 GJ/t)
CV natural gas = 40 000 kJ/m^3 (varies with source see Table A3).
Net heat content of gas = 0.9 * gross heat content.

Table A2 CV of coal

Coal	Toe/Tome
China	0.531
United States	0.634
India	0.441
Australia	0.614
South Africa	0.564
Russia	0.545
Indonesia	0.615
Poland	0.551
Kazakhstan	0.444
Ukraine	0.505

Table A3 CV of natural gas kJ/m^3

Country	Natural gas
Russia	37 578
United States	38 347
Canada	38 260
Iran	39 536
Algeria	42 000
United Kingdom	3979
Norway	40 029
Netherlands	33 320
Indonesia	40 600
Turkmenistan	37 700

Index

AAC already allocate capacity, 100, 202
Abu Dhabi, 12, 248
ACE Area Control Error, 201
active networks, 40, 120
Adjusted customer number, 117
AGC Automatic Generator
    Control, 181, 201
ancillary services, 22, 156, 179–198
Annuity, 38, 166, 190
arbitrage, 21, 151, 179, 226
ARIMA Auto Regressive IMA,
    232, 269
asset costs, 40
Asset utilisation, 41,105, 211
ATC Available Trans. Capacity,
    101, 269
auction emission credits, 76, 87
    interconnections, 137, 142, 207, 237
    energy, 153, 186
Australia, 34, 50, 84, 106, 183, 240, 278
Auxiliaries, 42, 46
availability, 11, 23, 26, 45, 66
    payments, 242
average costs, 7, 215
AVR Automatic Voltage
    Regulator, 182

back-casting, 170
Balancing market, 11, 26, 29, 144
Baltrel, 285
barrels of oil, 52, 277
base load profit, 226
Belgium, 4, 50, 81, 92, 164, 203
Benchmark, 114, 117, 170, 188
Benelux, 4, 100
bid ladder, 187
bid pricing, 26
bidding, 25, 139, 148, 223
bilateral contract, 91, 141, 223
    deals, 31, 241
    trade, 32, 110, 143, 247
biomass, 58, 62, 86
bituminous coal, 78, 83
black start, 186, 194
boiler efficiency, 46, 68
    fluidised bed, 259
BOO build own and operate, 232
BOT build operate and transfer, 232
BP British Petroleum, 265, 282
British Energy, 149, 276
brown coal, 51, 78, 170, 282, 298
BRP Balance Responsible Party, 31,
    110, 144

BSP bulk supply point, 110
BST Bulk Supply Tariff, 6, 32, 109, 130
Btu, 45, 52, 277
Bulgaria, 214, 274
business process, 19

Canada, 86, 279, 282
capacity auctions, 137, 142, 207, 237
    payments, 27, 249, 281
ÇAPEX, 99, 118
    non-load related, 99
    reinforcements, 118
capital costs, 43, 50, 119, 166, 190
carbon, 51, 57, 75, 250, 265, 283
CCGT, 44, 47, 165, 189
CCL Climate Change levy, 64
CCS Carbon Capture & Storage, 84,
    265, 281
CDCA Central Data collection
    Agent, 144
CDM Clean Development
    Mechanism, 77, 273
Centrel, 142
CERs Certified Emission
    Reductions, 273
CFB Circulating Fluidised Bed, 259
CfDs Contract for Differences, 10, 30
China, 12, 34, 50, 77, 139, 265, 279
clean coal, 74, 272, 282
CO_2, 51, 72, 172, 259, 278
coal CV, 43, 83, 243
coal gasification, 74, 266, 281
coal prices, 34, 561, 79, 174, 225, 274
co-firing, 58
Columbia, 279
Commodity, 93, 115, 268, 272
comparative generation costs, 52
competition, 8, 35, 50, 108, 138, 221,
    238, 287
connection charges, 219
constrained off, 36, 91
constrained on, 91
constrained schedule, 30

contracts, 10, 20, 49, 65, 128, 22, 259
conversion tables, 297
cost chain, 39, 56, 228
cost of debt, 66
cost of equity, 45, 65, 256
credit risk, 147
cross-border prices, 124
    capacity, 54, 196
    trading, 87, 142, 199, 237, 270
customer switching, 133
CV calorific value gas, 4, 243
Czech Republic, 275
Czechoslovakia, 208

Danish, 67
DCLF DC load flow, 95
Debt, 43, 65, 226
Decommissioning, 56, 65, 278
demand side participation, 28, 35, 240
    prediction, 11, 171, 285
    growth forecasting, 156, 163, 221
desalination, 246
dispatch, 21, 25, 90, 156, 187, 240
distributed generation, 72, 120, 210, 255
distribution, 5, 107, 111, 128, 210, 263
    owner, 6
    tariff, 22
domestic, 94, 107, 121, 128, 143
droop, 181
dynamic programming, 156, 222

E HV extended high voltage, 54,
    265, 285
EAU emission allowance unit, 82
EdeF, 276, 277
efficiency boiler, 46, 68
    gross, 46
    net, 46
    part load, 47, 189
EGEAS, 222
EHV supergrid, 54
Electrabel, 137
Elia, 92

ELV Emission limit values, 78
embedded generation, 5, 22, 118,
    163, 244
emergency power, 186
emergency reserve, 196
emissions, 55, 75, 172, 254, 272
end user cost chain, 42, 238
    charges, 121, 123
    prices, 96, 124, 131
Endesa, 141
end-user consortia, 141
ENEL, 137, 240, 254, 287
entry/exit, network, 30, 99, 118, 224
Eon Netz, 195
EOR Enhanced Oil Recovery, 265, 279
EPWR European Pressurised Water
    Reactor, 276
Equal lambda criteria, 100
Equity, 43, 65, 156, 226
ERGEG European Regulators Group for
    Electricity and Gas, 90, 201, 237
ERUs Emission Reduction Units, 273
Estonia, 98, 275
ETS Emission Trading Scheme, 76,
    254, 272
ETSO European Transmission System
    Operators, 97, 200
EU Directive 2003/87/EC, 76
EUR Enhanced Oil Recovery
European generation, 8, 11, 51, 54, 137
    Directive, 237
    markets, 33, 54, 100, 140, 199
Eurostat, 93
Eurostat customer type, 106
ex-ante, 19, 25
Exceltium, 141
Exchange APX, 142, 204
Exchange Powernext, 142
Exchanges EEX, 142
ex-post, 19, 26, 91

feed in tariffs, 62
FERC Fed. Energy Reg. Council, 90, 219

FGD Flue Gas Desulphurisation, 274
firm capacity, 176, 210
fixed operating costs, 44, 166
forecasting demand, 156, 163, 221
forecasting generation, 254
forecasting prices, 51, 156, 170
forward market, 223, 251
FPNs final physical notice, 144, 247
France, 4, 33, 50, 98, 108, 125, 140, 202
franchise, 6, 107, 130
freight, 34, 50, 272
    market, 286
frequency control, 105, 181, 201
fuel prices, 34, 43, 50, 72, 166, 243, 277
    supply security, 241, 253, 268, 279
futures, 21

gallenium selenide, 59
gas emissions, 76
gas prices, 34, 50, 66, 125, 153, 226, 259
gate closure, 29, 110, 142, 254
GDP Gross Domestic Product, 163
generation capital costs, 50
    fixed costs, 44, 113, 125, 159
    operating at margin, 53
    variable costs, 126, 152, 223
    variable operating costs, 44, 80
geothermal, 50, 84
Germany, 23, 50, 92, 124, 190,
    258, 275
global warming, 3, 55, 75, 255, 271
governance, 200
Greece, 32, 51, 81, 142, 170, 215, 275
Green Certificate, 55, 62
grid parity, 59
GRTN, 63
GSP, 145
GWh, 297

hedging risk, 10, 105
hedging strategy, 49, 106, 119,
    141, 146
Hungary, 98, 205, 214, 275

hydro energy, 66, 160
    ricing, 162
    run of river, 161
    storage, 160, 162, 221

Iberdrola, 4, 137
ICRP Investment cost related
    pricing, 95
IEM Internal Electricity Market, 200
incentive schemes, 17, 62, 273
indexation, 281
Indonesia, 279
Infrastructure, 5, 204, 264, 273
interconnection auction, 213
    capacity, 13, 99, 200
    Europe, 203
    pricing, 54
interest rate, 43
investment appraisal, 100, 156, 221
IPP Independent Power Producer, 13,
    15, 32
IT systems, 21, 145
Italy, 23, 51, 89, 92, 124, 137, 209, 215

Japan, 228
JI mechanisms, 273
Joule, 78, 267

Kingsnorth, 280
Kvar reactive energy, 6, 23, 182, 193, 219
Kyoto Protocol, 77, 273

Lagrangian relaxation, 156
Latvia, 275
Laufenberg, 142
LCPD Large Combustion Plant Dir.
    77, 272
LDC Load Distribution Curve, 159
least cost abatement, 3, 273
LECS levy exemption certificates, 64
LFC Load Frequency Control, 183, 206
Liberalisation, 3, 30, 82, 133, 225, 242
Lignite, 51, 78, 170, 224, 282

Liquidity, 23, 89, 110, 126, 138, 238, 253
Lithuania, 275
LMP locational marginal price, 105
load factor, 22, 41, 53, 71, 93, 107, 164
LOLP Loss of Load Probability, 26,
    132, 242
loop flows, 206
losses, 22, 41, 93, 112, 145, 186, 200, 215
LP mix, 222
LPX Leipzig Power Exchange, 142
LTI contract, 152, 225

Makeup, 13, 32, 147, 179
mandatory pool, 10, 30, 247
marginal generator, 24, 158, 167, 231
marginal pricing, 24
market development, 19, 104, 235
    mechanisms, 19, 23, 141, 189, 239
    multi market, 11, 31, 288
    operation, 82, 90, 118, 135, 141
    operator, 91
    performance, 231
    power, 137, 232, 247, 288
    simulation, 26, 158, 163
MCV market for green certificates, 62
Medring, 215, 285
merchant generator, 222
merit order, 25, 43, 102, 156, 170, 220
    Table 'A', Table 'B', 48
Metering, 21, 93, 110, 112, 126, 144
micro generation, 56, 68, 120, 270, 284
Middle East, 16, 32, 111, 236, 245
Miller field, 265
minimum off time, 148
minimum on time, 148
monopoly, 4, 14, 90, 125, 266, 286
MVar, 182
MW mile, 219

Namibia, 12
NAP National Allocation Plan, 80
national champions, 13
NBP National Balancing Point, 138

NERP nat. emission reduction plan, 78
NETA, 142, 247
Netherlands, 4, 50, 81, 109, 142, 182, 249
new entry, 24, 33, 53, 77, 121, 172, 216
new entry Europe, 176
New Zealand, 84, 137
Nordel, 142, 200
Nordpool, 20, 35, 91, 204, 240, 251
normal demand distribution, 165
North America, 219
Northern Ireland, 4
Norway, 57, 97, 204, 234
Nox, 77, 267
nuclear generation, 56, 80, 255, 269
    fuel, 278
    parks, 277
NUG non utility generator, 13
NW Europe, 93, 115, 125

OCGT open cycle gas turbine, 49, 259
Ofgem, 21, 63, 123
oil indexation, 35, 51, 259
oil prices, 34, 277
Oman, 12, 32, 248
OPEC, 271
open access, 27, 89, 104, 239, 248
operating costs, 42, 70, 112, 132,
    188, 210
operational efficiency, 3, 54, 238
OPEX, 114, 116
OTC Over The Counter, 11, 33, 146
outage planning, 11, 242

part load efficiency, 46, 189
participant, 89, 139, 179, 241
passive radial networks, 120, 263, 284
PDC Price Duration Curve, 169
Peaking, 49
Peaking contract, 128, 144
    generator, 126, 148, 159
    plant, 49, 127, 153, 223
    prices, 160, 174, 223
    profit, 226, 228

performance, market, 237
    assessment, 242
    criteria, 82, 218
    improvement, 238, 246
PJM Penns. NewJersey Maryland,
    90, 105
Planning, 9, 13, 99, 141, 172, 201, 218
plant costs, 225
plant margin, 14, 27, 156, 174, 210, 253
plant mix, 19, 27, 49, 125, 222, 253
Poland, 203, 214, 275
Polysilicon, 59
Pool, mandatory, 3, 30
portfolio generator, 148, 158, 222, 242,
Portugal, 51, 57, 81, 247
post market settlement, 27
power boards, 12
Powernext, 142
PPA Power Purchase Agreement,
    32, 226
price spikes, 34, 242
pricing bid, 25, 150, 159
pricing ex-ante, 19, 23
pricing ex-poste, 19, 26, 91
pricing marginal, 24
primary reserve, 189, 194
primary response, 183
project life, 41, 65, 139, 155
pumped storage, 162, 221
PWR Pressurised Water Reactor, 276

RAB regulated asset base, 111
reactive support, 183, 193, 219
REC renewable energy certificates, 85
recovery resources, 186
regulating reserve, 191, 194
regulation, 22, 77, 90, 116, 138, 201
regulator, 22, 90, 111, 204, 240
renewable, 50, 60, 85, 274
Renewables Directive, 274
Republic of Ireland, 4
Reserve, 35, 180, 199, 268
reserve margin, 202, 285

reservoirs, 57, 161
risk credit, 147
risk management, 146
risk price, 23, 50
risk regulatory, 83, 98
risk volume, 21, 50, 147, 247
ROC Renewable Obligation
    Certificate, 55, 63
Romania, 97, 214, 276
RPI retail price index, 20, 117
run down rate, 148
run of river, 161
run up rate, 148
Russia, 271
RWE Netz, 92

SBP System Buy Price, 144
Scheduling, 25, 201, 219, 241
SE Europe, 215
secondary reserve, 180
secondary response, 180
security of supply, 89, 130, 141, 277
SEP Protocol, 127
SHP small hydro plant, 57
SIEPAC project, 100
Simulation, 156
simulation market, 26, 158
single buyer, 11, 16, 32
Single Buyer Market, 50, 139, 222, 245
Slovenia, 164, 275
Slovakia, 208, 214
SMP Marginal Price, 27, 132, 171, 223
SO$_2$, 77, 267
Solar, 59, 85, 263, 284
South Africa, 10, 27, 34, 50
South Korea, 286
Southern Africa, 99, 216
spark spread, 150
spill, 32
split market, 92
spot markets, 146, 152
spot prices, 141, 172
SSP System Sell Price, 145

start up costs, 25, 148, 159
statistical forecasting, 170
Statoil, 282
Storage, 56, 120, 148, 160, 263
Supercritical, 258
super-peak, 127
supplier, 21, 107, 123, 141, 147
Switzerland, 57, 207, 215
Syngas, 267, 278
system gain, 181
system security, 14, 28, 179, 272, 280
system services, 23, 97

table A merit order, 48
table B merit order, 48
take or pay contract, 148, 225
tariff, 6, 62, 94, 112, 130
TARTAM, 139
Tennet, 92, 186, 204
Therm, 44, 256
thermal efficiency, 46, 68
tidal barrier, 57
tie-line bias frequency control, 181, 206
TLM transmission loss multiplier, 145
toe tons oil equivalent, 298
trader, 21, 146, 155
transmission constraints, 10, 27, 90, 156
transit horizontal network, 210
transit key, 210
transmission charge, 95
    owner, 22
    pricing, 28
    organisations, 90
triad, 6
TRM transmission reserve margin,
    101, 202
TTC total transmission capacity,
    100, 202
Turkey, 51, 215, 232
TWh terra watt hours, 43, 57, 65

UCG underground coal
    gasification, 284

UCTE 183, 200
unconstrained schedule, 30
unit commitment, 10, 30, 162
USA, 86
use of system, 20, 95, 101
utilisation, generation, 48, 159

variable operating costs, 42, 166
virtual power plant, 263
VLL value of lost load, 26, 132, 243
voltage control, 21, 105, 180
volume risk, 21, 50, 143

WACC, 43, 113
WASP, 222

waste to energy, 59, 70, 120, 176,
    255, 284
wave power, 59
wheeling, 99, 210
wholesale prices, 42, 10, 124,
    138
wind farms, 61, 67
wind off shore, 58, 67
wind on shore, 57, 120, 225
wind output, 195, 210
wind turbines, 58, 275

zonal pricing, 27
zone export, 105, 180, 219
zone import, 91, 211, 245